Frank Wedekind

≻─↭─◦─↮─≺

FOUR MAJOR PLAYS

A Smith and Kraus Book
Published by Smith and Kraus, Inc.
PO Box 127, Lyme, NH 03768

Cover and Text Design by Julia Hill Gignoux, Freedom Hill Design
Cover Illustration: Gustav Klimt

First Edition: March 2000
10 9 8 7 6 5 4 3 2 1

The Library of Congress Cataloging-In-Publication Data

Wedekind, Frank, 1864–1918.
[Plays. English. Selections]
Frank Wedekind : four major plays / translated by Carl R. Mueller. — 1st ed.
p. cm. — (Great translations series)
Contents: Spring's awakening — Lulu — The tenor — The Marquis of Keith.
ISBN 1-57525-209-0
1. Wedekind, Frank, 1864–1918—Translations into English. I. Title: Four major plays.
II. Mueller, Carl Richard. III. Title. IV. Great translations for actors series.
PT2647.E26 A26 2000
832'.8—dc21   00-029708

Frank Wedekind

FOUR MAJOR PLAYS

Translated by Carl R. Mueller

Great Translations Series

SK
A Smith and Kraus Book

was divided; he was torn between two divergent poles of life and thought: the conventional bourgeois morality on the one hand, and the new morality of sexual freedom and liberation on the other. The latter was his personal contribution to the way of the world, a world that in his day lay under the pall of sexual hypocrisy and repression, a world in which one thing was preached and another was desired.

In Frank Wedekind the desire for the expression of the repressed self was uncommonly strong; yet the bourgeois oppressiveness of commonplace morality was always with him, nagging and eating away at his conscience. Like the triumphant but tormented men of the Renaissance, and like his fellow countryman Johannes Faustus, Wedekind had two souls burning in his breast. It was one soul that furnished the impetus to express himself, and the other that rebelled against this impulse and was his eternal torment.

Born in Germany in 1864, Wedekind's life from almost his inception was one of uprootedness. His father was a German liberal and supporter of the 1848 Revolution, a doctor who wanted to establish an orthopedic clinic and watering-place but who, after a short time as a practical physician, migrated to Constantinople, joined the Turkish service, and traveled with various expeditions to the Tigris and Euphrates Rivers. Three years later he went from Palermo to Rome, which he found so agreeable that he remained there until the autumn of 1847.

Disenchanted with the Revolution of 1848 in its attempts at democratic action, he repaired to North America, where he settled as a doctor in San Francisco. Here he met and married a young actress from the local German-speaking theater who was almost half his age. Two years later, in 1864, they returned to Europe, where their second child, named Benjamin Franklin, in honor of the land of freedom that harbored them, was born. Once in Hanover, Frank's father, a man independently wealthy, retired from his medical practice and gave himself over to politics. His disgust with Bismarck and his new Reich drove the Wedekind family to Switzerland in 1872.

In Switzerland Frank and his brother Armin lived a reasonably happy childhood in Schloss Lenzburg in Canton Aargau. Because of the family's liberal tendencies, the Wedekind children were tutored privately and in boarding schools.

Frank was to have become a lawyer but forced permission to take a semester of literature and art courses. He matriculated at the University of Lausanne and majored in philology and French literature. In 1884 he and his brother went to Munich, a city that was to remain central for most of Wedekind's life.

1886 found him working as publicity agent for a soup manufacturing firm near Zurich. It was here he made the acquaintance of the young socialist-naturalist group of writers known as "Young Germany," among whom were Carl and Gerhart Hauptmann. Yet Wedekind had no leanings, even at that early age, toward the dull and photographic observation that was the religion of the naturalists. His interest lay not with the Fourth Estate of workers, but with the mysterious underworld, with adventurers, drifters, and artists, with asocial types—and children.

Wedekind and Hauptmann became enemies as a result of Hauptmann's breaking of a personal confidence imparted to him by Wedekind regarding his unhappy parental family life brought about by the separation of his parents and the effects such experiences have on the children involved. This information was worked by Hauptmann into his play *Das Friedensfest*. Wedekind retaliated with a satiric comedy in which he ridiculed the photographic realism of the naturalist school.

One salutary thing, however, did emerge from the meeting of Wedekind and Gerhart Hauptmann. It was Wedekind's good fortune to be introduced by Hauptmann to the long-neglected and only recently rediscovered early nineteenth century playwright and revolutionary Georg Büchner. This introduction to Büchner's plays furnished the young Wedekind with the stylistic basis upon which to found his future iconoclastic work: fragmented dialogue, frenetic, episodic scenes, a distortion of natural phenomena to arrive at the true center, and the disarmingly modern technique of isolation as seen in the tendency of characters to talk past rather than at one another.

While his naturalist brethren worked at their trade of observation, Wedekind spent six months wandering from country to country with a circus troupe. London, Paris, Munich, Leipzig, Berlin, Silesia, Switzerland, Austria, and Southern Germany—these were the places he visited, and where he wrote his first short sketches and stories.

THE WORK

In 1891 Frank Wedekind published his first drama, a children's tragedy, as he called it, which he titled *Spring's Awakening*. It was a trailblazer in many respects, and still is. It introduced a new kind of drama to the modern stage—what was early in the next century to be termed expressionism. It also spoke out loudly and yet with great compassion of the trials and ago-nies accompanying the awakening of puberty. Because of the moral repres-siveness and prudery of the time, *Spring's Awakening* met with violent antagonism and debilitating censorship regulations. The play was not given its first performance until 1906, under Max Reinhardt's direction, and then only in a bowdlerized version which plucked out the offending passages, in effect emasculating the work. It is interesting to note that the full text of the play was not allowed on the British stage until 1963.

The most startling, indeed disturbing, fact to Wedekind's contempo-raries was that he should flout morality and decency and the long-accepted and time-honored standards of the bourgeois establishment. Wedekind was saying to them that nature cannot lie, that nature is truth, and therefore nature is the supreme morality. In repressing its sexual instincts, or, at best, hiding beneath the cloak of a hypocritical double standard, Wedekind maintained that his age was poisoning itself; natural instincts were regarded as sinful; his contemporaries were subjugating naked beauty and enslaving its youth to fear, to ignorance, to frustration, to unhealthy and psycholog-ically dangerous attitudes. To Wedekind, nakedness and beauty and truth were one—the trinity of his universe.

Spring's Awakening is the story of adolescence at the point when the sexual urge is experienced for the first time, and when it is still mysterious and frightening—and wonderful—confusion and elation inexplicably intermingled in an inevitable paradox. The crux of the play is the opposi-tion the child meets from its elders at the moment when openness and understanding are the vital, life-giving factors which will determine its future course.

Wedekind's children in the play, Wendla, Melchior, and Moritz, are naïve; and it is from this naïveté that much of the play's beauty and strength derive. Their dialogue serves as a fresh breath of lyricism in the stuffy atmosphere of its age. Wedekind shows these children caught up in the most perplexing moments of their lives—the confusion that accompa-nies sexual awakening, questions regarding the nature of love and concep-tion—and the wall erected by parents and teachers against responding to these perfectly normal concerns.

The moral cowardice of the adult world that Wedekind indicts here results in Wendla's becoming pregnant and dying at the hands of an abor-tionist brought in by her mother who fears facing the consequence of her own culpable negligence in refusing to answer her daughter's plea for answers to her adolescent questions.

School and teacher, too, come under fire, and Wedekind typifies the latter as a pompous, overbearing, closed-eared, unfeeling piece of bureaucratic machinery. The language of the faculty is bloated, convoluted, grotesque, and, in the last analysis, ludicrous in its gross inhumanity; the language of the parents is earthbound and prosaic; and both contrast violently with the natural lyricism of the children's dialogue when they are free to discuss among themselves. Behind each of their sentences, however, lurks the instinctual fear which blazes forth when the wall of indifference threatens to reassert itself. When Hans Rilow locks himself in the lavatory with a reproduction of Palmo Vecchio's "Venus" and masturbates for one last time before destroying it because he has been taught the "evils" of that act, he is loaded with a sense of guilt that will only increase when he appropriates his next reproduction—after all, he says to his Venus, many have preceded you.

When Hans and Ernst pursue each other, scarcely knowing what it is they are after, and finally express themselves in a homosexual love scene of great delicacy, beauty, and humor, they protect themselves from their confusion and isolation by taking refuge in the "conventional" view of the future in which they see themselves as self-respecting, law-abiding, heterosexual bourgeois pillars of society, who, when they think back on "a night like this," will only laugh.

Parents are shown to be egocentric, sadistic, and self-justifying wardens of their offspring, from Martha who is beaten by her parents nightly and confined for the night to a sack on the floor; to the Gabors who—once they discover that not only did their fifteen-year-old son write a dialogue on "copulation" for his sexually frustrated and curious best friend Moritz who receives no answers from his parents, but that he has impregnated a fourteen-year-old girl—implicitly consider themselves towers of moral virtue by consigning their son to a reformatory for his manifest "moral depravity," where he will be taught with iron discipline what is lawful as opposed to what is interesting. In effect, they are seeing to it that their son Melchior will become the hypocritical, well-oiled machine which the bourgeois bureaucracy was, and still is, most comfortable with, assuming he survives in the first place. And he will become so, Wedekind implies, at the expense of his happiness and of his very existence. It is Wedekind's most explicit statement regarding the sins of parents against children: insistence on the death of natural instinct and desire. These men and women, these demons, parents and teachers and society Wedekind draws in various degrees of distortion and caricature. They are the evil spirits he is trying to exorcise by showing them the results of their actions and non-actions. In the final scene of the play Wedekind introduces himself in the guise of the Man in the Mask. The scene is a graveyard; it is night and the wind blows sky and earth. The ghost of Moritz (carrying on his arm the head he blew off when he committed suicide for having disgraced his parents by not being promoted) meets Melchior just escaped from the reformatory. Moritz tries to lure his best friend Melchior into taking his hand and thus join him in the realm of the dead. But each time, Melchior instinctively declines, no matter how distraught he is over Wendla's death by abortion. The sense of life is too urgent in him; it always was; whereas Moritz, in life, jumped at his own shadow.

At the crucial moment, the Man in the Mask, Wedekind, the Spirit of Life, appears and, wrapping Melchior in his arms, repossesses him for the world of the living—to life, to beauty, to truth—to nature, but also to the enervating struggle for an unfettered existence. The overwhelming sadness of Moritz's desire for Melchior to take his hand is sensed in the fact of Moritz's Olympian loneliness in death. He is so alone that he would think nothing of taking his friend's life only for one touch of a human hand held out to him in recollection of earthly love and affection.

Wedekind's intention is clear, and he shows the way to sanity as no one before him or after him had done with such clarity and direction. The convention of hypocrisy must fall to the trumpet blast of innocence and truth. To be sure, this is naïve—but not all that unattainable if only eyes and ears and understanding are engaged. Wedekind was never again to present his theme so freshly, so sympathetically, so tenderly, and at the same time so devastatingly, as in *Spring's Awakening*.

If censorship dogged Wedekind in regard to *Spring's Awakening*, it was to virtually destroy him with the creation of his next play, *Lulu*, which he completed in 1894. If it is possible to say that a single work, whether available for public consumption or not, is the foundation stone of the modern theater, then that work must inevitably be *Lulu*. Wedekind did in that monster tragedy in 1894 what Beckett and Pinter were to do more than half a century later. In this play Wedekind, in total disregard of public convention, not to say morality, lays bare the underside of life in a way that had never been seen on any stage. In the character of Lulu he presents for the first time the study of a woman struggling against the odds of male supremacy in a world in which the female was to be seen and not heard, a decorative motif in the life of the male. Lulu sits still for no one. She moves forward with unflinching rapidity and resolve. She refuses to be caught up in the repressive demands of the social collective. She forges her own path. In a word, she is larger than life. She is an enigma. She is all things and something different to every man she engages. She is fact, she is myth; she is corporeal, she is idea; she is realist, she is ideal. And, to pervert Goethe's final lines of *Faust*, she is the eternal-womanly that draws us downward.

Liberation is Lulu's goal, a goal she chases down the paths of experience with a vengeance. Sexual liberation, social liberation, political liberation, personal liberation, the liberation to be her own being. Nobody owns her, though every man she encounters tries mightily. Nobody can handle her, as every man she meets attempts. Nobody knows who or what she is, and that's the way she wants it. In Act Five, in the rat-trap attic of their demise in a London slum, Schigolch, on his last legs, remarks: "I don't understand women"; and Lulu's third husband, Alwa, who will not survive the night, adds in despair: "I never understood them"; to which, in all simplicity and supremacy in her final degradation, even though she will end the night dead, with her vulva taken as trophy by Jack the Ripper, Lulu comments: "I understand them." And in that understanding she speaks for all women who have suffered the indignity of having lived—if that is the right word—in a male world. These are the realities that the society of Wedekind's time could not allow and so they fought back tooth and nail. As a result, Wedekind neither saw his *Lulu* in print nor on the stage. It led him to begin again almost immediately with the same material. In 1895 he transformed the first half of the play into what he called *Earth Spirit;* and in 1903 he fashioned the second half into *Pandora's Box* (the original title of the "monster tragedy" here titled *Lulu*). In 1898 *Earth Spirit* was first performed in Leipzig. Finally, in 1913, Wedekind revised both plays once more, and these are the versions the theater world has come to know, and by which it judges the character of Lulu. They are the plays that served as the foundation stone of modern drama. But neither *Earth Spirit* nor *Pandora's Box* is the play that *Lulu* is. They have been tamed. They have been made acceptable (though only barely so). They have also become well-constructed plays in the conventional sense. It must be said, however, that they are plays, however tamed, of enormous theatrical power. They also have incidents which do not appear in the original one-play text, incidents as well as characters that are genuinely stunning. But the rawness and unvarnished honesty and horror of the original has been gone over with the equivalent of an air-brush. It is only a guess, but it is intriguing to speculate whether or not the "monster" referred to in the title of the original play is not Lulu, but Society.

In 1897 the one-act farce *The Tenor* appeared in print and on 10 December 1899 saw its first performance in Berlin. It is unquestionably one of the great farces in dramatic literature. Its hero Gerardo is the epitome of the self-serving egocentric matinee idol of the age (of any age), the great Wagner Singer of his generation, whom women of all sizes and shapes and ages pursue with a single intent: to bed him no matter what. The play is a tour-de-force of brilliant dialogue, wit, and situation, and it has successfully held the stage since the time of its first production.

The Marquis of Keith, of 1900, is rightly considered Wedekind's masterpiece of dramatic construction—even he thought so. It concerns the dealings of a would-be entrepreneur who is caught, as has been noted elsewhere, between two ethical premises: the life of the pleasure-seeking sensualist and that of the idealistic moralist. Keith, the free-and-easy, lighthearted insouciant, is done in by a system and a bourgeois society of ambiguous morality that is corrupt to the core. In the 1960s the play became and still is highly topical. The Marquis' fantasy is to build a cultural center of such magnitude and importance that all the world will turn in obeisance. We are still seeing those structures rising at a remarkable rate and at enormous expense. Munich, the scene of *The Marquis of Keith,* finally has a venue that would have tickled the Marquis' funny-bone.

From the proto-expressionism of *Spring's Awakening* to the classic construction of *The Marquis of Keith* and beyond, Wedekind never gave up his rabid pursuit of the multifarious dishonesty he saw as the cancer in the body-collective of the bourgeois world. We may have come a long way since his death in 1918, but his plays still resonate with a fervor and a truth in their struggle against a reality that is probably beyond alteration.

CARL R. MUELLER
Department of Theater
School of Theater, Film and Television
University of California, Los Angeles

A NOTE
ON THE TRANSLATION

Three of these four plays are presented in their original form without omissions. Only *Lulu* has been altered. The reason for this is fairly obvious when one looks at the original text. Wedekind wrote this play of monstrous length in three languages. The first three acts that transpire in Berlin are in German. Act Four takes place in Paris and Wedekind, in order to take various jabs at the ostentation and frivolousness of the upper-class Parisian public largely used French as his means to that end. Most of the act, however, is in German. The major reasons for omitting the scenes in French are that in translation they lose their main purpose and the additional characters that these scenes introduce are only peripheral. The loss is minor. For the most part, then, the omission required simple snipping away of excess. This process has required only the slightest bit of adaptation, particularly towards the end, in order to facilitate a cut without leaving a gap.

In addition to the above, very minor cutting has also been introduced throughout the play. This amounts to the elimination of a line or two from time to time when those lines have no currency in English and are therefore superfluous. Examples are puns that do not translate, but also lines whose meaning is either lost (even in the original) or are editorially inserted in the original only for the sake of completeness. Occasionally lines have been juggled to make better sense, though this is rare. Wedekind's play was neither published nor produced in his lifetime and reconstruction of it will always be problematic. Every editor (or editor/translator) is forced to make his own choice, and that is the situation here.

A large part of Act Five, on the other hand, is written in English, a natural choice since it takes place in London. But Wedekind's command of English was considerably less fluent than his ease in French. In large part the English is grammatically incorrect and even pidgin English and would sound exceedingly odd if juxtaposed against the English of the translation. Therefore wherever English lines could be salvaged, they have been. Where they do not make the grade, they have been altered to reflect the tone of the rest of the translation.

One further point. In Act Five a Dr. Hilti makes an appearance as one of Lulu's customers. He is Swiss and speaks a Swiss-German that is virtually incomprehensible even to a native German. Wedekind obviously intended this segment to serve as satire, and in German it does so splendidly. Unfortunately the linguistic satire does not translate, and any translator is faced with the decision to omit or not to omit. My choice has been not to exclude it. While the satire is lost in translation something equally important (perhaps even more important from a purely dramatic standpoint) comes through, namely, a very funny and happily incongruous sex scene which serves as "comic" relief between two grizzly sex scenes, the one with Kungu Poti that precedes it and in particular the play's final, Grand Guignol scene between Jack and Lulu. It is an old technique, ancient, in fact, going back as far as the plays of Sophocles. To have missed it would have been to damage the effect of the monster tragedy's ultimate outrage.

SPRING'S AWAKENING

A Children's Tragedy

1891

ACT ONE
SCENE ONE

Living room.

WENDLA: Mother, why did you make my dress so long?

MRS. BERGMANN: Because you're fourteen years old today.

WENDLA: Then I wish I could have stayed thirteen.

MRS. BERGMANN: Wendla, the dress is not too long. What do you expect? Is it my fault you grow an inch taller each spring? A grown girl doesn't go around dressed like a little princess.

WENDLA: But at least it fits me better than this old nightshirt.—Please, mother, just once more! Just for the summer. This old sackcloth will last till I'm fifteen. Let's put it away till next birthday. All I'd do now is step on the hem.

MRS. BERGMANN: Oh, I just don't know. I wish I could keep you just as you are. Other girls your age are awkward and plump, but look at you. Who knows what you'll be like when the others are grown?

WENDLA: Who knows? Maybe I won't even be here.

MRS. BERGMANN: Where do you get such thoughts!

WENDLA: Mother, don't be sad.

MRS. BERGMANN: *(Kissing her.)* My baby!

WENDLA: They come to me at night sometimes, when I can't sleep. And they don't make me feel at all sad, because I know I'll sleep better for it. Mother, is it a sin to think about such things?

MRS. BERGMANN: Oh, very well, hang the old sack in the closet and put on your princess dress. I'll stitch a hand of ruffling around the bottom.

WENDLA: *(Hanging the dress in the wardrobe.)* Mother! I'd rather be twenty all at once if you're going to do that!

MRS. BERGMANN: I just don't want you to catch cold. Time was when that dress was just right; but now—

WENDLA: But summer's almost here. Children don't get diphtheria in the backs of their knees, for heaven's sake. Besides, people my age don't feel the cold, not in their legs. Do you want me to be too warm? Be glad early some morning your little precious doesn't rip off her sleeves and come to you with no shoes or stockings. The day I put on that old sack I'll wear the Queen of the Fairies' clothes underneath. Don't scold me, mother, no one will see.

Sunday evening.

MELCHIOR: I'm tired of this game. It's boring.

OTTO: Then I guess we'll *all* have to stop!—You done your homework yet, Melchior?

MELCHIOR: Why do you have to stop?

MORITZ: Where are you going?

MELCHIOR: For a walk.

GEORG: But it's almost dark.

ROBERT: Done your homework?

MELCHIOR: Why shouldn't I go for a walk in the dark?

ERNST: Central America! Louis XIV! Sixty verses of Homer! Seven equations!

MELCHIOR: Damn homework!

GEORG: *And* Latin Composition!

MORITZ: Homework really messes things up.

OTTO: I'm going home.

GEORG: Me, too. Homework.

ERNST: Me, too. Me, too!

ROBERT: 'Night, Melchior!

MELCHIOR: Sleep tight! *(All leave except for MELCHIOR and MORITZ.)* Why were we ever born!

MORITZ: I'd rather be a cart horse than go to school. What do we have to go to school for anyway? So they can give us examinations! And why do they have to give us examinations? So they can fail us! Seven of us *have* to fail because the classroom only holds *sixty.*—You know, Melchior, ever since Christmas I just haven't felt right. Damn, if it wasn't for father, I'd pack my bag and take off for God knows where.

MELCHIOR: Can we change the subject?

(They walk.)

MORITZ: See that cat over there poking its tail in the air?

MELCHIOR: You believe in omens?

MORITZ: Not sure. Came from over that direction. Doesn't mean anything.

MELCHIOR: *(Philosophically.)* It's my opinion that that's the Charybdis one falls into once he's freed himself from the Scylla of religious delusion.—Let's sit down under that beech tree. There's a warm spring breeze from the mountains. I wish I was a young wood nymph so I could rock and swing all night in the treetops.

MORITZ: Unbutton your vest, Melchior.

MELCHIOR: Mmm, feel how it blows your clothes.

MORITZ: Almost dark. Can't even see your hand. Hey, where are you, Melchior—Melchior, will you tell me something? Do you think that—that our sense of shame is something we learn?

MELCHIOR: I thought about that the other day. I decided it must be something really deep in human nature. Imagine taking off all your clothes in front of your best friend. You wouldn't do it unless he did it, too—at the same time. Or maybe it's just what happens to be in fashion.

MORITZ: If I ever have children—both kinds—they'll sleep in the same room, even in the same bed, and morning and evening they'll help each other dress and undress. And in hot weather they'll wear nothing but a light-wool tunic tied with a leather strap. Growing up like that will make them a lot less embarrassed than we are most of the time.

MELCHIOR: You're right, Moritz! But what if the girls have babies?

MORITZ: Babies?

MELCHIOR: Well, it's like an instinct. I mean, if you raise a boy cat and a girl cat together from the start, all by themselves, with their instinct—I think the girl cat would get pregnant even if no one ever showed them how.

MORITZ: Maybe with animals it just happens.

MELCHIOR: It's the same with people. If your boys and your girls all sleep in the same bed, together, and all of a sudden the boys get those—you know—feelings? Well, I'll just bet that—

MORITZ: Maybe so, but—

MELCHIOR: It's exactly the same with girls. Not that a girl would actu-ally—well, I mean, who knows. But it's not impossible. And you can't ignore natural curiosity.

MORITZ: Can I ask you something?

MELCHIOR: What?

MORITZ: Promise you'll tell?

MELCHIOR: Sure.

MORITZ: The truth?

MELCHIOR: Shake hands on it.—Well? What is it, Moritz?

MORITZ: You done the essay yet?

MELCHIOR: Scaredy cat! No one can hear.

MORITZ: Of course, my children would have to work all day on the farm or in the garden, or play games that take a lot of exercise. And they'll have to ride and tumble—but most of all not sleep in soft beds, like we do. We're so weak. I think people who sleep on hard beds never dream at all.

MELCHIOR: From now on, after grape harvest, I'll sleep in nothing but my hammock. I already shoved my bed behind the stove. It folds up. Once last winter I dreamed that I whipped my dog Ruff so hard he couldn't move. That's about the worst I ever dreamed.—Why're you looking at me like that, Moritz?

MORITZ: You felt it yet—?

MELCHIOR: What?

MORITZ: You know—

MELCHIOR: Here?

MORITZ: M-hm.

MELCHIOR: —Sure!

MORITZ: Me, too—

MELCHIOR: I've known about it for a long time now.—Almost a year.

MORITZ: It felt like a bolt of lightning!

MELCHIOR: Did you have a dream?

MORITZ: Short one. Legs in sky-blue tights climbing over the teacher's desk. At least I *thought* they'd climb over. I only caught a glimpse.

MELCHIOR: Georg dreamed about his mother.

MORITZ: He told you *that?!*

MELCHIOR: Out on the Gallows Road.

MORITZ: *God,* if only you knew what I've been *through* since that night!

MELCHIOR: Guilty conscience?

MORITZ: Guilty *conscience?!* I thought I was *dying!*

MELCHIOR: *Jesus!*

MORITZ: I thought I'd breathed my last. Thought I had some internal ailment. Finally I calmed down, but only because I started writing my memoirs. Oh, Melchior, these last weeks have been hell.

MELCHIOR: I was kind of ready for it when it happened to me. A little ashamed, maybe. But that's about all.

MORITZ: And you're almost a whole year younger.

MELCHIOR: Don't let it get you down, Moritz. There's no set age for the first time. You know that big Lämmermeier kid? Straw-colored hair? Nose like an eagle's beak? He's three years older than me, and Hans Rilow told me that all he still dreams about is sponge cake and apricot jelly.

MORITZ: What does Hans Rilow know?

MELCHIOR: He asked him.

MORITZ: *Asked* him?! God! I could *never* ask anybody *that!*

MELCHIOR: You asked *me*, didn't you?

MORITZ: I guess.—Maybe Hans even made out his Last Will and Testament.—It's like they're playing some weird game on us, and we're supposed to be grateful. God, I never asked for *any*thing like *that!* Why couldn't I just sleep straight through it? My parents could've had a hundred children better than me. But somehow *I* came along, and I *don't know how*, and so it's *all my fault.* Melchior, how did we get *into* this mess?

MELCHIOR: You really don't know?

MORITZ: How could I? I see how hens lay eggs, and they say mother carried me under her heart, but what the hell does that *mean?* I still remember when I was five, I got embarrassed when the Queen of Hearts was turned up, with her dress cut *clear* down to *here.* Well, I got over that. But today it's all I can do to talk to a girl without thinking something disgusting. And I *swear*, Melchior, I don't know *what!*

MELCHIOR: I can tell you if you want. I got it from books and pictures, and from just watching nature. Boy, will you be surprised! It turned me into an atheist. I even told Georg, and he wanted to tell Hans, but Hans had learned about it from his governess when he was only a baby.

MORITZ: I've gone through the encyclopedia from A to Z and it's all words, *words!* Not *one explanation!* God, and the *shame!* Why have an encyclopedia that doesn't answer the most obvious question in the world!

MELCHIOR: You ever watched two dogs run down the street?

MORITZ: *No! God! No!* Not today, Melchior! Please! I've still got Central American History and Louis XIV to think about! Not to mention the sixty verses of Homer, seven equations, and Latin Composition. I'd only fail tomorrow. If I don't keep my nose to the grindstone, I'll *never* make a go of it.

MELCHIOR: Come home with me. In forty-five minutes I'll finish the Homer, the equations, and *both* our Latin essays. I'll put a few mistakes in yours and no one'll ever guess. Mother'll make us some lemonade and we'll have us a nice cozy chat about reproduction.

MORITZ: I *can't!* How can I have a cozy chat about reproduction? But you can do me a favor. Write down everything you know, short and clear as you can, and stuff it between my books tomorrow during gym class.

I'll take it home without knowing and discover it all at once. And I couldn't keep from reading it if I was dead tired. And, well, if you think it'd help, you could make some drawings in the margins.

MELCHIOR: You're just like a girl! All right. At least it won't be dull. One more thing, Moritz.

MORITZ: What?

MELCHIOR: You ever seen a girl?

MORITZ: Oh, sure!

MELCHIOR: Everything?

MORITZ: Everything there is!

MELCHIOR: Then I won't have to draw you any pictures.

MORITZ: It was during the shooting match at the Anatomy Museum. If anybody'd found out, I'd've been kicked out of school. Beautiful! Just beautiful! And so true to nature!

MELCHIOR: I was in Frankfurt last summer with my mama— You going, Moritz?

MORITZ: Homework. 'Night.

MELCHIOR: See you!

SCENE THREE

THEA, WENDLA, and MARTHA walk along arm in arm down the street.

MARTHA: This water sure gets into a person's shoes!

WENDLA: And the wind blows your face!

THEA: And your heart goes bumpety-bump!

WENDLA: Let's go out to the bridge. Ilse said the river's full of trees and bushes. And the boys have a raft there. I heard where Melchi Gabor almost drowned last night.

THEA: Oh, he can swim!

MARTHA: You better bet!

WENDLA: But if he didn't, he'd surely have drowned.

THEA: Your braid's coming undone, Martha. Your braid's coming undone!

MARTHA: Oh, pooh, let it! It does that all the time. Drives me crazy. They won't let wear it short, like yours; they won't let me wear it loose, like Wendla's; and they won't let me wear bangs! And besides that, they make me do my own hair. All because of my crabby old aunts.

WENDLA: Tomorrow I'll bring scissors to religion class, and while you're reciting, I'll cut it off.

MARTHA: Good heavens, Wendla! Father would beat me to a pulp, and mother'd lock me up in the coal shed for three whole nights!

WENDLA: What does he beat you with, Martha?

MARTHA: Sometimes I think they'd miss it if they didn't have a horrid little brat like me around.

THEA: Oh, Martha!

MARTHA: Well, didn't you want to thread a sky-blue ribbon through your petticoat like us?

THEA: Pink satin. Mother says pink suits my pitch black eyes.

MARTHA: Blue is my special color. One night mother pulled me out of bed by the braids—like this—and I landed flat on my hands on the floor. Mother comes up to pray with us every night—

WENDLA: If I were you, I'd have run away a long time ago.

MARTHA: "So there, you see, that's what it'll come to," she says. "You see, you see! Oh, she'll learn soon enough, she will—just you wait! At least I can't blame my mother later when something goes wrong—"

THEA: (Laughs.) Hoo! Hoo!

MARTHA: I don't even know what she was trying to say, do you?

THEA: I don't. Do you, Wendla?

WENDLA: I would have asked her.

MARTHA: I lay there on the floor and screamed till my father came in, and he tore off my petticoat and I ran to the door. "There, you see!" I wanted to run out on the street like that just to show them—

WENDLA: I don't believe a word of it.

MARTHA: I froze. They locked me up. I had to sleep all night in a sack.

THEA: I couldn't sleep in a sack if my life depended on it.

WENDLA: I wish I could sleep in your sack for you sometime.

MARTHA: If only they didn't beat you.

THEA: Didn't you almost smother?

MARTHA: Your head sticks out. They tie it under your chin.

THEA: Then they beat you?

MARTHA: No. Only when there's something special.

WENDLA: What did they hit you with, Martha?

MARTHA: Anything that's handy. Does your mother say it's a sin to eat a piece of bread in bed?

WENDLA: No, of course not.

MARTHA: I almost think they enjoy it. When I have children, I'll let them grow up like the weeds in our rose garden. No one ever bothers about them, and they grow like mad, while the roses bloom worse every summer.

THEA: When I have children, I'll dress them all in pink—pink hats, pink dresses, pinks shoes. Except for their stockings that will be as black as night. And when I go walking with them, they'll parade along ahead of me. What about you, Wendla?

WENDLA: How do you know you'll even have any?

THEA: Why shouldn't we?

MARTHA: That's true, you know. Aunt Euphemia doesn't have any.

THEA: Silly goose! That's because she's not married!

WENDLA: Aunty Bauer was married three times and never had any.

MARTHA: If you ever have children, Wendla, which would you rather have, boys or girls?

WENDLA: Boys! Boys!

THEA: I want boys, too.

MARTHA: Me, too. I'd rather have twenty boys than three girls.

THEA: Girls are so boring.

MARTHA: If I hadn't been born a girl, I sure wouldn't want to be one now.

WENDLA: That's a matter of taste, Martha. I wouldn't want to be anything else. Not even a prince. But I still want only boys.

THEA: That's crazy, Wendla, really crazy.

WENDLA: It must be a thousand times more wonderful to be loved by a man than by a girl.

THEA: Are you saying the forest commissioner loves his wife more than she loves him?

WENDLA: Of course. He's a proud man, and proud of being forest commissioner, because it's all he has. And his wife is absolutely ecstatic because she gets a million times more from him than she's actually worth.

MARTHA: Aren't you proud of yourself, Wendla?

WENDLA: That would be silly.

MARTHA: I'd be proud if I was in your shoes.

THEA: Just look at how she walks—how she dresses—how she holds herself! If that's not pride—

WENDLA: But why? I'm so happy just being a girl that if I weren't I'd kill myself so that next time—

(MELCHIOR walks by and greets them.)

THEA: He's so handsome!

MARTHA: I always think of the young Alexander going to school to Aristotle.

THEA: Oh, God! Greek History! All I remember is how Socrates lay in a barrel while Alexander sold him a donkey's shadow.

WENDLA: They say he's third in his class.

THEA: Professor Knochenbruch says that if he wanted to he could be first.

MARTHA: He has such a beautiful forehead. But his friend has a more soulful look.

THEA: Moritz Stiefel? He's a dumbbell!

MARTHA: I always get along with him.

THEA: He's always embarrassing people. At Hans' children's party he offered me some chocolates. But they were all warm and gooey, Wendla! Isn't that just— Well, he said he'd kept them in his pants pocket too long.

WENDLA: Melchi Gabor told me that evening that he doesn't believe in anything—not in God, or in an afterlife, or in anything else in this world!

SCENE FOUR

Park in front of the high school.

MELCHIOR: Where's Moritz?

GEORG: Boy, is he in for it!

OTTO: One of these days he'll go too far.

LÄMMERMEIER: I wouldn't be in his shoes for anything.

ROBERT: He's sure got some nerve!

MELCHIOR: What're you talking about?

GEORG: Don't look at *me!*

LÄMMERMEIER: How should *I* know?

OTTO: Me, either.

MELCHIOR: I said I want to know!

ROBERT: All right! All right! Moritz Stiefel broke into the faculty room.

MELCHIOR: The faculty room?

OTTO: The faculty room. Right after Latin class.

GEORG: He was the last one to leave. Stayed behind on purpose.

LÄMMERMEIER: I turned the corner and saw him open the door.

MELCHIOR: Go to hell!

LÄMMERMEIER: Unless *he* gets there first.

GEORG: The Headmaster must have left the key in the lock.

ROBERT: Or Moritz has a skeleton key.

OTTO: I wouldn't put it past him.

LÄMMERMEIER: He'll be lucky just to be detained on Sunday.

ROBERT: It'll go in his record.

OTTO: He'll be lucky not to be expelled.

HANS: There he is!

MELCHIOR: White as a sheet!

(MORITZ appears in a state of excitement.)

LÄMMERMEIER: Naughty, naughty, Moritz! What you did!

MORITZ: I didn't! I didn't!

ROBERT: You're shaking.

MORITZ: With happiness! With joy! God!

OTTO: Did they catch you?

MORITZ: I've been promoted, Melchior! Oh, Melchior, I've been promoted! I don't believe it! But there it was, in the record book! I must've read it over twenty times! I've been promoted! *(Smiling.)* I feel like my head's going round in circles! Oh, Melchior, you don't know the hell I've been through, not knowing!

HANS: Congratulations, Moritz. Be glad you got away with it.

MORITZ: You don't know, Hans—it was like my whole life depended on it. I've crept by that door for three weeks now like it was the gates of hell. Then today I noticed it wasn't quite shut. Nothing—nothing in the world could've held me back. So there I was—in the middle of the room—I open the record book—I page through it—I find it—and all that time—I'm shaking—

MELCHIOR: *What* "all that time"?

MORITZ: All that time the door behind me is wide open! I don't know how I ever got out of there and down the stairs! God, I'm trembling, look!

HANS: Did Ernst Roebel get promoted?

MORITZ: Sure, Hans. Ernst Roebel's up the same as me.

ROBERT: You're a liar, Moritz. The classroom only holds sixty people. Counting Roebel, that makes sixty-one.

MORITZ: I know what I know, Robert. Ernst Roebel's moved up the same as me, except for both of us it's provisional. During the first term they'll decide which of us has to go. Poor Roebel! I *know* I'll make it. I couldn't handle it if I didn't.

OTTO: Bet you five marks you fail.

MORITZ: With *what?* You haven't got any money. Besides, I wouldn't want to clean you out. But, God, I'll work like hell! I can say this now, you can believe it or not, 'cause I don't care. If I hadn't been promoted, I'd've shot myself.

ROBERT: Liar!

GEORG: Coward, Moritz!

OTTO: You couldn't kill a fly!

LÄMMERMEIER: Try this! *(Punches MORITZ.)*

MELCHIOR: *(Hits LÄMMERMEIER.)* Come on, Moritz, let's go to the forester's!

GEORG: You really stupid enough to believe that?

MELCHIOR: None of your business! Don't listen to 'em, Moritz! Let's go!

(PROFESSORS HUNGERGURT and KNOCHENBRUCH pass by.)

HUNGERGURT: I simply don't understand, dear colleague, how my best pupil can be so attracted by the very worst of them.

KNOCHENBRUCH: Unbelievable! Simply unbelievable!

SCENE FIVE

Sunny afternoon. MELCHIOR and WENDLA meet in the forest.

MELCHIOR: That you, Wendla? What're you doing up here all by yourself?—I walked in the forest for three hours and never met a soul, and suddenly you come along out of the trees.

WENDLA: It's me, Melchior.

MELCHIOR: If I didn't know you were Wendla Bergmann, I'd've taken you for a wood-sprite that fell from the trees.

WENDLA: It's only Wendla Bergmann. What are you doing here?

MELCHIOR: Thinking.

WENDLA: I'm looking for woodruff. Mother's making May wine. She was coming with me, but then Aunty Bauer came, and she doesn't like climbing, so I came by myself.

MELCHIOR: Found any woodruff?

WENDLA: A whole basketful. Over there under the beech trees it's thick as clover. Right now I'm trying to find my way out. I guess I'm lost. What time is it?

MELCHIOR: Half-past three.—When do they expect you home?

WENDLA: Is that all it is? I lay down in the moss beside the brook and just dreamed for the longest time. Time passed so quickly I thought it must be evening already.

MELCHIOR: If they're not expecting you, let's sit down for a while. My favorite place is under the oak tree over there. Lean your head against the trunk and look up through the branches. It almost hypnotizes you. The ground's still warm from the morning sun.—I've wanted to ask you something for weeks now, Wendla.

WENDLA: I have to be home before five.

MELCHIOR: We'll go together. I'll carry the basket and we can strike out through the bushes and be at the bridge in ten minutes. The most amazing thoughts come to you when you lie here like this with your head propped in your hand.

(They both lie beneath the oak.)

WENDLA: What did you want to ask me, Melchior?

MELCHIOR: I've heard that you spend a lot of time visiting poor people. That you take them food and clothing, and even money. Why do you do that? Because you want to? Or does your mother tell you to?

WENDLA: Mostly because mother tells me. They're poor families with lots of children. And when the father can't find work, they freeze and go hungry. And we have so many things at home that we don't need. But how do you know about that?

MELCHIOR: Do you like going?

WENDLA: Oh, yes! You should know that without asking.

MELCHIOR: But the children are dirty, the women are sick, the houses filthy, and the husbands hate you because you don't have to work.

WENDLA: That's not true, Melchior. And even if it was, that's all the more reason to go.

MELCHIOR: What do you mean, all the more reason?

WENDLA: All the more reason to go. It makes me happy to help them.

MELCHIOR: You go to those poor people because it makes you *happy?*

WENDLA: I go to them because they're poor.

MELCHIOR: And if it didn't make you happy, you wouldn't go?

WENDLA: Is it *my* fault if it makes me happy?

MELCHIOR: And I suppose you think it'll get you into heaven! I've thought a lot about this for a long time now. Is it the miser's fault that visiting sick, dirty children doesn't make him happy?

WENDLA: Oh, but I'm sure it would give you the greatest happiness.

MELCHIOR: And so that's why the miser's condemned to hell! I'm going to write up an essay on that and give it to the Pastor. He's the one who started me thinking about it. He just loves the idea of *sacrifice!* And if he doesn't have an answer, I'll stop going to catechism class, and I won't be confirmed.

WENDLA: Why hurt your poor parents like that? Let them confirm you. They don't cut your head off. If only it wasn't for those awful white dresses of ours and the baggy pants *you* have to wear, we might even enjoy it.

MELCHIOR: There's no such thing as self-sacrifice! There's no such thing as selflessness! The good are happy and the bad are unhappy—and you, Wendla Bergmann, can shake your curls at me all you want!— What were you dreaming about earlier?

WENDLA: Just silly things—foolishness—

MELCHIOR: With your eyes open?

WENDLA: I dreamt I was a poor, poor little beggar girl who had to be out on the street by five every morning. And I had to beg all day long, whether it was rainy, or windy, or whatever. And I was always around rough, hard-hearted people. And when I came home at night, shivering with hunger and cold, I hadn't collected enough money to suit my father and he beat me—beat me—

MELCHIOR: You get those ideas out of crazy fairy tale books. Brutal people like that don't exist anymore.

WENDLA: You're *wrong*, Melchior, they *do!* Martha Bessel gets a beating night after night so that the next day you can still see the *welts!* It makes me so furious I cry at night in my pillow. I've been thinking of how to help her for months now. I'll do *any*thing to change places with her for a *whole week.*

MELCHIOR: Somebody ought to report her father to the police. They'd take her away from him.

WENDLA: I've never been beaten in my life, Melchior. Not one time. I can't even imagine what it's like. I've hit myself, though, just to find out how it must feel, inside. It must be horrible.

MELCHIOR: I don't think it ever improved a child.

WENDLA: What?

MELCHIOR: Being beaten.

WENDLA: Like with this switch. Look how strong and slender it is.

MELCHIOR: A thing like that could draw blood.

WENDLA: Would you hit me with it once?

MELCHIOR: Who?

WENDLA: Me.

MELCHIOR: What's wrong with you, Wendla?

WENDLA: What difference does it make?

MELCHIOR: Be quiet! I'm not going to hit you!

WENDLA: Even if I say it's all right?

MELCHIOR: Don't be silly!

WENDLA: Not even if I begged you, Melchior?

MELCHIOR: Wendla! You're crazy!

WENDLA: I've never been beaten in my life!

MELCHIOR: How can you beg for a thing like that?

WENDLA: Please! Please!

MELCHIOR: I'll teach you how to say please! *(Beating her with the switch.)*

WENDLA: Oh, God! I don't feel it!

MELCHIOR: No wonder with all those skirts on!

WENDLA: Then beat my legs!

MELCHIOR: Wendla! *(Beating her harder.)*

WENDLA: You're not even *touching* me! Not even *touching!*

MELCHIOR: There! I'll show you! There! There! I'll show you! Bitch! Bitch!

(In a rage of passion, tears streaming down his face, MELCHIOR throws aside the switch and begins beating WENDLA with his fists. Suddenly he jumps to his feet, grasps his head in his hands, and runs sobbing into the forest.)

END OF ACT ONE

ACT TWO
SCENE ONE

Evening in Melchior's study. The window is open; a lamp burns on the table.
MORITZ and MELCHIOR are seated on the sofa.

MORITZ: I feel a lot better now, just worked up a little. I slept through Greek. I'm surprised old Zungenschlag didn't pull my ear. God, I was almost late again this morning! I woke up thinking about verb forms! And during breakfast and walking to school I conjugated till I was blue in the face. I must have dozed off at about three this morning. The pen left a blot on my notebook. When Mathilda woke me, the lamp was still smoking and the blackbirds in the lilacs outside my window were chirping for all they were worth. Then all of a sudden I felt miserable again. I put on a collar and ran a brush through my hair. Still it makes you feel good when you've won a victory over yourself.

MELCHIOR: Can I roll you a cigarette.

MORITZ: Thanks, I don't smoke.—I only hope I can keep up this pace. I'll work my butt off if I have to. Ernst has failed six times since school started. Three times in Greek, twice in Knochenbruch's class, and the last time in Literature. I only failed five times—but I won't fail again. At least if Ernst fails, he won't shoot himself. His parents aren't sacrificing everything for him like mine are. He can go off any time he wants and be a mercenary, or a cowboy, or a sailor. But if I fail, my father'd have a heart attack and my mother'd end up in an institution. I just can't let that happen. Before the exam I prayed to God to let me die. It was all I could think of. Anyway, I made it. But I just can't fail again. And if I do, well, I'll just see if I can't manage to break my neck.

MELCHIOR: Life's no easy matter, Moritz. I wouldn't think twice about hanging myself from one of those branches out there.—Where's mother with the tea?

MORITZ: At least it'll calm me down. I'm shaking, Melchior! It's like I'm not in my body. It's all like a dream. I see the quiet garden down there in the moonlight, like a part of eternity. I see misty figures slip from bushes, glide and disappear, breathless and busy. It's like they're holding a council under the chestnut tree there. Let's go down, Melchior.

MELCHIOR: We'll have tea first.

MORITZ: There's a breeze in the branches. It's like my grandmother telling the story of "The Queen without a Head." She was a beautiful,

beautiful queen, beautiful as the sun, more beautiful than all the other girls in the kingdom, except that she was born without a head. She couldn't eat, couldn't drink, couldn't laugh or see—and she couldn't kiss. The only way she could make herself understood to the court was with her soft little hands. And she tapped out declarations of war and death sentences with her delicate feet. Then one day she was conquered by a king who had two heads. And these two heads were always getting into each other's hair so neither could get a word in edgewise. So the chief court magician took the smaller head and set it on the queen's shoulders, and to everyone's surprise it fit perfectly. And so the king and queen got married, and the two heads no longer got in each other's hair. Instead, they were always kissing each other on the forehead, and the cheek, and the mouth, and lived happily ever after.— How stupid! Whenever I see a beautiful girl, I see her without a head—and then all of a sudden I see myself as the queen without a head. Maybe someday they'll put another head on my shoulders.

MRS. GABOR: *(Enters with the steaming tea which she places on the table in front of them.)* Here you are, children. Enjoy your tea. Good evening, Mr. Stiefel. How are you?

MORITZ: Fine, thanks, Mrs. Gabor. I was just watching the dance down in the garden.

MRS. GABOR: Child, what is it? You don't look well.

MORITZ: Nothing. I've been getting to bed too late.

MELCHIOR: He worked all last night, mother.

MRS. GABOR: You should be more careful, Mr. Stiefel. Take better care of yourself. School can never take the place of your health. Go on long walks. At your age that's more important than knowing perfect Middle High German.

MORITZ: Thanks, I will. I can study while I'm walking. But I ought to do my written work at home.

MELCHIOR: We can do it here, together. It'll be easier for us both.

MRS. GABOR: What's the book, Melchior?

MELCHIOR: *Faust.*

MRS. GABOR: Have you read it?

MELCHIOR: Not all the way through.

MORITZ: We just started the "Walpurgis Night" scene.

MRS. GABOR: I think you should have waited another year or two.

MELCHIOR: It's the most beautiful book I've ever read. Why shouldn't I read it?

MRS. GABOR: Because you don't understand it.

MELCHIOR: How do you know? Anyway, I know I don't understand it as deeply as I will someday.

MORITZ: And we always read together. That makes it easier.

MRS. GABOR: You're old enough to know what's good for you and what isn't, Melchior. You're free to do whatever you can answer for to your conscience. And I look forward to the time when I don't have to deny you anything. But even the best can harm you if you're not ready for it. Well, I'll always choose to put my trust in you rather than in some vague educational principles.—If you need anything else, I'll be in my room. *(Goes out.)*

MORITZ: Your mother meant that part where Gretchen has a baby.

MELCHIOR: We hardly gave that a second thought.

MORITZ: Faust himself couldn't have cared less.

MELCHIOR: Besides, how can a little scandal be the high point of a masterpiece like *Faust?* Faust could have promised to marry her and then just walked off, and he wouldn't have been any less guilty in my eyes. And Gretchen could have died of a broken heart instead of going insane and killing her baby and being executed. The way people go crazy over the subject, you'd think the whole world revolves around the penis and the vagina!

MORITZ: That's how I've felt since I read your essay. It slipped out of my French grammar just after vacation started. God, I must've read most of it with my eyes closed! The way you explained it was like I knew it all before I was born, and then forgot it when I came into the world. What hit me hardest was the part about girls. I'll never forget that. Believe me, Melchior, it's better to suffer wrong than to do it. To have to endure such a sweet wrong and still remain innocent has got to be the highest form of happiness.

MELCHIOR: I couldn't care less about happiness that's given as charity!

MORITZ: Why not?

MELCHIOR: I don't want anything I haven't had to fight for!

MORITZ: But would that still be happiness, Melchior? Oh, Melchior, girls enjoy themselves like the gods in heaven! A girl protects herself by her very nature. She keeps herself free from bitterness till the last moment. And then, then, all at once, she feels heaven descend upon her like a soft cloud. A girl is afraid of hell even at the moment she sees paradise spread before her. Her emotions are as fresh as water springing from a rock. A girl lifts up a chalice that no earthly being has touched, a flaming, flickering chalice of nectar that she drinks at a single gulp—I think the satisfaction that a man receives at a time like that must be hollow and dull by comparison.

MELCHIOR: Think what you like, just keep it to yourself, okay? I don't like thinking about it—

SCENE TWO

Living room.

MRS. BERGMANN: *(Hat on, her shawl around her shoulders, and a basket on her arm, enters, her face beaming.)* Wendla dear! Wendla!

WENDLA: *(In a petticoat and stays, comes through a side door, right.)* What is it, mother?

MRS. BERGMANN: You're up already! What a good girl.

WENDLA: Where've you been so early in the morning?

MRS. BERGMANN: Hurry and get dressed. I want you to go to Ina's and take her this basket.

WENDLA: *(Finishes dressing during the following.)* You were at Ina's? How is she? Is she better?

MRS. BERGMANN: Ina had a visit last night. From the stork, Wendla, just imagine. And he brought her a fine new baby boy.

WENDLA: A boy! Oh, I'm so glad! That must be why she had influenza for so long.

MRS. BERGMANN: A really splendid boy.

WENDLA: I've got to see him! That means I'm an aunt for the third time now. One girl and two boys.

MRS. BERGMANN: And what fine boys! That's what happens when you live so close to the church roof. Tomorrow it will be two years exactly since your sister walked up the aisle in her white wedding dress.

WENDLA: Were you there when the stork brought him, mother?

MRS. BERGMANN: He had just flown out of sight.—Wouldn't you like to pin a rose here in front?

WENDLA: Mother! Why didn't you get there earlier!

MRS. BERGMANN: I think he might have left something for you, too— a brooch perhaps.

WENDLA: I'm so disappointed!

MRS. BERGMANN: I said he brought a brooch for you, Wendla!

WENDLA: I don't need any more brooches!

MRS. BERGMANN: Then don't complain! What more do you want?

WENDLA: I want to know if he flew in through the window or down the chimney.

MRS. BERGMANN: You'll have to ask Ina that. Ina will tell you all about it. She talked to him for a whole half-hour.

WENDLA: I'll ask her when I get there.

MRS. BERGMANN: Don't forget now. And tell me all about it when you come home. In through the window or down the chimney.

WENDLA: Or maybe I'll ask the chimney-sweep. He should know better than anyone.

MRS. BERGMANN: No, Wendla! What would the chimney-sweep know about storks! All he does is babble about things he doesn't under-stand.—Why are you staring down at the street like that?

WENDLA: It's a man, mother! Three times the size of an ox and with feet the size of steamships!

MRS. BERGMANN: (Rushing to the window.) Don't be silly, child! That's impossible!

WENDLA: (Simultaneously.) He's holding a bed frame under his chin and fiddling "The Watch on the Rhine."—Oh! He just went around the corner!

MRS. BERGMANN: Oh, Wendla! You're still such a child! Frightening your simple-minded mother like that! When will you get some sense in that head of yours! I've almost given up hope.

WENDLA: So have I, mother. It's sad how little I know. Here I have a sis-ter who's been married for two-and-a-half years, and I'm an aunt for the third time, and I don't even know how it happens.—Don't be cross with me, mother. Who else can I ask? Please tell me. I'm so ashamed of myself. Please, mother, say something. Don't scold me. How does it happen? I'm fourteen years old. How can you still expect me to believe in the stork?

MRS. BERGMANN: What's gotten into you? The things you think of! How can you expect me to—

WENDLA: But why? Why not? How can it be ugly when it makes every-one so happy?

MRS. BERGMANN: Dear God!—Come here, child, I'll tell you.—Oh, but just not today, Wendla. Whenever you say, but just not today—

WENDLA: Today, mother! Right now! How can I be calm when you're so upset?

MRS. BERGMANN: I can't, Wendla!

WENDLA: I'll kneel here at your feet and put my head in your lap—and then you'll put your apron over my head and talk and talk like you were the only one in the room. I won't move, I won't cry, I'll just listen.

MRS. BERGMANN: Heaven knows, Wendla, it's not my fault. God can see into my soul.—Well, all right, child—come here—I'll tell you how you came into the world.

WENDLA: *(From beneath the apron.)* I'm listening!

MRS. BERGMANN: *(Beside herself.)* It's no use! I can't! I can't answer you! I deserve to have you taken away from me—

WENDLA: Oh, God!

MRS. BERGMANN: To have a child—do you understand, Wendla—?

WENDLA: Hurry, mother, I can't stand it!

MRS. BERGMANN: To have a child—a person must—must love the man she's married to—she must love him—as one can only love a husband. She must love him so completely, with all her heart, that—that there are no words to describe it. She must love him, Wendla, in a way that at your age you could never love— So now you know.

WENDLA: God—God—

MRS. BERGMANN: Now you know the trials that lie ahead of you.

WENDLA: And that's all?

MRS. BERGMANN: So help me!—Now take the basket and go to Ina's. She has some chocolates for you, and some cakes.—Come here, child. Let me look at you again. There now! Laced boots, silk gloves, sailor's blouse—and a rose for your hair.—But your dress is much too short now, Wendla.

WENDLA: Have you bought the meat for lunch yet, mother?

MRS. BERGMANN: God bless you.—The first chance I get, I must sew a hand of ruffling around the bottom.

HANS RILOW enters with a light in his hand, locks the door behind him and lifts the lid.

HANS: Hast thou prayed tonight, Desdemona? *(Pulls out a reproduction of Palmo Vecchio's "Venus" from inside his shirt.)* It doesn't look like you've been praying, my pretty—just lying there waiting for anyone who might come along—like you waited for me in Mr. Schlessinger's shop-window.—Those limbs, those hips, those breasts—waiting for me. How could the old master have endured painting you—only fourteen years old!—Will you visit me in my dreams? In my dreams I'll take you in my arms, I'll kiss you till your breath is gone.—You mustn't think I'm killing you for any frivolous reason. My nights will be lonely without you. And I'm not murdering you because I've grown tired of you. How could I ever have enough of you? But you're sucking the life out of my bones, you're crooking my back, you're robbing me of my youth. It's you or me. And I'm the stronger.—Oh, you're not the first I've had—or had to murder. There was "Psyche" and "Io" and "Galatea"— and even a little "Cupid"—and then the one I abducted from my father's secret drawer; and the "Leda" I found in my brother's note-book. Six, six of them have gone on this downward path to oblivion. Let that be some comfort, and don't beg me with your eyes, don't antagonize me.—It's for *your* sins you must die, not for mine. It's my only defense against myself.—Once you're out of my life, my conscience will be free and I'll get my strength back again—until someone else takes your place. But at least I'll be cured for a while. Another three months, my love, and your naked body would have begun eating away at my brain like the sun at a ball of butter.—There's no other way. It's looking at you, lying there, like that, that makes me kill myself like this!—One more kiss on your radiant body, your child-like, budding breasts, your sweetly rounded—oh, your cruel knees—

It is the cause, it is the cause, my soul.

Let me not name it to you, you chaste stars!

It is the cause!

(The picture falls into the depths; he closes the lid.)

SCENE FOUR

Hayloft. MELCHIOR lies on his back in the fresh hay. WENDLA climbs up the ladder.

WENDLA: So *this* is where you ran off to hide? Everyone's looking for you. The wagon's gone off again. You ought to be helping. There's a storm blowing up.

MELCHIOR: Get away from me! Get away!

WENDLA: What's the matter? Why are you hiding your face?

MELCHIOR: Get out! Get out! I'll throw you down the ladder!

WENDLA: I wouldn't leave now for anything. *(Kneels beside him.)* Come out to the meadows, Melchior. It's so dark and stuffy in here. So what if we get soaked to the skin? What do we care? It's so dark and stuffy in here. So what if we get soaked to the skin? What do we care?

MELCHIOR: The hay smells so good. The sky outside must be black as death by now. All I can see in here is the red poppy burning there on your dress—here—and your heart beating—

WENDLA: Don't kiss me, Melchior—don't kiss me—

MELCHIOR: Your heart—I hear it—beating—

WENDLA: You have to love a person—that you—kiss—don't—don't—

MELCHIOR: There's no such thing as love!—It's all selfishness and ego! I don't love you any more than you love me.

WENDLA: Don't—don't, Melchior—

MELCHIOR: Wendla!

WENDLA: Oh, Melchior! Don't—don't—

SCENE FIVE

MRS. GABOR sits, writes.

MRS. GABOR: Dear Mr. Stiefel,

I write to you with great sadness. I have considered and reconsidered your request for the last twenty-four hours. Believe me when I say that I am unable to provide you with the passage money to America. In the first place, I don't have that much on hand; and in the second, if I did, I couldn't in any good conscience help you to carry out so rash and serious a plan. Please do not see in my refusal any failure in my affection towards you. I am, of course, prepared to write your parents to convince them that you have done everything possible during this school term, and that to punish you for your failure to be promoted would not only be unjust, but a blow to both your mental and physical health. Quite frankly, my dear Mr. Stiefel, I consider your implied threat to take your own life in the event that you are unable to flee to be a momentary loss of judgment which has somewhat alienated my sympathies. Your attempt to make me seem responsible for your possible commission of a grievous sin seems very much like blackmail. Such behavior is the least I should have expected of you. I realize, however, that the shock you have suffered may well have made you unaware of your action.—I hope that by now you find yourself in a better frame of mind. Accept the matter as it stands. I do not believe that it is in any way proper to judge a young man by his school marks. We have too many examples of very bad students becoming remarkable men, and, conversely, of excellent students distinguishing themselves in no particular way whatever. I assure you, however, that your misfortune will in no way be allowed to alter your relationship with Melchior. I will always be pleased to see my son in the company of a young man who—let the world judge him as it may—has won from me my fullest sympathy. And so, my dear Mr. Stiefel, be brave. If we all committed suicide as the solution to our problems, soon there would be no one left in the world. Let me hear from you again soon, and accept these heartfelt greetings from your ever steadfast and motherly friend,

Fanny G.

SCENE SIX

The Bergmann garden in morning sunlight.

WENDLA: Why did you slip from the room? To look for violets. Because mother can see me smiling. Why can't you keep your lips together anymore? I don't know. I really don't know. There are no words.—The path is like a plush carpet. Not a stone. Not a thorn. My feet aren't even touching the ground.—Oh, God, I slept so sweetly last night. This is where they used to be. I feel as solemn as a nun at communion.—Dear little violets.—All right, mother, I'll put on my old sack-dress.—Oh, God, why doesn't someone come that I can throw my arms around his neck and tell him everything!

Scene Seven

Twilight. The sky is slightly overcast. The path snakes its way through the low brush and reeds. Nearby, the river is heard flowing past.

MORITZ: It's better this way. I don't belong to them. Let them beat their heads together if they want to. I'll just close the door behind me and step out into the open. I don't like being pushed around. I never pushed before. Why should I push now? I don't have a contract with God! However you look at this business, they still forced me. It's not my parents' fault. Besides, I think they're prepared for the worst. They were old enough to know what they were doing when they brought me into the world. If I hadn't been a baby at the time, I'd have chosen to come as someone else. Why should I have to suffer because of them! I think I must be crazy. If someone gives me a mad dog as a present, then I give him his dog back. And if he doesn't want to take back his mad dog, then I act like a properly kind person and—
    I think I must be insane!
    A person is born completely by accident, but after mature consideration he's not allowed to— It's enough to make you want to shoot yourself. At least the weather seems considerate. It's looked like rain all day long, but now it's nice again. A strange peace reigns over nature. Nothing shrill—nothing disturbing. Heaven and earth are like a transparent spider's web. And everything seems to feel so fine. The countryside is lovely as a lullaby. "Sleep, little princeling, sleep!" as Miss Prudentia sang. It's a pity the way she held her hands—so awkward. The last time I danced was at the St. Cecilia's Day Picnic. Her silk dress was cut down back and front. Down to her waist in back, and so low in front it drove you out of your mind. She couldn't have had anything on underneath.—That might be something to keep me here. More for curiosity's sake. That must be an extraordinary feeling—like being swept along in a flood. How can I ever go back and tell them I haven't— Imagine being born human without ever knowing the most human of feelings.—You're from Egypt, sir, and haven't seen the pyramids?

I don't want to cry again. I don't want to think of my funeral. Melchior will put a wreath on my coffin. Pastor Kahlbauch will comfort my parents. Headmaster Sonnenstich will cite examples from history.—I probably won't get a gravestone. I'd like an urn of snow-white marble on a base of black granite. But thank God I won't miss it. Memorials are for the living, not the dead.

I'd need at least a year to say good-bye to everyone I can think of. I don't want to cry again. I'm satisfied just to be able to look back without bitterness. All the wonderful evenings I spent together with Melchior—under the willows at the river, at the forester's cottage, by the ruins of the old castle.—When the time comes to do it, I'll think as hard as I can about whipped cream. Not that whipped cream will keep me from doing it, but it'll stop me up so it won't run all out in my pants—and it has a pleasant aftertaste.—I always thought people were worse than they are. But I've never met anyone who didn't try his best. I feel sorry for them for having to put up with me.

I go to the altar like a sacrifice for next year's harvest. Here I stand, drinking life to the dregs, drop by drop—the mysterious terror of taking off. I weep with the sadness of my fate. Life turned me a cold shoulder. I see solemn, friendly eyes beckon to me from the other side: the headless queen, the headless queen—sympathy waiting for me with gentle arms.—Your commandments are for children! I've earned my free ride! When the shell pulls back, the butterfly flutters away. Mirages no longer torment us. Why should I play these mad games with illusion? The mists are dissolving. Life is a matter of taste.

(ILSE, her clothes torn and with a bright kerchief around her head, enters and grabs MORITZ from behind by the shoulders.)

MORITZ: Ilse!

ILSE: What are you looking for?

MORITZ: Why did you scare me?!

ILSE: What are you looking for? What did you lose?

MORITZ: Why did you scare me like that?!

ILSE: I'm just coming from town. On my way home.

MORITZ: I don't know what I lost.

ILSE: Then looking won't do much good.

MORITZ: Damn you! Damn!

ILSE: I haven't been home for four days.

MORITZ: Sneaking up on me like that!

ILSE: I'm wearing my dancing slippers. Mother'll be surprised when she sees me. Come with me as far as the house.

MORITZ: Where have you been knocking around this time?

ILSE: Oh, all over the place. She'll be furious.

MORITZ: Were you posing for someone?

ILSE: One of them's painting me as a saint on a Corinthian column. He's a nut. I step on a tube of paint and he wipes his brush in my hair. I slap him one and he throws his palette at me. I knock over his easel, he comes after me with his painting stick, leaping over the divan, the tables, chairs, around the whole studio. Then I spot a sketch behind the stove. I tell him to behave or I'll tear it to pieces. He swore a truce then but ended up just kissing and kissing and kissing me like a demon.

MORITZ: Where do you sleep when you stay in town?

ILSE: Last night we were at "Karl's," and the night before at "The Red Garter," and Sunday at "The Copper Kettle." We had champagne at "Pandinsky's." And Adolar drank from an ashtray and almost wore out his guitar. I was so drunk they had to put me to bed.—Do you still go to school, Moritz?

MORITZ: No. No—I'm getting out this term.

ILSE: About time, too. It's amazing how time flies when you're earning money. Do you still remember how we used to play cops and robbers? Wendla Bergmann and you and me and the others? When you used to come out and drink warm goat's milk at our house? What's Wendla doing? I saw her watching the flood not long ago. And Melchi Gabor—does he still look so melancholy? We used to stand across from each other in music class.

MORITZ: He philosophizes.

ILSE: Wendla came over not long ago and brought my mother some preserves. I was posing for Landauer that day. For a Madonna and Child. He's not only an idiot, he's disgusting.—Do you have a hangover?

MORITZ: From last night. We sopped it up like sponges. I staggered home at five this morning.

ILSE: I can tell.—Were there any girls?

MORITZ: Sure. Arabella the Andalusian Beer Nymph! The innkeeper left her alone with us the whole night.

ILSE: You look like it. I never get a hangover. At Carnival last year I didn't get into bed or out of my clothes for three days and nights. I just went from one party to another without stop. Henry found me the third night.

MORITZ: Was he looking for you?

ILSE: He stumbled over my arm. I was passed out in the snow. That's how I happened to move in with him. I didn't leave his house for two weeks. God, what a time that was! In the morning I had to throw on his Persian bathrobe and in the evening traipse around in a black page's costume. He must have photographed me in a million different positions, from Ganymede to a female Nebuchadnezzar on all fours. And all the while he raved on about murder, and shooting, and suicide, and coal smoke. Early every morning he brought a pistol to bed, loaded it, pointed it at my breast, and threatened to shoot. And he would, too, Moritz, he would have, too. Then he'd put the thing in his mouth like a peashooter. They say it heightens your instinct of self-preservation. Ugh! That bullet would have gone straight through my spine!

MORITZ: Is Henry still alive?

ILSE: What do I know!—In the ceiling over the bed there was a big mirror. That little room seemed tall as a tower and bright as an opera house.—You saw yourself hanging down live from the sky. Oh, and the terrible dreams I had.—God, o God, won't it ever be daylight!—Goodnight, Ilse. When you're asleep you're so beautiful I could murder you!

MORITZ: Is this Henry still alive?

ILSE: Thank God, no!—One day when he was out buying some absinthe I threw on my coat and slipped into the street. Carnival had ended. The police picked me up and asked what I was doing in men's clothes? They took me to the station. And Nohl, Pandinsky, Oikonomopulos, and the whole Priapia gang came and bailed me out and took me home to Adolar's. I've stuck kind of close to them ever since. Nohl's a pig, Pandinsky's a monkey, Oikonomopulos's a camel, and then there's all the rest—but that's why I love them, and I wouldn't need another soul even if the world was made up of angels and millionaires!

MORITZ: I have to get back, Ilse.

ILSE: Come as far as the house.

MORITZ: But why? What for?

ILSE: For some warm goat's milk. I'll curl your hair and tie a little bell around your neck. And we even have a rocking horse you can play with.

MORITZ: I have to get back. I've still got the Sassanids, the Sermon on the Mount and the Parallelepipedon on my conscience.—Good night, Ilse.

ILSE: Sweet dreams!—Do all of you still go down to the wigwam where Melchi Gabor buried his tomahawk?—Brr! By the time any of you are fit for anything, I'll be ready for the junk heap! *(Hurries off.)*

MORITZ: *(Alone.)* Just one word and I could have—*(Calling.)* Ilse! Ilse!— Thank God she can't hear me. I'm not in the mood. For something like that you have to be really clearheaded and feel good. Too bad to lose the chance though!—I'll tell them there was a huge crystal mirror over my bed, and that I made her prance in front of me in long black stockings and patent-leather boots, and very long kid gloves and black velvet around her neck, and how I lost control and smothered her in the pillow. And I'll smile when they talk about sex—I'll scream!—I'll scream!—I want to be you, Ilse! You!—Phallopia!—Oblivion! Blackness! Nothingness!—It's draining my strength!—This child of happy fortune!—This child of light and sun!—This glorious temptress crossing my path of misery!—Oh!—Oh!

(In the bushes at the river's edge.) I've come back again without even trying—the grassy bank. The high tapers look like they've grown since yesterday. But the view between the willows is just the same. The river flows like molten lead.—Just so I don't forget—*(Takes Mrs. Gabor's letter from his pocket and sets fire to it.)* The sparks—back and forth.—Before I struck the match I could still see the grass and a streak of light on the horizon. It's dark now. I won't go home anymore.

END OF ACT TWO

ACT THREE
Scene One

Faculty room. On the walls hang portraits of Pestalozzi and J. J. Rousseau. Around a green table, over which burn several gas lamps, sit PROFESSORS AFFENSCHMALZ, KNÜPPELDICK, HUNGERGURT, KNOCHEN-BRUCH, ZUNGENSCHLAG, and FLIEGENTOD. HEADMASTER SONNENSTICH sits at the upper end of the table on an elevated chair. HABEBALD, the school porter, cowers near the door.

SONNENSTICH: Has any of you gentlemen any further remarks to make?—Gentlemen! If we find ourselves in a position which prevents us from circumventing the necessity of applying to the Ministry of Education for the expulsion of our delinquent pupil, then it is for the most weighty of reasons. It is for the reason that we have no alternative but to atone for the evil that has already befallen us, and, similarly, in order to defend our institution in future against like catastrophe. It is for the reason that we must chastise our delinquent pupil for the demoralizing influence which he has exerted upon his fellow classmates. And, above all else, it is for the reason that we must strive to hinder him from exerting a similar influence upon the remainder of his classmates. It is for the reason, gentlemen—and this is perhaps the weightiest of all the reasons—it is for the reason that we must defend our institution against the ravages of a suicide epidemic such as has already spread through various other schools, and which to date has defied all efforts to instill in the pupil—by means of the educative process—a sense of duty towards an educated existence.—Has any of you gentlemen any further remarks to make?

KNÜPPELDICK: I am no longer capable of preventing myself from arriving at the conclusion that the time has come at last to open a window somewhere in this room.

ZUNGENSCHLAG: An a-a-atmosphere p-p-prevails here that resembles the subter-ter-teranean ca-ca-catacombs, or the a-a-archives of the law courts in old Wetzler.

SONNENSTICH: Habebald!

HABEBALD: Yes, sir!

SONNENSTICH: Open the window! God be praised there is sufficient atmosphere outside.—Has any of you gentlemen any further remarks to make?

FLIEGENTOD: If it is the collective opinion of my most eminent colleagues that a window be opened, then I shall in no manner whatsoever hinder that design. However, my sole regard is that the window to be opened be not immediately behind my back.

SONNENSTICH: Habebald!

HABEBALD: Yes, sir!

SONNENSTICH: Open the other window instead!—Has any of you gentlemen any further remarks to make?

HUNGERGURT: Without wishing to obscure the controversy regarding the window with my own impositions, I wish merely to draw attention to the fact that the other window has been walled up since the autumn holidays.

SONNENSTICH: Habebald!

HABEBALD: Yes, sir!

SONNENSTICH: Leave the other window closed!—I feel the necessity, gentlemen, to put the matter to a vote. I will ask those of my colleagues who are in favor of opening the window in question to rise. *(Counting.)* One. Two. Three—*(Counts again.)* One. Two. Three.—Habebald!

HABEBALD: Yes, sir!

SONNENSTICH: You will leave the one window which is capable of being opened closed as well!—If I may venture an opinion concerning the atmosphere, I should say that it leaves nothing to be desired.—Has any of you gentlemen any further remarks to make?—Gentlemen! Let us suppose that we fail to apply to the Ministry of Education for the expulsion of our delinquent pupil—we may be certain then that that same Ministry of Education would hold *us* responsible for the evil that has befallen us. Of the various schools affected by the suicide epidemic, those in which twenty-five percent of the pupils have been ravaged by the epidemic have been suspended by the Ministry of Education. It is our duty, as protectors and guardians of our institution, to defend it against any such shattering blow. It is a matter of eternal regret that we are unable to consider any of our delinquent pupil's qualifications as mitigating circumstances. Although a procedure of leniency in regard to our delinquent pupil was justifiable, yet, under the circumstances, and insofar as the institution is at the moment in grievous straits—it is *not*, gentlemen, in *any way* justifiable. We find ourselves in need, therefore, to pass judgment upon our delinquent pupil ourselves.—Habebald!

HABEBALD: Yes, sir!

SONNENSTICH: You may bring him up!

(HABEBALD goes out.)

ZUNGENSCHLAG: If it has be-be-been determined that the prevailing a-a-atmosphere leaves li-li-little to be-be-be desired, then I propose that during the summer holidays the other window be walled up as well!

FLIEGENTOD: If our esteemed colleague Professor Zungenschlag finds the premises not suitably ventilated, then I should like to propose that our esteemed colleague have a ventilator installed in his frontal cavity.

ZUNGENSCHLAG: Th-th-this is an outrage! I ne-ne-needn't countenan-an-ance a-a-any such insolence! I am m-m-m-master of m-my f-f-f-f-f-f-five senses!

SONNENSTICH: I must request of my colleagues Professors Fliegentod and Zungenschlag, that they endeavor to maintain a reasonable degree of decorum. It appears to me that our delinquent pupil is on his way up the stairs.

(HABEBALD opens the door. MELCHIOR enters, pale but composed, and stops in front of the assemblage.)

SONNENSTICH: You will step closer!—Mr. Rentier Stiefel, after being informed of his son Moritz Stiefel's impious deed, set about to search among his son's effects, in hope of somehow discovering a trace of the cause of that most despicable outrage. In doing so, he came upon—in a place which seems to bear no relevance to the present situation—a handwritten document which, even though it does not illuminate the source of the despicable outrage, does, in any event, provide us with an all too lucid presentation of *this* delinquent pupil's state of moral degradation. The document in question is twenty pages in length, handwritten, in dialogue form, entitled *Copulation,* supplied with life-sized illustrations and rank with such shameless indecencies that would meet the most perverted demands which an abandoned libertine might make of pornographic literature.

MELCHIOR: I—

SONNENSTICH: You will hold your tongue!—After the father of our now deceased pupil had delivered into our hands the aforementioned document, we assured that distracted man that we would at all costs discover its author. We therefore set about comparing the handwriting of the profligate's fellow pupils, and have come to the unanimous conclusion among the faculty, as well as with the professional opinion of our esteemed colleague in calligraphy, that the handwriting contained in this document bears the most strikingly convincing similarity to *yours!*

MELCHIOR: I—

SONNENSTICH: You will hold your tongue!—Regardless of the crushing fact of the similarity which has been attested to by unimpeachable authorities, we feel ourselves justified for the present in abstaining from any further measures, until we have first circumstantially interrogated the delinquent pupil concerning his crime against decency and the resulting instigation to self-destruction which arose therefrom.

MELCHIOR: I—

SONNENSTICH: You will answer the precisely formulated questions which I will put to you one after the other with a single and unassuming Yes or No.—Habebald!

HABEBALD: Yes, sir!

SONNENSTICH: The document! *(HABEBALD brings the document.)*—I shall ask our secretary Professor Fliegentod to record all that occurs from here on as nearly verbatim as possible. *(To MELCHIOR.)* Are you acquainted with this document?

MELCHIOR: Yes.

SONNENSTICH: Is the handwriting of this document your handwriting?

MELCHIOR: Yes.

SONNENSTICH: Does this obscene document owe its conception to you?

MELCHIOR: Yes. But, sir, would you please show me just one obscenity in it?

SONNENSTICH: You will answer the precisely formulated questions which I will put to you with a simple and unassuming Yes or No!

MELCHIOR: I wrote nothing but what is a very well known fact to all of you.

SONNENSTICH: The insolence!

MELCHIOR: Please show me where there is one offense against decency.

SONNENSTICH: If you have any idea of making a fool of me—! Habebald!

HABEBALD: Yes, sir!

SONNENSTICH: This is Langenscheidt's *Manual for the Three-Hour Course in Agglutinative Volapük!!*

MELCHIOR: I—

SONNENSTICH: I shall ask our secretary, Professor Fliegentod, to close the minutes.

MELCHIOR: I—

SONNENSTICH: You will hold your tongue!—Habebald!

HABEBALD: Yes, sir!

SONNENSTICH: Take him downstairs!

Cemetery. Pouring rain. PASTOR KAHLBAUCH, holding an open umbrella, stands at the foot of an open grave. At his right are RENTIER STIEFEL, his friend ZIEGENMELKER, and UNCLE PROBST. At his left are HEADMASTER SONNENSTICH and PROFESSOR KNOCHEN-BRUCH. SCHOOLBOYS complete the circle. ILSE and MARTHA are seen at a slight distance, in front of a half-ruined gravestone.

KAHLBAUCH: He who rejects the Grace with which the Eternal Father has blessed him born in sin shall die the death of the spirit.—He who lives in willful carnal denial of the honor due the Godhead and serves the cause of iniquity shall die the death of the body.—But he who wantonly denies the cross which the All-Merciful has laid upon him for his sin's sake, verily, verily I say unto you, he will die the Everlasting Death. *(Throws a shovelful of earth into the grave.)* But let us who wander continuously upon the path of thorns give praise and thanks unto the All-Merciful God for His inscrutable elections to Grace. For as surely as this soul died a three-fold death, just as surely will the Lord God lead the righteous into bliss and Eternal Life.

RENTIER STIEFEL: *(Voice choked with tears, throws a shovelful of earth into the grave.)* He was no son of mine! He was no son of mine! I never liked him even as a child!

SONNENSTICH: *(Throws a shovelful of earth into the grave.)* Suicide, as the most serious conceivable offense against the moral world order, is also the most serious conceivable proof for that moral world order, in that the suicide relieves that moral world order of the need to pass judgment upon him, and in doing so gives proof of its very existence.

KNOCHENBRUCH: *(Throws a shovelful of earth into the grave.)* Dissolute—dissipated—debauched—depraved—and degenerate!

UNCLE PROBST: *(Throws a shovelful of earth into the grave.)* How can a child treat his parents so unfeelingly—?

ZIEGENMELKER:—his father, his father who for all these years entertained no higher thought than the welfare of his child!

KAHLBAUCH: *(Pressing RENTIER STIEFEL's hand.)* We know that for them who love the Lord all things work together for good. Corinthians I, 12:15.—Think of the mother in sorrow and seek to replace him she has lost with redoubled love.

SONNENSTICH: *(Pressing RENTIER STIEFEL's hand.)* Very likely we would not have been able to promote him in any case.

KNOCHENBRUCH: *(Pressing RENTIER STIEFEL's hand.)* You may entrust yourself to my guidance. What miserable weather! Enough to make one's bowels growl. We must get after it at once with a hot grog. Such weather can affect the heart.

RENTIER STIEFEL: *(Blowing his nose.)* He was no son of mine—he was no son of mine—

(RENTIER STIEFEL is led off by PASTOR KAHLBAUCH, HEADMASTER SONNENSTICH, PROFESSOR KNOCHENBRUCH, UNCLE PROBST, and ZIEGENMELKER.—The rain has let up.)

HANS: *(Throws a shovelful of earth into the grave.)* Rest in peace, old boy. Give my best to all my murdered brides, and to God. Poor little dumbbell. They'll probably put a scarecrow on your grave for all your angelic simplicity—

GEORG: Did they find the pistol?

ROBERT: Why should they want to look for a pistol?

ERNST: Did you see him, Robert?

ROBERT: It's a goddamned fraud! *Who* saw him? *Who?*

OTTO: That's right! They threw a cover over him.

GEORG: Was his tongue hanging out?

ROBERT: My God, his eyes! That's why they covered him up.

OTTO: Horrible!

HANS: Are you sure he hanged himself?

ERNST: They say his whole head was blown off.

OTTO: Oh, go on! I don't believe it!

ROBERT: I even held the noose in my hands! Can you imagine not covering a hanged body?

GEORG: What a vulgar way to go!

OTTO: He still owes me five marks. We made a bet on whether he'd fail or not.

HANS: It's all *your* fault he's lying there! You called him a liar!

OTTO: Go to hell! You think I don't have to study all night, too? If he'd learned his Literary History of Greece, he wouldn't have had to kill himself!

ERNST: Done your essay yet?

OTTO: Just the introduction.

ERNST: I don't know what to write.

GEORG: Weren't you there when Affenschmalz made the assignment?

HANS: I threw together something from Democritus.

OTTO: Have you finished your Virgil for tomorrow?

(The BOYS go off. MARTHA and ILSE approach the grave.)

ILSE: Hurry! Hurry! The grave diggers are coming!

MARTHA: Wouldn't it be better to wait, Ilse?

ILSE: Why? We'll bring fresh ones. We'll keep bringing fresh flowers all the time. They'll grow all over the place.

MARTHA: I guess you're right. *(Tosses an ivy wreath into the grave. ILSE opens her apron to let a shower of fresh anemones fall onto the coffin.)* I'll dig up roses in the garden at home. I know they'll beat me for it, but at least they'll be able to blossom.

ILSE: And I'll water them every time I come by. I'll bring forget-me-nots from the brook and irises from home.

MARTHA: It's going to be just beautiful.

ILSE: I had just crossed the bridge when I heard the shot.

MARTHA: The poor thing.

ILSE: And I know why he did it, too, Martha.

MARTHA: Did he say anything to you?

ILSE: Parallelepipedon! But don't tell anyone.

MARTHA: Cross my heart.

ILSE: Here's the pistol.

MARTHA: So that's why they didn't find it.

ILSE: I took it from his hand when I passed the next morning.

MARTHA: Give it to me, Ilse! Please give it to me!

ILSE: No, I want to keep it as a remembrance.

MARTHA: Ilse? Is it true that he's buried there without a head?

ILSE: He must have loaded it with water. The high tapers were all splattered with blood. His brains were hanging from the willows.

SCENE THREE

The Gabor house.

MRS. GABOR:—They needed a scapegoat! They couldn't stand up to their own guilt, so they blamed it on him! Foolish old pedants! What am I supposed to do now that Melchior's fallen into their nets? Help them carry out the execution?

MR. GABOR: I've watched your ingenious method of education for fifteen years now without a word, even if it was contrary to everything I believed in. A child is not a plaything. A child deserves our serious attention. But I thought that your charm and intelligence might take the place of my more serious principles. Obviously I was mistaken. I'm not blaming you, Fanny. But it's time we make amends for the wrongs we've done him.

MRS. GABOR: And the reformatory is your way of doing that? I'll fight you until there's not another drop of blood left in me. You might as well sentence him to death. If he's not a criminal now, he'll become one there. What else can happen? And I'm not aware of doing him any wrong. My only crime is having given him character and nobility. What has he done that's so terrible? I'm not making excuses for him, but it's not his fault that he's been hounded out of school. And if it was his fault, he's surely paid for it. Theoretically you may be perfectly correct. But I will not allow my only son to be violently hounded to his death!

MR. GABOR: That's not for us to say, Fanny. It's a risk that we accepted along with our happiness. The weak fall by the wayside. And in the last analysis it's not the worst thing possible when the inevitable comes when it must come. Heaven save us from that! Our duty at this moment is to steady the waverer as long as reason prevails. You say that it's not his fault that he has been hounded out of school. I suppose that if he hadn't been hounded out it wouldn't be his fault either!—You're far too easy going, Fanny. Matters that can fundamentally damage character mean nothing to you. Women aren't meant to judge such things. A person capable of writing what Melchior wrote must be rotten to the core. His very marrow is tainted. Any half-way healthy organism couldn't possibly have sunk to such a level. None of us are saints; we all stray from time to time; but what he has written involves a *principle*. What he has written is not the result of an accidental lapse. It proves beyond any doubt that his action was deliberate, and that he has a depraved inclination towards immorality for immorality's sake. As a jurist I have no choice but to call him spiritually corrupt. Is there any remedy for his condition? I don't know. But for the sake of our conscience, we must act at once. There's no other hope. No more arguing now, Fanny. I know how difficult this must be for you. I know how you idolize the boy; he's the mirror of your own gentleness. But you must be selfless now for your son's sake.

MRS. GABOR: How can I fight a thing like you? You have to be a man to talk like that! You have to be a man to be so blinded by dead, unfeeling words! You have to be a man not to see something staring you in the face!—I've dealt with Melchior from the first as responsibly and thoughtfully as was humanly possible, because I knew how impressionable he was. And are we now to be blamed for this coincidence, this accident? Tomorrow a tile could fall from a roof and hit you on the head, and your friend comes along—your father, and instead of tending to your wounds he steps on your face!—I will not stand by and see my child massacred! If I do, then I am not his mother.—It's inconceivable. It's beyond belief. What is so terrible about what he has written? The proof of his innocence, of his artlessness, of his childish immaturity, is that he *could* write such a thing. If that deed is morally corrupt, than you know nothing about human nature. Then you are an unfeeling bureaucrat and unspeakably narrow. If Melchior goes to the reformatory because you send him there, then our marriage is over. And then I will do everything in my power to save him from that destruction.

MR. GABOR: You might as well give in now as later, Fanny. It's not easy coming to terms with misfortune. But I'll stand by you. And when your courage gives out, I'll help to make your burden lighter. It's a dismal, cloudy future ahead. And losing you would make it even worse.

MRS. GABOR: I'll never see him again—never see him. How can he survive such coarseness? He'll never come to terms with filth. He'll cut himself free. He has Moritz's horrible example to give him strength. And if I do see him again, he won't be the same. No freshness, no laughter, no purity. No determination. Everything I cherished in him. If some wrong demands punishment, blame me. You can do what you want with me, but don't touch that child.

MR. GABOR: He *sinned!*

MRS. GABOR: He did *not* sin!

MR. GABOR: *He sinned!* I'd have done anything to have saved your boundless love for him.—A woman came to me this morning so beside herself that she was hardly able to talk—to show me this letter written to her—to her fifteen-year-old daughter. The woman said she opened it out of foolish curiosity. The girl wasn't at home. In the letter Melchior admits to being troubled with guilt for his treatment of her. He says that he sinned against her, etcetera, etcetera, and that he will assume full responsibility. He tells her not to worry even if there are serious consequences. He's already attempted to find help for her, and his expulsion from school has made that easier. His former error, he says, might well lead to their happiness—and more of the same hogwash!

MRS. GABOR: That's impossible!

MR. GABOR: The letter's a forgery. A simple case of deception. Someone trying to turn to his own account the well-known fact of Melchior's expulsion. I haven't spoken with the boy yet—but take a good look at the handwriting. Notice the style.

MRS. GABOR: This is an unheard of, shameless trick!

MR. GABOR: That's what I'm afraid of!

MRS. GABOR: No, no, never!

MR. GABOR: It will be all the better for us. The woman stood there wringing her hands, asking me what she should do. I suggested that she try keeping her daughter from tumbling about in haylofts. Fortunately she left the letter with me. If we send Melchior off to another school, where he'll be free of even *parental* supervision, inside of three weeks it will have happened all over again. He'll be expelled. And that "freshness" and "purity" of his will eventually grow accustomed to it. Tell me, Fanny! Where shall I send the boy?!

MRS. GABOR:—To the reformatory—

MR. GABOR: To the—?

MRS. GABOR:—reformatory!

MR. GABOR: He'll have there all the things that were denied him at home: iron discipline, principles, and moral constraint. And he will have no alternative but to submit. Besides, the reformatory is not as terrible a place as you might imagine. It emphasizes the development of Christian thought and feeling. The boy will be taught to desire what is *good* rather than what is *interesting*, and to act not according to his *natural instincts*, but according to what is *lawful*. Half an hour ago I received a telegram from my brother confirming what that woman told me. Melchior has confided in him and asked for two hundred marks to escape to England.

MRS. GABOR: *(Covers her face.)* Merciful heaven!

Reformatory. A corridor.

DIETER: Here's a coin.

REINHOLD: So?

DIETER: I put it on the floor. You stand around. Who hits it first wins.

RUPERT: You want in, Melchior?

MELCHIOR: No thanks.

GASTON: Oh, *he* couldn't play with *us!* He's just here for a vacation.

MELCHIOR: *(To himself.)* I shouldn't stay by myself like this all the time. They're always watching me. But if I don't play their little game, I'll go crazy. Being shut up like this makes them suicidal. If I break my neck it's all right! If I break out of here it's all right! I win either way. Rupert's becoming my friend; he knows his way around here. I'll tell him about all the dirty parts in the Bible.—He's got the sorriest face in my squad.

RUPERT: I'm coming!

HELMUT: Me, too!

GASTON: When? Next Christmas?

HELMUT: Coming! Coming! O-God-o-God!

(They all cheer him on.)

RUPERT: *(Picking up the coin.)* Thanks a lot!

HELMUT: Give it here, you bastard!

RUPERT: Stick it!

HELMUT: Prick!

RUPERT: *(Punches him in the face.)* How's that! *(Runs away.)*

HELMUT: *(Running after him.)* I'll kill 'im!

THE OTHER BOYS: *(Running after them.)* Go on! Get 'im! Get 'im! Give it to 'im! Give it to 'im!

MELCHIOR: *(Alone, turns to the window.)* That's where the lightning rod goes down the side of the building. I'll have to wrap a handkerchief around it.—Every time I think about her I almost go crazy—and I just can't get Moritz out of my mind.—I'll get a job in a newspaper office. They pay by the hundred lines. I'll sell newspapers! Gossip, articles— local news—ethics—psychology—it's hard to starve these days what with soup kitchens and— This building is sixty feet high and the plaster's peeling.—She hates me! She hates me! I took away her freedom! No matter what happens now, it can't be anything but rape. Maybe as time passes she'll—O God, I hope!—There'll be a new moon in a week. Tomorrow I'll grease the hinges. By Saturday at the latest I'll need to know who has the key. Sunday evening during chapel I'll arrange to have a fit. I hope to God nobody else gets sick! It's so clear, it seems like it's already happened. I'll slip quietly over the sill—swing—grab— I'll have to wrap a handkerchief around it when I— Here comes the Grand Inquisitor. *(Goes off left.)*

(DR. PROKRUSTES enters with a LOCKSMITH.)

PROKRUSTES: True, the windows are on the fourth floor, and there are thorn bushes planted below, but what do degenerates know about thorn bushes! Last winter we had one fall out of a skylight on us, and then we had all the bother of picking him up, carting him off, and burying him.

LOCKSMITH: You say you want a wrought-iron grating?

PROKRUSTES: Wrought-iron, of course. And since it can't be fitted into the wall, it will have to be riveted.

SCENE FIVE

A bedroom. MRS. BERGMANN, INA MÜLLER, and DR. BRAUSEPUL-VER. WENDLA in bed.

DR. BRAUSEPULVER: How old are you exactly?

WENDLA: Fourteen and a half.

DR. BRAUSEPULVER: I have been prescribing Blaud's purgative pills for fifteen years now with astonishing success. I much prefer them to cod-liver oil and iron tonics. Begin with three or four pills daily and increase the dosage as rapidly as possible. I prescribed that the Baroness Elfriede von Witzleben increase her dosage by one pill every three days. But the Baroness misunderstood and increased it by three pills *every* day. Well, in less than three weeks the baroness was in good enough health to go off to the Pyrmont Spa with her lady *maman* to complete the cure. I will excuse you, of course, from tiring walks and special diets. But you must promise me, my dear, that you will move about as much as possible and that when your desire for food returns you will ask at once. Your heart palpitations will soon cease, along with the dizziness, headaches, chills, and indigestion. Within a week of beginning her cure the Baroness Elfriede von Witzleben was enjoying an entire roast chicken with potatoes in their jackets for breakfast.

MRS. BERGMANN: May I offer you a glass of wine, Doctor?

DR. BRAUSEPULVER. Thank you, no. My carriage is waiting outside. You needn't take this too seriously. In a few week's time our little patient here will be up and about as chipper as ever. Good day, Mrs. Bergmann. Good day, child. Good day, ladies. Good day.

(MRS. BERGMANN escorts him to the door.)

INA: *(At the window.)* Your plane trees are changing color already. Can you see them from your bed? They come and go so quick; it's hardly worth being happy over them, their beauty is so brief. But I must leave soon myself. My husband will be waiting for me outside the post office, and before that I must drop in at the tailor's. Little Mucki's getting his first pair of long pants, and Karl needs a new wool suit for winter.

WENDLA: Sometimes I feel so happy—there's so much joy and bright sunshine. I never knew I could be so happy. I want to go out and walk in the meadows at sundown and look for primroses along the river bank, and then sit down and just dream. And then I get a toothache and think I'm going to die tomorrow. I get hot and cold, and every-thing in front of me goes black, and then the monster flies in.—And when I wake up, I see mother crying. It hurts me so much, I just can't tell you, Ina.

INA: Shall I raise your pillow a bit?

MRS. BERGMANN: *(Returning.)* He thinks the vomiting will leave soon, and then you can get up. I think you'll be getting up soon, too, Wendla.

INA: The next time I see you you'll be jumping around like a jack-rab-bit.—Good-bye, mother. I have to hurry to the tailor's. God bless you, Wendla dear. *(Kisses her.)* Hurry now and get better.

WENDLA: Good-bye, Ina. And bring some primroses when you come again. Good-bye. Say hello to your boys from me. *(INA goes out.)* What did he tell you out there, mother?

MRS. BERGMANN: Nothing. Except that even the Baroness von Witzleben had fainting spells. That's how it is when—

WENDLA: When what?

MRS. BERGMANN: You're to drink milk and eat meat and vegetables as soon as your appetite returns.

WENDLA: When what, mother?

MRS. BERGMANN: He said you're— Be quiet, Wendla—be quiet.—You—

WENDLA: Tell me, mother—what—?

MRS. BERGMANN: It will be better soon. He said so.

WENDLA: It won't. It won't!—I'm going to die, mother.

MRS. BERGMANN: No, no, no—you won't have to die—you won't—

WENDLA: Then why are you crying?

MRS. BERGMANN: You're pregnant, Wendla.—You won't have to die.— You have a baby.—You're going to have a baby.—How could you—!

WENDLA: But I haven't—

MRS. BERGMANN: Don't lie to me! I know! I just—I just couldn't tell you.—Oh, Wendla—

WENDLA: But that's impossible—

MRS. BERGMANN: Wendla, what have you done!

WENDLA: I don't know! We were lying there—I never loved anyone in the world except you, mother.

MRS. BERGMANN: My baby—

WENDLA: Why didn't you tell me—

MRS. BERGMANN: Don't make it worse, child. Stay calm. And don't lose hope. How could I tell a fourteen-year-old girl such things? I'd rather believe the sun could fall from the sky! I did the same to you as my mother did to me.—We must trust in the goodness of God, Wendla; we must trust in His mercy and do our part! Look, child, nothing's happened yet. And if we don't lose heart, God will not desert us.—Be *brave*, Wendla, be *brave!*—You sit looking out your window, hands folded in your lap, sure that everything is for the best, and the world crashes at your feet and breaks your heart—Why are you trembling?

WENDLA: Someone knocked.

MRS. BERGMANN: I didn't hear anything, dear. *(Crosses to the door and opens it.)*

WENDLA: Oh, but I heard it so clearly.—Who's out there?

MRS. BERGMANN: No one.—Just Mr. Schmidt's mother from over on Garden Street.—You've come just in time, Mother Schmidt.

MEN and WOMEN working in a hillside vineyard. The sun is setting behind the mountains. The clear sound of bells floats up from the valley. HANS RILOW and ERNST ROEBEL are rolling around in the dry grass at the top of the vineyard beneath overhanging rocks.

ERNST: I think I overdid it.

HANS: Let's not be sad.—It's a pity the way time flies.

ERNST: You see them hanging there, but you just can't stuff another one down—and then tomorrow they're in the winepress.

HANS: Being tired is just as bad as being hungry.

ERNST: Oh, I just can't eat any more.

HANS: Just one more fat, shining, beautiful grape!

ERNST: My stomach can't stretch any farther.

HANS: If I bend down the shoot, it'll swing back and forth between our mouths. We won't even have to move. Come on, Ernst. We'll bite off the grapes and let the stalks swing back to the vines.

ERNST: Why do we make resolutions when all we do is break them?

HANS: And then there's the gorgeous fiery sky at sunset—and the evening bells—what more can I ask out of life?

ERNST: Sometimes I imagine myself a worthy pastor, with a motherly wife, a well-stocked library, and duties to perform and positions to hold in the community. For six days you meditate, and on the seventh you speak. And when you go for a walk, school children come up and shake hands with you. And when you get home you find the coffee steaming, and the cake is brought in, and girls bring apples to you through the garden gate. Can you imagine anything more wonderful, Hans?

HANS: I'm always thinking about half-closed eyes, parted lips, and Turkish draperies. I don't believe in suffering for love, and pity, and all that. Do you know why our parents go around looking so serious all the time? They're just trying to hide how stupid they are. I *know.* When I become a millionaire I'll build a monument to God.—Think of the future as a milk-pudding with sugar and cinnamon. One person spills it all and howls, and the other stirs it into a mess till he sweats. Why not just skim the cream off the top? Or don't you think we can learn how?

ERNST: Let's skim it off!

HANS: And what's left we'll throw to the chickens.—I've gotten out of more scrapes than I can even remember—

ERNST: Let's skim it off, Hans!—Why are you laughing?

HANS: Are you starting in again?

ERNST: Well, somebody has to.

HANS: Thirty years from now, when we think back on an evening like this, it might seem beautiful beyond words.

ERNST: Can it get that way by itself?

HANS: Why not?

ERNST: If a person were all alone, he could burst out crying—

HANS: Let's not be sad. *(Kisses ERNST on the mouth.)*

ERNST: *(Kisses him back.)* I left the house thinking I'd only talk to you and go right back home.

HANS: I was waiting for you.—Virtue isn't such a bad suit of clothes if you've got the body to wear it.

ERNST: It sure hangs loose on us though.—I could never have been happy if I hadn't met you. I love you, Hans, like I've never loved anyone before—

HANS: Let's not be sad!—When we think back on this in thirty years, we might even make fun of it all. But right now it's so beautiful—the mountains glowing in the sun, the grapes hanging down into our mouths, and the breezes stroking the rocks like a playful kitten—

SCENE SEVEN

Bright November night. Dry leaves rustle on bushes and trees. Ragged clouds scurry across the moon. MELCHIOR clambers over the churchyard wall.

MELCHIOR: *(Jumps down inside.)* That pack of hounds will never find me here. While they're searching the whorehouses for me, I can catch my breath and find out where I am. My coat's nothing but rags. No money in my pocket. I couldn't defend myself against a baby. I'll push farther into the woods tomorrow when it's light.—What did I stumble over? A cross. So cold. Flowers all frozen. All barren. Land of the dead!— This is worse than getting through that skylight! I wasn't prepared for this. If I'd known, I'd have stayed where I was.—Why did it have to be Wendla? Why not me? Why not the guilty one?—I'd have broken rocks and starved. What's there to keep me honest now? One crime leads to another—deeper and deeper—I'm too weak to even kill myself. I wasn't *bad!* I *wasn't* bad! I *wasn't!* God, I wish I were dead!

Don't be silly. You'd never have the guts. Or if I could go insane—tonight! I'll look over there where the new graves are. The wind sounds different with every stone it touches. Decaying wreaths dangling by long ribbons. A horrible forest of scarecrows across the graves. Enough to frighten the devil. What's this? A new grave—evergreen all around it—weeping willows groping at the inscription like a giant's fingers.—Not a star.—*(Reads.)*

Here rests in God
WENDLA BERGMANN
Born 5 May 1878
Died of Anemia
27 October 1892
Blessed are the pure in heart.

I murdered her! I murdered her! I don't want to cry! Have to get out of here! Got to get—

MORITZ: *(With his head under his arm, comes stomping across the graves.)* Melchior! Wait up! Don't go! We might not meet again for a long time! You have no idea how much depends on time and place.

MELCHIOR: Where did you come from?

MORITZ: Over there. By the wall. You knocked over my cross. My grave's beside the wall. Give me your hand, Melchior—

MELCHIOR: You can't be Moritz Stiefel!

MORITZ: Give me your hand. You won't be sorry. I know. It will never be this easy again. This is a strange meeting. Lucky, too. I came up for it specially.

MELCHIOR: Don't you sleep?

MORITZ: Not what *you* call sleep. We sit high up on church towers and roof tops—whenever we want.

MELCHIOR: Because you're not at peace?

MORITZ: Just for the hell of it. We glide around May poles and into lovely forest chapels. We hover over crowds and disaster areas, over gardens and festivals. In people's houses we crouch behind stoves and bed curtains.—Give me your hand.—We spirits have no contact with one another, but we see and hear what goes on in the whole world. We know that everything that man does and strives for is a waste of time. That's always good for a laugh.

MELCHIOR: What good does it do?

MORITZ: What good *should* it do? Nothing can touch us anymore, good *or* bad. We exist far above the concerns of this world, each one only for himself. We have nothing to do with each other, because that would be too boring. And none of us possesses anything he would hate to lose. We're way above joy and grief, and that's that. But it's the living we despise more than anything; we can't even pity them. They amuse us; we smile at their tragedies; and then we meditate on the subject.— Give me your hand. If you give me your hand, you'll laugh yourself silly for being so afraid.

MELCHIOR: Doesn't it disgust you?

MORITZ: We're above all that. We smile. And I was a mourner at my own funeral. I had a wonderful time. I wailed louder than anybody, and then doubled up with laughter. It's being so far above it that makes us able to swallow all that crud. I suppose they laughed at me, too, before I gave myself the big promotion.

MELCHIOR: I guess I don't really *want* to laugh at myself.

MORITZ: The living don't deserve to be pitied. I never realized that before, but now I see through the deception so clearly. I'll never understand how people can be so naïve.—How can you still hesitate, Melchior? Give me your hand. In the blink of an eye you'll be sky-high above yourself. Your life is a sin of omission.

MELCHIOR: Can the dead forget?

MORITZ: We can do anything.—Give me your hand.—We can pity the young for thinking that being scared out of their wits is being an idealist; and pity the old who break their hearts believing in their superiority. We see the emperor tremble at the strains of a street ballad, and a clown at the mention of the Last Judgment. We see through the actor's make-up and watch the poet put on his mask in the dark. We watch the satisfied man in his destitution and the capitalist with his trouble and toil. We observe lovers blushing in front of each other, knowing that each will be both deceiver and deceived. We see parents bringing children into the world just so they can tell them how lucky they are to have them as parents. And then we see those same children go out and do the same thing all over again. We can drop in and see stupid, innocent kids climbing the walls for love and affection; and the next minute watch a common whore reading her Bible. We see God and the Devil playing at one-upmanship with each other, and know for a fact that they're both drunk out of their skulls. It's peace, Melchior. It's contentment.—Just reach out your little finger to me. You might be a gray old man before the chance comes again.

MELCHIOR: If I agree with you, Moritz, it's only because I hate myself.

Because I'm an outcast. I can't be courageous anymore. I don't know what it means to be honorable. And there's nothing, *nothing* to stand in the way of my death. I hate myself, Moritz, I despise myself—

MORITZ: Then what are you waiting for?

MAN IN THE MASK: *(Enters; to MELCHIOR.)* You're in no condition to make such a decision! You're shivering! You're hungry! *(To MORITZ.)* And you, leave him alone!

MELCHIOR: Who are you?

MAN IN THE MASK: You'll know soon enough. *(To MORITZ.)* Get away from here! What are you doing here anyway? Why don't you put your head to its proper use!

MORITZ: I shot it off.

MAN IN THE MASK: Then stay where you belong. Your time is past. We have no need of your graveyard stench. Look at your fingers! They're crumbling!

MORITZ: Please don't make me leave. Let me stay—just for a while. I promise I won't cause any trouble. It's so gruesome down there.

MAN IN THE MASK: Then why all the bragging? It's all talk, a lie! Well, if it means that much to you, all right. But just be careful what you say. And keep your deadman's hands out of our business.

MELCHIOR: Are you going to tell me who you are?

MAN IN THE MASK: No, but I suggest you put yourself in my hands. And the first order of business is to survive.

MELCHIOR: Are you—my father?

MAN IN THE MASK: Wouldn't you know your father by his voice?

MELCHIOR: No.

MAN IN THE MASK: At the moment your dear father is seeking consolation in the strong arms of your mother.—I can open the world to you. If you're confused now, it's because you're miserable. With a hot meal in your belly, you'll see things differently.

MELCHIOR: *(To himself.)* They can't *both* be the Devil. *(Aloud.)* Not with what I'm charged with!

MAN IN THE MASK: That depends on the meal. I can tell you this much: that girl would have given a splendid birth; she was built magnificently for it. It was Mother Schmidt's abortion pills that killed her.—I can surround you with all kinds of people. I can help you broaden your horizons beyond your wildest dreams. I can show you all the interesting things of this world.

MELCHIOR: Who are you? Who are you? I can't trust myself to someone I don't even know.

MAN IN THE MASK: Then I'm afraid you'll never know me.

MELCHIOR: Is that true?

MAN IN THE MASK: It's true. Besides, you have no choice.

MELCHIOR: I can give my friend here my hand any time I want.

MAN IN THE MASK: Your friend here is a fake and the most pitiable of creatures.

MELCHIOR: So what? But either you tell me who you are or I *will* give him my hand!

MAN IN THE MASK: Well?

MORITZ: He's right, Melchior, I was bragging. Take his advice. Use him for all he's worth. If he's masked, he's masked; at least you know where you stand.

MELCHIOR: Do you believe in God?

MAN IN THE MASK: That depends.

MELCHIOR: Can you tell me who invented gunpowder?

MAN IN THE MASK: Berthold Schwartz, a Franciscan monk, at Freiburg in Breisgau, around 1330.

MORITZ: God, I wish he hadn't!

MAN IN THE MASK: In which case you would have hanged yourself.

MELCHIOR: What do you think of morality?

MAN IN THE MASK: Do I look like a school boy?

MELCHIOR: How should I know?

MORITZ: Don't argue! Please don't argue! I was looking forward to sitting here and taking part in your plans, but if all you're going to do is argue, I'll take my head under my arm and go.

MELCHIOR: Timid old Moritz. You never change.

MAN IN THE MASK: The ghost is right. We must never lose sight of our dignity. I think of morality as the real product of two imaginary forces: *Duty* and *Desire:* what I *ought* to do and what I *want* to do. The end product is *Morality*, and its reality is undeniable.

MORITZ: Why didn't you tell me that sooner! Morality is what made me kill myself—for my parents's sake. "Honor thy father and thy mother that thy days may be long." The old saying didn't fare too well in my case!

MAN IN THE MASK: Don't deceive yourself, my friend. Morality would no more have killed your parents than it would have killed you. Seriously considered, they would have raged and stormed at you out of the sheer, healthy, physical need to do so.

MELCHIOR: That might be right as far as it goes, sir. But I also know that if I had given my hand to Moritz, morality alone would have been responsible.

MAN IN THE MASK: And the reason that you didn't is that you are not Moritz.

MORITZ: I don't think the difference is that important. You could just as easily have come upon *me* in the elder grove with the pistol in my hand.

MAN IN THE MASK: Ah, you don't remember me, then. Even at the last moment you vacillated between life and death. But this is hardly the place to prolong so profound a debate.

MELCHIOR: Good-bye, Moritz. I don't know where this man is leading me, but at least he's alive—

MORITZ: Don't blame me for trying to destroy you, Melchior. It's just that I liked you so much. I'd be happy to moan and groan for the rest of my days if we could go out somewhere together again, just once more.

MAN IN THE MASK: Each of you has his own share. *(To MORITZ.)* You, the comforting knowledge that you possess nothing—*(To MELCHIOR.)* and you, the enervating doubt about all things. *(To MORITZ.)* Good-bye.

MELCHIOR: Good-bye, Moritz. And thanks for letting me see you again. Just think of all those happy, carefree days we spent together for fourteen years. And I promise you, Moritz, no matter what happens—however many times I might change—whether fortune is good to me or bad—I'll never forget you—

MORITZ: Thanks—thanks, Melchior.

MELCHIOR:—and if I ever get to be an old man with gray hair, maybe you'll be closer to me than all the other people in my life.

MAN IN THE MASK: Come, child! *(Links arms with MELCHIOR and they disappear across the graves.)*

MORITZ: *(Alone.)* So here I sit, with my head on my arm. The moon hides its face and then uncovers it again, and doesn't look a jot the wiser. I guess I'll go back to my little plot of ground, set up my cross that the clumsy fool knocked over, and when everything's in place, I'll stretch out on my back, warm myself with my own putrefaction, and smile—

END OF PLAY

LULU

1894

LULU
SCHIGOLCH
DR. GOLL
DR. FRANZ SCHÖNING *editor-in-chief*
ALWA SCHÖNING *his son by his first marriage*
EDWARD SCHWARZ *portrait painter*
COUNTESS MARTHA GESCHWITZ
RODRIGO QUAST *an acrobat at the Belle Union Circus-Theater*
MARQUIS CASTI-PIANI
PUNTSCHU *banker*
MR. HOPKINS
DR. HILTI
KUNGU POTI
JACK
DR. BERNSTEIN
GENDARME
HENRIETTE *maid*
FERDINAND *servant*

TIME AND PLACE
The mid-1890s; Berlin, Paris, London

ACT ONE
BERLIN

*A spacious artist's studio. Upstage left, the main entrance. Downstage left a
side door leading to the bedroom. Center, slightly left and upstage, a plat-
form. Behind it a Spanish screen. In front of it a Smyrna carpet. Downstage
right, two easels. On the upstage easel, in a working frame, the pastel portrait of a forty-year-old woman in an evening gown. Against the downstage
easel leans a canvas with its back to the audience. Stage left, an easy chair.
In front of the easels is an ottoman with Turkish cushions. Thrown across it
is a tiger skin. Far upstage there is a stepladder. The window of the studio is
presumed to be downstage of the proscenium. Mid to late morning.*

SCHÖNING: *(Studies the pastel portrait while holding a photograph.)* I don't
know. I just don't see it. What I wanted you to paint. It's a woman, all
right. In an evening gown. But it's not my wife. Not really. The woman
I admired. Looked up with childlike awe. The woman I respected half
of my life. Just not—there.

SCHWARZ: A model is always better than a photograph.

SCHÖNING: She'd never have sat for you. For anyone, for that matter.
Too high-minded. Life for her was a passing thing. Nothing to be hon-
ored. But, then, what do I know! Too much the good wife and mother
was what she was. No need for that sort of homage. That's what I don't
see in this.

SCHWARZ: Is it in the photograph?

SCHÖNING: A suggestion, perhaps. I know I drew it to your attention. I
don't know. Memories. They still haunt me. Always will, I guess.

SCHWARZ: I took your word as gospel. Even combed the streets for a
model of how I saw her. I needed something to grab hold of. Flesh and
blood.

SCHÖNING: What do I know. Maybe it *is* good. I'm the last one to judge.
People who didn't know her well would recognize her. Yes.

SCHWARZ: How do you like the hair?

SCHÖNING: Good. Good. And the left hand. How you've set it off from
the material! And you've changed the lighting!

SCHWARZ: That I stole. A dancer at the Odeon.

SCHÖNING: *(Indicating the photograph.)* Look at that. That look. The
noble brow. Imagine she's talking to you. Eyebrows arched, head lowered, the sheer honesty of her gaze. She's nobility itself. Nothing com-

mon would ever approach it. That's what I don't see in this. And yet it's here. *(Indicates the photograph.)* The luminous eyes. The indefinable calmness of her closed lips.

SCHWARZ: Step back a bit. Far as possible.

SCHÖNING: *(Backs up slowly and knocks over the canvas leaning against the downstage easel.)* I beg your pardon.

SCHWARZ: *(Picking up the canvas.)* Not at all.

SCHÖNING: *(Recognizing the portrait.)* Wha—what?

SCHWARZ: You know her?

SCHÖNING: No. She sits for you?

SCHWARZ: Since Christmas. *(Lifts the picture onto the easel. It is of a woman dressed as Pierrot. She holds a long shepherd's crook in her hand.)* There's so much still to do.

SCHÖNING: In this costume?

SCHWARZ: Surprised? First class all the way.

SCHÖNING: *(With a glance at SCHWARZ.)* Congratulations! Indeed!

SCHWARZ: *(Registering frustration.)* Christ!

SCHÖNING: Problems?

SCHWARZ: Problems! Her husband brings her and I end up entertaining the old goat for two hours! He's all gaga over "Art"! Just my luck!

SCHÖNING: How did it happen?

SCHWARZ: The old buffoon just shows up one day. Fat, doddering old troll! Would I paint his wife? Christ, I'll paint anything! So ten the next morning in flies this vision, driven on by the old pig himself! I nearly collapsed! Then in comes some lout in livery carrying a package. Where's the changing room? Well, really! So I open my bedroom door. Good thing the bed's made. In she whisks, and papa pig stands guard. Two minutes later, out steps Pierrot. *(Takes a deep breath.)* A fairy tale! Perfect head to toe! And that impossible costume! She could have been born in it! The grace! The way she lifts her feet, buries her elbows in the pockets, tosses her head! Doesn't even know she's doing it! Jesus, sometimes the blood just shoots straight to my head!

SCHÖNING: You need to get hold of yourself. Build up a resistance against such attacks.

SCHWARZ:*(Shaking his head.)* You haven't seen her! Resistance? So tell me! Just seeing a naked breast disgusts me! Resistance!

SCHÖNING: There's more to this than nakedness.

SCHWARZ: Whatever you say. Perhaps less.

SCHÖNING: Look more deeply, my boy. But first you need a steady hand. I understand her. The soul evaporates in the heat and from outside falls back onto the body as dew. The spirit and the fig leaf are one.

SCHWARZ: I'll show it to you! One moment. *(Goes out left.)*

SCHÖNING: *(Alone, to himself.)* Poor boy, he needs to get out more often.

SCHWARZ: *(Returns with a white satin costume.)* She wore it at a Freemason's Ball.

SCHÖNING: *(Admiringly.)* M—hm!

SCHWARZ: *(Unfolding the costume.)* Cut down low front and back.

SCHÖNING: The gigantic pompons!

SCHWARZ: *(Feeling the pompons.)* Black silk thread.

SCHÖNING: Crows in snow!

SCHWARZ: *(Holding up the costume by the shoulder straps.)* She's naked underneath.

SCHÖNING: One piece.

SCHWARZ: Waist and legs.

SCHÖNING: And no lacing or stays.

SCHWARZ: Doesn't need them.

SCHÖNING: Then how—?

SCHWARZ: Through the top!

SCHÖNING: Aha!

SCHWARZ: She wears nothing between this and her body.

SCHÖNING: And if it slips from her shoulders?

SCHWARZ: No way!

SCHÖNING: But how can it not!

SCHWARZ: She raises her right arm.

SCHÖNING: But these—these legs—

SCHWARZ: Yes?

SCHÖNING: Too long.

SCHWARZ: She hikes the left one up.

SCHÖNING: Yes.

SCHWARZ: That's her pose. Holds it with her hand. Above the knee.

SCHÖNING: As if she's just tucked it up.

SCHWARZ: Enchanting.

SCHÖNING: The right leg falls onto the shoe.

SCHWARZ: All the way to the tip.

SCHÖNING: White satin shoes.

SCHWARZ: Black silk stockings.

SCHÖNING: Transparent. What else!

SCHWARZ: *(Sighing.)* Which I will have to paint!

SCHÖNING: Only death comes free.

SCHWARZ: Besides that—she flirts.

SCHÖNING: How admirable!

SCHWARZ: You don't believe me!

SCHÖNING: I can see it!

SCHWARZ: *(Turning to the picture.)* Will you look at that arm—

SCHÖNING: What an elegant stretch!

SCHWARZ: She holds the shepherd's crook as high as she can.

SCHÖNING: It lifts the figure.

SCHWARZ: Armpits in full view.

SCHÖNING: Yes.

SCHWARZ: And so natural.

SCHÖNING: Is that flirting?

SCHWARZ: Wait. The arm's a jewel. Every curve emphasized. The hollow of the elbow pulled taut. The bright blue veins. The gentle radiance across it, flickering with light!

SCHÖNING: I can just imagine—little as there is to see.

SCHWARZ: Then the armpit!

SCHÖNING: Yes.

SCHWARZ: Directly in the center—there—of the most intense matte flesh tone—two coal-black little locks!

SCHÖNING: Which are also missing.

SCHWARZ: Dyed, of course.

SCHÖNING: Where did you get that dreadful idea?

SCHWARZ: Where did I get it? They're darker than the hair on her head, darker than her eyebrows, whereas her body hair—

SCHÖNING: Continue.

SCHWARZ: *(Folding the costume.)* Well—she pays a great deal of attention to it.

SCHÖNING: I was about to say—

SCHWARZ: Please.

SCHÖNING: And the old man stands guard?

SCHWARZ: Our kind, you know—ah, well—*(Takes the costume back into the bedroom.)*

SCHÖNING: *(Alone, to himself.)* Our kind—

SCHWARZ: *(Returning, looks at the clock.)* By the way, if you'd like to meet her—

SCHÖNING: No.

SCHWARZ: They should be along any moment.

SCHÖNING: I'll have to make do with the counterfeit. *(Turning to the pastel portrait.)* I'll be indebted if you'd also design the frame.

SCHWARZ: Whatever you say. A few immortelles—

SCHÖNING: I'll leave that to you. As I said, the picture has all one could ask for. Come see me soon.

SCHWARZ: *(Accompanying him.)* Thank you.

SCHÖNING: Don't trouble yourself. *(Goes upstage left and in the doorway runs into DR. GOLL and LULU. Half to himself.)* Good God!

SCHWARZ: *(Hurrying toward them.)* May I introduce—

GOLL: *(Measuring SCHÖNING with a glance.)* What are you doing here?

SCHÖNING: *(Extending LULU his hand.)* Mrs. Goll.

LULU: How charming!

SCHÖNING: *(Giving GOLL his hand.)* I've been looking at my wife's portrait.

GOLL: I beg your pardon. Hm!

LULU: Surely you're not leaving already?

SCHÖNING: I just thought—well, that your sitting was about to begin.

LULU: Exactly!

GOLL: No matter. Stay.

SCHÖNING: How can I refuse?

GOLL: *(Putting down his hat and stick.)* Besides, I need a word with you.

LULU: *(Giving her hat and coat to SCHWARZ; to SCHÖNING.)* Imagine! The Duchess of Villa-Franca passed us in her coach!

GOLL: *(Inspecting the pastel portrait.)* Should have lived more! Lived! A good heart, though. *(While lighting a cigarette.)* Her problem was she lacked a stimulus. But who knows—

SCHÖNING: Don't we all?

GOLL: Not you, certainly!

SCHÖNING: Our problem is we don't go looking for it. Too lazy to give ourselves a good rest.

LULU: Then upset the cart, why don't you?

SCHÖNING: I lack the stimulus.

GOLL: Go on now, Elly. Get dressed!

LULU: Now it's my turn.

GOLL: Why else are we here! Schwarz is already licking his brush.

LULU: We each have our turn. I thought it would be more fun.

SCHÖNING: You at least have the pleasure of amusing others.

LULU: *(Going left.)* Just you wait.

SCHÖNING: *(Opening the bedroom door for her.)* Mrs. Goll—if you would be so kind. *(Pulls the door shut behind her.)*

GOLL: I decided to christen her Elly.

SCHÖNING: Why not Mignon?

GOLL: Possibly. I didn't dig that deeply. In love, you see, I prefer the unfinished, the helpless, the creature not yet ready to do without a fatherly friend—

SCHÖNING: *(Lighting a cigarette.)* In which case it doesn't pretend to be taken seriously—

GOLL: Nor does it pretend to take one over—

SCHÖNING: And the advantages remain the same—

GOLL: On the contrary.

SCHÖNING: If only it didn't take so long to learn that! About all one can do is continue to feel well.

GOLL: My whole day is spent battling the Grim Reaper—and what a bore that is—and, as you know, I have no children. There are needs, alas, we can never be weaned of, however rapidly one's mind is going dotty. *(To SCHWARZ.)* But tell me, how's your little dancer getting on?

SCHWARZ: She sat for me only as a favor. I met her on an outing of the Saint Cecilia Society.

GOLL: *(To SCHÖNING.)* I think we can expect a change in the weather.

SCHÖNING: Could Mrs. Goll be having trouble changing?

GOLL: Undressing is easier than dressing. The stays down the back, don't you know. Next time I'll play the maid.

SCHÖNING: A healthier style of dress might be the answer.

GOLL: It's the unhealthy ones that grab my interest. *(Calling.)* Nellie!

SCHWARZ: *(Hurries to the door and calls through the keyhole.)* Mrs. Goll.

LULU: *(From inside.)* Coming, coming!

GOLL: *(To SCHÖNING.)* I don't understand these blockheads.

SCHÖNING: *(While SCHWARZ is looking through the keyhole.)* I envy them. They have their "ego"—the only inexhaustible source of pleasure. They sleep in peace at night wrapped in their own arms. You don't judge a man who's scratched together a living painting since he was a boy! Take him up! Make him a success! An exercise in arithmetic is all! I'd do it myself, but don't have the moral energy. For me it would be a rascally schoolboy prank like discovering America. The day will come when everything is lit by electricity! Why bother? Too big a bite—

LULU: *(Enters from the bedroom as Pierrot.)* Voilà!

SCHÖNING: *(Looking at her in amazement.)* It's infernal!

LULU: *(Coming nearer.)* Well?

SCHÖNING: Almost unbearable.

LULU: How do you like me?

SCHÖNING: There are no words.

LULU: No?

SCHÖNING: None!

GOLL: Quite a sight!

SCHÖNING: Yes.

LULU: And don't think I don't know it!

SCHÖNING: A little more consideration might have—

LULU: I do my duty.

SCHÖNING: You've painted yourself.

LULU: I what?! Do I look sunburned?

SCHÖNING: Not at all.

LULU: Under my snow-white wig?

SCHÖNING: You've never shone more brightly.

GOLL: She has deliciously white skin. I've told our artist to do as little work on the skin as possible. I'm no great fan of this modern daubing.

SCHÖNING: Depends on the dauber.

GOLL: It might be just the thing for a piece of meat in a butcher's window.

SCHWARZ: *(Busy at the easel.)* Impressionism solved more interesting problems than the saccharine daubers of the seventies.

SCHÖNING: Everything has two sides.

SCHWARZ: According to you.

SCHÖNING: *(To SCHWARZ.)* Even narrow-mindedness.

GOLL: *(To LULU as she embraces and kisses him.)* Your slip's showing. Pull it down. He'll paint it.

LULU: I don't know why I wore it. It's such a bother. *(Mounts the platform; to SCHÖNING.)* What would you say, Doctor, if you had to stand still as a tree for two hours?

SCHÖNING: I? I'd sell my soul to be a little creature the likes of you.

GOLL: *(Sits down left.)* Come over here. From here she looks even lovelier.

LULU: *(Assuming her pose.)* I'm lovely from all positions—*(Bending back her head.)* At least have a little pity!

SCHWARZ: The right knee a bit forward—that's fine. The satin settles gently. But never the same way twice.—At least the light's bearable today.

GOLL: More panache, man, more panache! Hold your brush toward the tip. A heavy hand just won't do. She's not a monument.

SCHWARZ: I want concentrate every expression into a single fleeting moment.

SCHÖNING: Treat her as a still life.

SCHWARZ: Exactly.

SCHÖNING: Paint snow on ice. Any deeper and nature defeats you.

SCHWARZ: Exactly, exactly.

SCHÖNING: Think of the setting as a salver for the main course.

GOLL: Art must let us appreciate the subject's spiritual side. Exhibitions are full of pictures that—that make you want to castrate yourself!

SCHÖNING: Then why go?

GOLL: I ask myself the same question. Maybe this beastly weather.

SCHÖNING: Little Miss O'Murphy's making her debut at the National.

GOLL: As a Peruvian Pearlfisher. Prince Polossow took me.

SCHÖNING: Some pearl!

GOLL: His beard has gone black again from sheer rapture.

SCHÖNING: She'll drain him dry as hay and spend it on her Anton.

GOLL: Or on that dunce she runs around with. The pigs.

SCHWARZ: *(Stepping back occasionally while painting.)* Last autumn I could have rented another studio. What frightened me was the moving. As soon as the sun comes out, the courtyard wall sends in warm reflections.

GOLL: *(To LULU.)* You're digging in your pockets!

LULU: They're empty.

SCHÖNING: Looking for your hanky?

SCHWARZ: Besides, the heating's not the best. In winter the air's so dry you've got a headache by noon.

GOLL: Then open a window! Poor man! Nothing healthier than a roaring fire with wide-open windows!

SCHWARZ: *(Under his breath.)* A spit of barbecue might help.

GOLL: *(To SCHÖNING.)* The opera has a new hit.

SCHÖNING: That's a surprise.

GOLL: Go see it. I prescribe it.

SCHÖNING: Thanks. I take chloral hydrate.

GOLL: Forget the chloral hydrate. Go see it. It won't ruin your stomach and doesn't go out of style as fast.

LULU: I—I think someone knocked.

SCHWARZ: Excuse me. *(Goes to the door and opens it.)*

GOLL: *(To LULU.)* A friendlier smile won't hurt. He doesn't know the difference. What's your sugar-snout for, after all! *I'm* the one who has to listen to his grumbling.

SCHÖNING: Think of sugared almonds—of strawberry-creme—

GOLL: That's only for children!

ALWA: *(Still behind the Spanish screen.)* May a friend of the arts barge his way in?

SCHÖNING: You?

LULU: It's Alwa Schöning!

GOLL: Well, let us see you!

ALWA: *(Coming forward, extending his hand to GOLL.)* How are you, Dr. Goll!

GOLL: Don't be shocked.

LULU: Mr. Alwa has seen his share of models.

ALWA: *(Having turned around quickly.)* Ah!

LULU: You recognize me?

ALWA: Who could forget you, having admired you in such a costume! *(To SCHÖNING.)* How are you?

SCHÖNING: Fine, thanks. And you?

ALWA: I was hoping to ask you to the dress rehearsal.

SCHÖNING: Today? Already?

LULU: The premiere's on Sunday.

GOLL: Oh? How do you know?

LULU: You read it to me in the paper.

GOLL: *(To ALWA.)* Tell me, my boy, what's your play called?

ALWA: Zarathustra.

GOLL: Zarathustra.

SCHÖNING: What am I to do there?

GOLL: I thought he was in a madhouse.

ALWA: You mean Nietzsche.

GOLL: Right. I always confuse the two.

ALWA: Of course I got my material from his books.

SCHÖNING: You'll be needing a special beat for the lame cripple's dance.

GOLL: Your play is a dance?

ALWA: But Nietzsche—forgive me—is the most divine genius of the dance the world has yet seen!

GOLL: Then I must have someone else in mind.

ALWA: Oh, Lord, save me.

GOLL: I thought he was a philosopher.

SCHÖNING: He believed everyone else was limping, and that set him dancing for joy.

ALWA: You know him, then!

SCHÖNING: He revolts me. The nauseating spectacle of him hopping about with his crutches! You'll never find *me* making a ballet out of it.

GOLL: I don't understand that.

SCHÖNING: The entire second act is based on his *Song of the Dance.* Young girls on a forest clearing. Eros asleep by a well. Zarathustra and his disciples emerge from the bushes. And then the dew falls—

GOLL: Goodness! Who composed the music?

ALWA: Me. I did. The First Act takes place in a city named the Many-Colored Cow. You see the Tightrope Dancer, you see the Matrons and Young Virgins—

GOLL: Not bad. Hm.

ALWA: You see the Wild Dogs, the Twisted Magistrate, the Little Girls!

GOLL: The Little Girls—

ALWA: You see the Last Man, the Red Judge, the Grunting Hog, the Pale Criminal, the Illustrious Wise Men, the Daughters of the Desert, the Watchers of the Night.

GOLL: That must be the grandest ballet ever to tread the boards.

ALWA: And you see—you see Zarathustra as night comes on bury the blood-stained body of the Tightrope Dancer in the market place.

GOLL: No problem there, don't you know. That's why we call ourselves realists. Congratulations!

ALWA: The Third Act gave me some trouble. The best is the scene with the Fire Hound spewed out of the Fire Mountain with the Imps. The Imps are concealed in dark sacks from the waist up. All you see are legs.

GOLL: Legs! Legs! That's real stage genius, I must say!

ALWA: In the final act they appear in reverse.

GOLL: One must be careful not to waste one's talents.

ALWA: Act Four. Zarathustra's Homecoming. Scene change. He draws the snake from the shepherd's throat. The birth of the Superman! Corticelli dances the Superman with such—

GOLL: She's always been a bit superhuman.

SCHÖNING: Corticelli?

GOLL: Music of the spheres!

SCHÖNING: She's lived a little, too. As long as her mother lived she danced with her legs. Once free, she danced with her head. She now dances with her heart.

GOLL: *(To ALWA.)* Let's hope you haven't thrown a dark sack over her!

ALWA: The Superman?! You can blame the police for the little she *does* wear!

GOLL: God be praised!

ALWA: But that's not the secret of her Superman.

GOLL: Hm.

ALWA: The Superman, you see, Dr. Goll, is symbolized by a head of curls arranged into two wings and a broad ruff around the neck. Under this ruff is the ineffable stuff of the soul that strives not merely onward but upward. But how to put that on stage!

SCHÖNING: My boy, my boy, beware of the madhouse.

GOLL: Hm. Will Corticelli be rehearsing, too?

ALWA: They'll all be rehearsing. The Wild Dogs, the Imps, the Little Girls—décolleté clear down to their souls. The Twisted Magistrate, the Grunting Hog.

GOLL: Ah, what a splendid fellow!

ALWA: Come with us, then.

GOLL: Impossible.

SCHÖNING: Besides, we haven't much time to lose.

ALWA: Do come, Doctor. In the last act you'll see Zarathustra in front of his cave, and the Two Eagles, the Snake, the Two Kings, and the old Pope.

GOLL: I'm only interested in the Superman.

ALWA: Well, then, come along. You'll love the Feast of Asses. It's the closing scene.

GOLL: I can't. I can't—

ALWA: But why? Afterward we'll drop in at Peter's and you can go wild expressing your amazement.

GOLL: She'll be—she'll be at Peter's?

ALWA: The whole bunch will be there.

GOLL: Don't pressure me—just don't pressure me. Please.

ALWA: You certainly won't be missing anything here.

GOLL: When I get back that ass will have bungled my picture!

ALWA: It can always be done over.

SCHÖNING: He doesn't lose his head that easily.

GOLL: The next time, gentlemen.

LULU: Reserve us a box for Sunday.

SCHÖNING: Of course, of course.

ALWA: *(Taking his arm.)* The Daughters of the Desert are slipping into their tights.

GOLL: Blasted daubing. It just doesn't do, don't you see. You have to explain every brush stroke to these people.

ALWA: Good-bye, Mrs. Goll.

LULU: Tell us about it afterwards!

GOLL: But do take my carriage.

SCHÖNING: We'll return it at once.

GOLL: *(To ALWA.)* And give my best to the Daughters of the Desert!

ALWA: They're sure to get after us for not bringing you along. *Allons!*

GOLL: *(To LULU.)* I'll be back in five minutes.

ALWA: The desert is growing.

GOLL: *(Taking his hat and stick.)* But I probably won't be going on to Peter's.

SCHÖNING: Good-bye.

ALWA: Stay nice and still now. Don't move. *(Urging GOLL and SCHÖNING toward the exit.)* The desert is growing. Woe to him who hides deserts in himself! *(Goes off with GOLL and SCHÖNING.)*

LULU: He usually doesn't leave me alone for a minute.

SCHWARZ: *(Painting.)* Wouldn't you like to rest a bit?

LULU: I'm afraid.

SCHWARZ: I've never had a model stay still for so long.

LULU: He could come back at any moment.

SCHWARZ: Hm. All my kind ever knows is skies of lead—not even a thunderstorm to break the monotony. Or over there—in the bright warm glow of the sun—the eternal stench of decay.

LULU: I'd never have dreamt it.

SCHWARZ: It would be a difficult choice.

LULU: Better not to have a choice.

SCHWARZ: What would you never have dreamt?

LULU: That he'd have gone off with them.

SCHWARZ: Sour grapes!

LULU: Paint!

SCHWARZ: Straighter on the left. That's fine.

LULU: I could stand here like this for half my life.

SCHWARZ: *(Painting.)* I'm on your hip just now.

LULU: Corticelli certainly must do something well.

SCHWARZ: Ugh! She's the same as all the rest!

LULU: You know her, then?

SCHWARZ: God forbid! She can fill a theater just by gyrating. Why else would they pay her a gigantic salary? One flap of her mini-skirt pulls in more than I make on a picture I've worked on for almost a year.

LULU: I feel—I really don't know—

SCHWARZ: What's wrong? You're pale.

LULU: It's the first time he's ever left me alone with a stranger.

SCHWARZ: But doesn't Dr. Goll make house calls?

LULU: That's why Lisa's around.

SCHWARZ: Your housekeeper?

LULU: I don't know where she comes from. She's kept house for him for fifty years.

SCHWARZ: But you do help out from time to time?

LULU: No. At night she puts me to bed and in the morning she dresses me. She bathes me and sees to my hair and drinks absinthe all day long.

SCHWARZ: Pfui!

LULU: But when I pour myself even a *tiny* glass, she boxes my ears.

SCHWARZ: And your husband allows this?

LULU: He takes her side.

SCHWARZ: How do you put up with this?

LULU: I read. To myself. French mostly.

SCHWARZ: Throw her out on the street—the bitch! You're the wife, you have every right!

LULU: And then what?

SCHWARZ: Then? Then—

LULU: I'm nothing without her. Who'd dress me for my dancing lessons?

SCHWARZ: Can't you do that yourself?

LULU: I don't know myself well enough.

SCHWARZ: How does she dress you?

LULU: In as little as possible.

SCHWARZ: Jesus!

LULU: I don't have the inventive genius to choose.

SCHWARZ: Who teaches you dancing?

LULU: He does. *(SCHWARZ lets his brush sink.)* Paint!

SCHWARZ: *(Painting.)* I'd give anything to see him show you a step!

LULU: He knows all the dances. Czardas. Samaqueca. Shimmy. Russian Dance. Sailor's Dance.

SCHWARZ: I'd die laughing!

LULU: He tells me how to dance, that's all. I dance by myself. He plays the violin.

SCHWARZ: And then you dance in costume?

LULU: I have two rooms full of costumes.

SCHWARZ: *(Drawing his breath.)* The world's a curious place.

LULU: Yes, and I'm glad it is.

SCHWARZ: So when do you dance?

LULU: After dinner.

SCHWARZ: Every evening?

LULU: Yes.

SCHWARZ: Tell me about it. It's easier painting when you talk.

LULU: We were in Paris last winter. Every evening a different dancer. And no sooner do we get home, I'm supposed to be able to do it. It was dreadful.

SCHWARZ: There must be a lot of misery in Paris.

LULU: We'd go out only at night. All day long he spent at the École de Medicine, and I stayed home and slept. Or sat at the fireplace.

SCHWARZ: Then you didn't see much of Paris—

LULU: Toward the end I took lessons. With Eugénie Fougère. My legs were sore for six months. She also showed me her costumes.

SCHWARZ: What are your costumes?

LULU: There's one that's a Fisherboy. I wear heavy wooden clogs when I dance in it. A shirt of coarse linen, open all down the front, with short white sleeves, and a pair of little shorts. But very wide. Made of coarse wool.

SCHWARZ: And the old goat sits there in front of you?

LULU: There's nothing to be seen.

SCHWARZ: Aren't you disgusted?

LULU: Why?

SCHWARZ: You call that a marriage?

LULU: Dr. Schöning comes every Thursday. And once we even had Prince Polossow over. I dressed as Eve.

SCHWARZ: I see—

LULU: High red boots with laces. Violet stockings. And my hair in a Grecian knot—and with a red ribbon around it.

SCHWARZ: (Sinking back.) I can't do anymore.

LULU: Paint!

SCHWARZ: My arm is stiff.

LULU: It never got stiff on you before.

SCHWARZ: And the lighting's changed.

LULU: Then rearrange the curtains.

SCHWARZ: Whatever I paint I'll scratch out the minute you've gone.

LULU: So what?

SCHWARZ: There are no reflections. The light's all wrong.

LULU: You never took a break before.

SCHWARZ: This is more than I can—! The picture won't be any better for that! I don't understand! How do you put up with it?

LULU: I have it easy.

SCHWARZ: I believe it. In that Pierrot costume. How do you not freeze!

LULU: You should first see me at home.

SCHWARZ: During your dancing lessons?

LULU: All day long—when he works at home—I'm almost always in my chemise.

SCHWARZ: Only a chemise?

LULU: It's a warm house. I'm used to it.

SCHWARZ: You learn something new every day!

LULU: I let my hair hang free—with a loop. Yesterday I wore a dark green blouse with white bows.

SCHWARZ: Coarse linen?

LULU: Silk! Everything! Long light-green stockings, and my white ballroom shoes. A pink bow in my hair. And garters. Pink. A very delicate pink.

SCHWARZ: Sounds like a brothel!

LULU: It's comfortable. In winter especially. When the salon is wonderfully warm. You can breathe.

SCHWARZ: You can do that anywhere.

LULU: In this Pierrot costume, too. I feel so good in it.

SCHWARZ: So?

LULU: *(Breathing in.)* Just watch.

SCHWARZ: Stop that! *(Jumps up, throws his brush and palette aside, and paces the floor excitedly.)* The bootblack's only concern is her feet. And his dye doesn't eat up his earnings. Tomorrow when I'm broke, no woman's going to ask me if I know how to eat oysters!

LULU: *(Pleading.)* Paint! Please!

SCHWARZ: What drove the old goat to the rehearsal?

LULU: He won't be much longer. I like it better with three people, too.

SCHWARZ: *(Having returned to the easel, painting.)* But it peels off! It peels off! It peels off!

LULU: The costume's not my idea. He designed it and the theater wardrobe master cut the pattern. I didn't mean to insult you.

SCHWARZ: This is enough to kill a man's soul! *(Lets the brush sink.)* I can't do it! I can't!

LULU: Paint! I beg you!

SCHWARZ: With colors dancing in front of my eyes!

LULU: Pretend!

SCHWARZ: I see fiery flashes.

LULU: He'll be here any minute. For your own sake, paint!

SCHWARZ: *(Begins again.)* Of course! Do I have a choice? Tomorrow they'll say I'm immoral! Only the medical profession can allow itself *that* luxury! *(Paints.)*

LULU: *(Breathing heavily.)* Thank God.

SCHWARZ: The artist is a martyr to his profession. No doubt about that.—The left pant leg. A bit higher, if you could.

LULU: Higher still?

SCHWARZ: Just a fraction.

LULU: I can't. You'd see skin.

SCHWARZ: *(Goes to the platform.)* Let me.

LULU: *(Pulling away.)* I can't.

SCHWARZ: But why?

LULU: Because my stockings aren't that long.

SCHWARZ: *(Takes her by the hand.)* I'll show you.

LULU: *(Throwing the shepherd's crook in his face.)* Don't touch me! *(Hurries toward the main door.)*

SCHWARZ: *(Following her.)* Where do you think you're going?

LULU: You won't get your hands on me for a long time.

SCHWARZ: Can't you take a joke? *(Forcing her into the corner, left.)*

LULU: *(Fleeing to the right.)* Of course I can, like a trooper. I can take anything. Just don't get near me. Force will get you nowhere.

SCHWARZ: *(Stepping to the rear.)* Please.

LULU: *(Returning to the platform.)* Get to work. You have no right to annoy me.

SCHWARZ: *(Drawing nearer.)* Don't change your pose.

LULU: First sit down at your easel. *(Flees behind the ottoman as SCHWARZ makes to grab her.)*

SCHWARZ: *(Trying to go right around the ottoman.)* Not before I've punished you!

LULU: First you'll have to catch me!

SCHWARZ: *(Trying to grab her from the left.)* You'll see soon enough.

LULU: *(Evading him by going right.)* Oh, you will, will you! *(Teasing him.)* Chicky-chicky-chicky—

SCHWARZ: If it's the last thing I do! *(Groping, right, around the ottoman.)*

LULU: *(Evading him to the left.)* Here-here-here-here!

SCHWARZ: *(At the upper end of the ottoman.)* You'll pay for that!

LULU: *(Opposite him, standing upright.)* Get to work. You won't catch me. That's a promise.

SCHWARZ: *(Pretending maneuvers both right and left.)* Just one minute more.

LULU: In a long dress I might not be able to defend myself.

SCHWARZ: You silly fool.

LULU: But in this Pierrot costume—

SCHWARZ: Just you wait.

LULU: I have almost nothing on under it.

SCHWARZ: *(Throwing himself across the ottoman.)* Got you!

LULU: *(Throws the tiger skin over his head.)* There! *(Jumps across the plat-form and clatters up the stepladder.)* I shine! I shine! Like the sun! I behold all the cities of the world!

SCHWARZ: *(Unwinding himself from the tiger skin cover.)* Damned skin!

LULU: *(Holding herself up with her left hand, she stretches her left arm high in the air.)* I grasp the clouds! I stick stars in my hair!

SCHWARZ: *(Clatters up after her.)* I'll shake it till you fall!

LULU: *(Climbing higher.)* Stop or I'll topple the ladder!

SCHWARZ: How beautiful you are!

LULU: I'll kick in your skull.

SCHWARZ: There's the lightning!

LULU: Take your claws off my legs!

SCHWARZ: One kick out of you, and I'll tear you to—

LULU: God save Poland! *(Knocks over the ladder, is thrown onto the plat-form, and throws the Spanish screen across SCHWARZ's head as he strug-gles, groaning, to his feet. She rushes downstage.)* The Children of Heaven are dashing across the field! *(At the easel, right, following SCHWARZ's movements.)* I told you, didn't I, you'd never catch me!

SCHWARZ: *(Extricating himself from the cover.)* Stay away from the picture!

LULU: I want to whistle away like the wind with a pack of dogs!

SCHWARZ: *(Coming downstage.)* If you can. *(Tries to grab her.)*

LULU: Stay clear of my body, or—*(As SCHWARZ grabs at her.)* that's what happens! *(Throws the easel and the pastel portrait at him, so that the por-trait falls crashing to the floor.)*

SCHWARZ: Oh, dear God!

LULU: *(Upstage and to the right of him.)* You put that hole in it yourself.

SCHWARZ: My studio rent! My trip! My trip to Norway!

LULU: Why did you chase me like that!

SCHWARZ: Who cares! *(Hurls himself at her.)*

LULU: *(Jumps across the ottoman, across the fallen ladder, strides downstage across the platform, and performs a somersault on the carpet.)* A ditch! A ditch! Don't fall in! *(Jumps up, stomps through the pastel portrait, and falls.)*

SCHWARZ: *(Falling on top of her.)* Got you!

LULU: *(Wriggling her way free and escapes.)* You squashed me! *(SCHWARZ rises and follows her upstage.)* Leave me alone now. I feel sick.

SCHWARZ: *(Stumbling over the Spanish screen.)* I will show you no mercy for this!

LULU: *(Out of breath, comes downstage.)* I feel—ah—I feel—I feel—oh, God! *(Sinks onto the ottoman.)*

SCHWARZ: *(Gasping for breath.)* Dear God! This woman! *(Goes upstage, locks the door, and returns.)* The world—is a filthy place. And I'm to think of a salver to serve her on. Easily said. *(Lying down beside her.)*

LULU: *(Opening her eyes.)* I fell down.

SCHWARZ: The world—is a filthy place.

LULU: Deep down—

SCHWARZ: Are you all right?

LULU: Storm.

SCHWARZ: *(Kisses her bare arm.)* Take off your clothes.

LULU: It's too cold.

SCHWARZ: Please. *(Tries to strip off her costume.)*

LULU: Don't.

SCHWARZ: Then come.

LULU: Where?

SCHWARZ: Into the bedroom.

LULU: He could come back.

SCHWARZ: Just for a moment.

LULU: Why?

SCHWARZ: I love you.

LULU: *(Shuddering.)* Oh.

SCHWARZ: *(Pulling up her pant legs.)* Sweet.

LULU: *(Holding back his hand.)* Don't.

SCHWARZ *(Kissing her.)* Then come.

LULU: No, here—

SCHWARZ: Here—

LULU: If you like—

SCHWARZ: Then let me undress you.

LULU: Why?

SCHWARZ: To love you.

LULU I'm yours!

SCHWARZ: Please.

LULU: I'm yours!

SCHWARZ: Oh, God.

LULU: If you like.

SCHWARZ: You're cruel.

LULU: Why don't you want me?

SCHWARZ: Please, my sweet.

LULU: I'm yours!

SCHWARZ: Be nice.

LULU: I want to be nice.

SCHWARZ: Then take off your clothes.

LULU: But why?

SCHWARZ: Your Pierrot costume!

LULU: But I'm already yours!

SCHWARZ: Nelly.

LULU: What's wrong with my Pierrot costume?

SCHWARZ: Nelly. Nelly.

LULU: My name isn't Nelly.

SCHWARZ: Your Pierrot costume.

LULU: My name is Lulu.

SCHWARZ: I'd call you Eve.

LULU: If you like.

SCHWARZ: Be nice, then.

LULU: If you like.

SCHWARZ: Eve.

LULU: What should I—?

SCHWARZ: Take off your clothes.

LULU: Why?

SCHWARZ: You're playing with me.

LULU: You don't want to.

SCHWARZ: I—

LULU: I'm yours.

SCHWARZ: But, Eve—

LULU: Then why not?

SCHWARZ: Please.

LULU: You don't like me.

SCHWARZ: Merciful heaven.

LULU: Come.

SCHWARZ: Eve. Eve.

LULU: Well, then don't.

SCHWARZ: You—*(Rises, jumps up, confused, bewildered.)* Oh, God. Oh, God, oh, God! Dear God in heaven!

LULU: *(Screaming.)* Don't kill me!

SCHWARZ: It happens! Everything happens!

LULU: *(Raising herself halfway.)* I think—that you have never—made love!

SCHWARZ: *(Turning quickly toward her, blushing deeply.)* Nor you.

LULU: I?

SCHWARZ: How old are you?

LULU: Eighteen. And you?

SCHWARZ: Twenty-eight. It sounds crazy. It sounds crazy. I know. It sounds insane. But—everything—happens—

GOLL: *(Outside.)* Open this door!

LULU: *(Has jumped to her feet.)* Hide me! Oh, God! Hide me!

GOLL: *(Pounding at the door.)* Open this door!

SCHWARZ: Merciful heaven! *(Starts toward the door.)*

LULU: *(Restrains him by the arm.)* Surely you won't—

GOLL: *(Pounding at the door.)* Open this door!

LULU: *(Has sunk down in front of SCHWARZ and clings to his knees.)* He'll beat me to death! Hide me!

SCHWARZ: Where? Where?

(The door falls into the studio with a crash. GOLL, red faced and with bloodshot eyes, rages toward SCHWARZ with his stick raised.)

GOLL: You dogs! You dogs! You—*(Falls forward onto the floor.)*

(SCHWARZ stands there trembling, with wavering knees. LULU has fled to the main door. Pause. He approaches GOLL.)

SCHWARZ: Dr.—Dr.—Dr. Goll—

LULU: *(In the doorway.)* Straighten up the studio first.

SCHWARZ: Keep quiet!

(Pause.)

LULU: *(Daring to come forward.)* He can't be—

SCHWARZ: *(Lifting GOLL's head.)* Dr. Goll. *(Stepping back.)* He's bleeding.

LULU: He probably hit his nose.

SCHWARZ: Help me get him onto the ottoman.

LULU: *(Steps back.)* No—no—

SCHWARZ: *(Trying to turn him around.)* Dr. Goll. Dr. Goll.

LULU: *(Unmoving.)* He—he's kicked the bucket.

SCHWARZ: A stroke—it might be a stroke. At least give me a hand here.

LULU: Not even the two of us could lift him.

SCHWARZ: *(Standing up.)* Fine kettle of fish this could turn out!

LULU: He weighs a ton.

SCHWARZ: He needs a doctor. *(Getting his hat.)* Be good enough to straighten the place a bit. *(Leaving.)* I guess I can just pack in the other picture, too! *(Goes out.)*

LULU: *(Remains some distance away.)* All at once—he'll jump up. *(Whispering.)* Kiss-kiss!—*(Both hands at her temples.)* He's not about to give himself away. *(She describes an arc upstage of him.)* He's shit his pants—and—doesn't even feel it! *(Standing upstage of him.)* Kiss-kiss! *(Touching him with the tip of her shoe.)* Little piggy! *(Pulling back.)* He really means it. *(Staring straight ahead of her.)* He won't be training me anymore. *(Goes thoughtfully to the right.)* He's fed up with me. What will I do? I have clothes—*(Turns toward the bedroom.)*—but I don't know how to dress myself. I can undress myself. That I can do. *(Comes downstage and bends very low.)* What a strange face! If he walked in right now looking like that—ha! *(While rising.)* And no one here. To close his eyes.

SCHWARZ: *(Rushing in.)* Still not conscious?

LULU: *(Coming forward from left.)* What will I do?

SCHWARZ: *(Bending over GOLL.)* Dr. Goll.

LULU: I don't think he'll be coming round again.

SCHWARZ: Dr. Goll.

LULU: He's had it.

SCHWARZ: Have some respect!

LULU: He never had an inkling of such a thing.

SCHWARZ: *(Trying to sit him up.)* He weighs two hundred pounds.

LULU: And before he's aware, he's cold as a stone.

SCHWARZ: *(Rolls GOLL onto his back.)* Dr. Goll. Doctor. *(To LULU, pointing at the ottoman.)* Get me that cushion.

LULU: *(Handing SCHWARZ the cushion.)* What if I dance a Samaqueca for him?

SCHWARZ: *(Pushing the cushion beneath GOLL's head.)* The doctor will be here in a second.

LULU: But I should be found alone with him.

SCHWARZ: I sent the house manager.

LULU: Medicine can't help him now.

SCHWARZ: You do what you can.

LULU: He never believed in it.

SCHWARZ: Don't you at least want to change?

LULU: If only there was someone here to help me.

SCHWARZ: For God's sake, you can do that yourself!

LULU: No.

SCHWARZ: Can *I* help you?

LULU: Just close his eyes first.

SCHWARZ: Dear God. Do you really think he's—?

LULU: Hm.

SCHWARZ: I don't know.

LULU: If not, then—

SCHWARZ: I've never seen anyone die before.

LULU:—then it doesn't matter.

SCHWARZ: You're a monster!

LULU: And you? *(SCHWARZ looks wild-eyed at her.)* Someday *I'll* be in his shoes.

SCHWARZ: Will you shut up!

LULU: *And* you!

SCHWARZ: You have no need to tell me that!

LULU: Do it!

SCHWARZ: What?

LULU: It'll soon be too late.

SCHWARZ: It's *your* job.

LULU: Me? Hm. Ah!

SCHWARZ: Why me?

LULU: He's staring straight at me.

SCHWARZ: Me, too. Straight at me.

LULU: What kind of a man are you? You're afraid to.

SCHWARZ: *(Pressing GOLL's eyes shut.)* This is the first time in my life I've ever—

LULU: What about for your parents?

SCHWARZ: No.

LULU: You were away?

SCHWARZ: No.

LULU: You were afraid.

SCHWARZ: *(Vehemently.)* No!

LULU: *(Shrinks back.)* I didn't mean to insult you.

SCHWARZ: They're still living.

LULU: Then at least you still have someone.

SCHWARZ: Oh, God! They're poor as beggars!

LULU: So was I once.

SCHWARZ: You?

LULU: Now I'm rich.

SCHWARZ: *(Looks at her, shaking his head.)* You make me shudder! *(Pacing the floor excitedly, talking to himself.)* How can she help it?

LULU: *(To herself.)* What am I to do?

(Long pause. LULU stands there motionless, looking at GOLL. SCHWARZ looks at her from the side.)

SCHWARZ: *(Grasping both her hands.)* Look at me.

LULU: What do you want?

SCHWARZ: Look at me.

LULU: What do you want to see?

SCHWARZ: Your eyes. *(Leads her toward the ottoman and indicates her to sit beside him.)* Look me in the eyes.

LULU: I see myself reflected as Pierrot.

SCHWARZ: *(Jumps up and pushes her away.)* Damn! Damn it to hell!!

LULU: I have to change.

SCHWARZ: *(Holding her back.)* One question. Just one question,

LULU: I can't answer you.

SCHWARZ: *(Pulls her back down onto the ottoman.)* Can you—can you—

LULU: Yes.

SCHWARZ: What! Tell the truth?

LULU: I don't know.

SCHWARZ: You *have* to be able to tell the truth!

LULU: I don't know.

SCHWARZ: Do you believe in a Creator?

LULU: I don't know. Leave me be. You're insane.

SCHÖNING: *(Holding her back.)* Is there anything you can swear by?

LULU: I don't know.

SCHWARZ: Then what do you believe in?

LULU: I don't know.

SCHWARZ: Isn't there a soul in your breast?

LULU: I don't know.

SCHWARZ: Are you still a virgin?

LULU: I don't know.

SCHWARZ: Dear God in heaven! *(Gets up and goes left wringing his hands.)*

LULU: *(Without moving.)* I don't know.

SCHWARZ: *(With a glance at GOLL.)* He knows.

LULU: *(Coming up to him.)* If there's anything you want to know—

SCHWARZ: Everything—I want to know everything!

LULU: Since my marriage, I've had to dance every night God gave me— half naked.

SCHWARZ: I don't want to hear! That tells me nothing!

LULU: Why don't I just—

SCHWARZ: What?

LULU: You can still—

SCHWARZ: Aren't you ashamed!

LULU: You asked.

SCHWARZ: Get out! Get out! Get dressed! *(LULU goes off into the bedroom. He looks at GOLL.)* She can't help it. I could lift her out of this mess. Wake her soul. She wouldn't hesitate. She's depraved—totally depraved. My parents, my poor parents. I'm miserable—with all this happiness! Do I love her? Does she love me? Me? She loves me. She's said so. I love her. She loves me. Loves me. The first time—that I'll have been married. I'm miserable. I want to change. Change places with you. Get up—old man—I'll give her back to you—your puppet. You can have my youth—throw my youth in, too. I just haven't got what it takes to live. To love. You can start all over again. With my strengths—my untapped strengths—you can catch up with me. You can. His mouth is open already. Mouth open and eyes shut. Like children. If I were that far gone—like children—I'm not a child—I never was. *(Groaning.)* I—*(Kneels down and ties GOLL's mouth shut with his handkerchief.)*—I'm an old maid! I pray heaven. I pray to heaven. To heaven. To make me capable of happiness. To give me the courage. And the power. And the glory. To be just a little bit happy. For her sake. Only for her sake.

LULU: *(Opens the bedroom door.)* Now if you'd be so kind as to—

END OF ACT ONE

ACT TWO
BERLIN

A small, very elegant salon. Upstage left, the main entrance. Side doors left and right. Above the fireplace on the back wall hangs the portrait of Lulu as Pierrot in a splendid brocade frame. Downstage right, several armchairs around a Chinese table. Numerous pictures, some of them unfinished, in attractive gold frames. Stage right, a carved ebony writing table. SCHWARZ sits in an armchair downstage right, with LULU on his knee. His brush and palette lay beside him on the carpet.

LULU: *(In a Nile-green silk dressing gown with a deep decolletage, trying to evade his advances.)* It's bright daylight.
SCHWARZ: *(Embracing her.)* You're mine.
LULU: You're terrible.
SCHWARZ: What can I do?
LULU: You're murdering me.
SCHWARZ: It's your fault.
LULU: *(Hides her face in his chest.)* Wait.
SCHWARZ: Till when? Christmas?
LULU: Just till evening.
SCHWARZ: It's evening already.
LULU: When I can have all of you.
SCHWARZ: What more do you want?
LULU: You—you—
SCHWARZ: And here I am.
LULU: Till we're free.
SCHWARZ: Isn't it the same?
LULU: No.
SCHWARZ: Please.
LULU: Like children.
SCHWARZ: Like children.
LULU: It's a sin.
SCHWARZ: Then let's sin.
LULU: You can do that by yourself.
SCHWARZ: I've never done such a thing. *(Trying to hike up her dress.)*
LULU: *(Secures her dress below her knees, so that her dark-green slippers fall from her feet.)* Let me tell you something.
SCHWARZ: You're not being nice.

LULU: *(Kisses him.)* You get sweeter—

SCHWARZ: I'm too sweet.

LULU: Not by a long shot.

SCHWARZ: Says you.

LULU: You know.

SCHWARZ: I only have to hear you walk—

LULU: *(Kisses him.)* Darling.

SCHWARZ:—to say the hell with it.

LULU: Then I'll go barefoot.

SCHWARZ: That's all I need.

LULU: I wouldn't want to wear you down.

SCHWARZ: I'd die happy.

LULU: *(Kisses him.)* And what's left for me?

SCHWARZ: *(Shaking himself.)* Oh—Eve—

LULU: Wait. Let me tell you something.

SCHWARZ: Hot off the wire?

LULU: A surprise.

SCHWARZ: Surprises give me the shakes. I go around paralyzed every day afraid the world will end. Mornings I wake up afraid by evening you'll be bitten by a mad dog. I had the jitters all day, afraid of a revolution. And tomorrow I'll be all a-shiver thinking an insect bite or some such thing could end our happiness. I can't look at a newspaper. It's all I can do to go out of the house. *(LULU rests against his chest and whispers in his ear.)* Not possible!

LULU: *(Sits up smiling.)* Ugh!

SCHWARZ: You're a mother?

LULU: Not yet.

SCHWARZ: *(Embracing her passionately.)* Eve! Eve! My Eve!

LULU: I wish I could have gone on a little longer just drifting in a clear blue sky.

SCHWARZ: No. You've made me so happy!

LULU: *(Covering her face.)* You're heartless!

SCHWARZ: Not true!

LULU: If only I could have waited.

SCHWARZ: *(Caressing her.)* Thank you. Thank you, my sweet. Oh, thank you—

LULU: *(Pulling herself together.)* It's all your doing.

SCHWARZ: No. Yours. Yours ten times over.

LULU: We won't argue about it.

SCHWARZ: And to think of all you did to—

LULU: Too late now.

SCHWARZ: It's certain, then?

LULU: Two weeks.

SCHWARZ: But to keep it a secret so long.

LULU: Half the nights I cried myself to sleep.

SCHWARZ: The only blessing we lacked!

LULU: I did everything I could.

SCHWARZ: Shame on you. I can deal with it in cold blood. I'm not afraid. I've fed two mouths for quite a while now. Just be brave. It will turn out, you'll see. I'm ranked higher today than almost any other painter. Art dealers scramble all over each other when I show up with a picture. What's the use of it all if not for my family?

LULU: I mean nothing to you.

SCHWARZ: I have you to thank for it. For everything. You've blessed my life in ways I can't say. And this just goes to prove it. You've taught me who I am. And now the world knows it. My confidence, my joy in creation, my pride as an artist, I owe it all to you—all—and I thank you. Do you mean anything to me? How can you ask! You're my happiness. It's all your doing, even if you have no idea—you just can't help it. You flower for me—you wither for me. For me! For me! Your body lives for me! Rejoice in your happiness. It's all you have. I fished you out of the mire at a mighty cost to myself, but I was man enough! And now I'm afloat in happiness. My fame grows greater by the day, and—whether you like it or not—every year you'll add another jewel to my treasury.

LULU: I need some air.

SCHWARZ: And I have to get back to work. The model's waiting. *(Picks up the brush and palette from the floor, kisses LULU.)* Till—this evening.

LULU: *(Looking at him.)* It terrifies me.

SCHWARZ: My Iphigenia still needs work. Everything that would make it mine, to be honest. Well, everything a work of mine ought to be. I've got till the end of March. Not to mention the five commissions from America.

LULU: *(Rocking on his knee.)* Mad at me?

SCHWARZ: *(Putting the brush and palette down again.)* I'm an artist— which is my excuse for a lot of things. And—you are one fearsome disruption.

(LULU shudders.)

SCHWARZ: True! No two ways about it!

LULU: I'm losing my figure.

SCHWARZ: That's no surprise.

LULU: That's right. Laugh.

SCHWARZ: God knows it isn't my fault.

LULU: Whose, then?

SCHWARZ: Your beauty's.

LULU: I'll be ripped apart.

SCHWARZ: Why are you so sweet?

LULU: You're inhuman.

SCHWARZ: I can't help it.

LULU: I can't be anything but what I am. I can't be anything but a woman—when you're here.

SCHWARZ: Yes. You're a woman, all right!

LULU: I wish I were ugly!

SCHWARZ: Oh, save me!

LULU: Just once for—three weeks.

SCHWARZ: Some disaster *that* would be!

LULU: I'd imagine myself young again. A little child. A total innocent. I'd find something to look forward to. Look forward to growing up. I could laugh again, just thinking of it. How beautiful it would be. To be a little virgin for a while.

SCHWARZ: *(Stroking her hair.)* Dear God.

LULU: I want so much to play in the streets again—

SCHWARZ: The world's a brutal place. Brutal! You're a sacrifice. Give in to it. To your death sentence. What a blissful death.

LULU: Often I just want to scream.

SCHWARZ: I've noticed. Why do I frighten you?

LULU: I wouldn't wish it on anyone.

SCHWARZ: It isn't just your skin.

LULU: My poor skin.

SCHWARZ: What, then? What could it be?

LULU: It's getting so wrinkled.

SCHWARZ: You'll get used to it.

LULU: I hardly know the difference between a silk sheet and the mattress webbing.

SCHWARZ: And it's not your twisting and turning—however beautifully you do that.

LULU: My skin was so delicate. When I'd run my fingertips across my knees, they left rosy streaks.

SCHWARZ: I once thought it was how you kissed me.

LULU: Or maybe my underwear?

SCHWARZ: Oh, save me!

LULU: Well, then, I won't wear any.

SCHWARZ: And it's not how you kiss.

LULU: *(Kisses him.)* No?

SCHWARZ: You're very frugal.

LULU: *(Kisses him.)* With my kisses?

SCHWARZ: And just where did you learn that?

LULU: Before I was born.

SCHWARZ: Silly goose.

LULU: From my little mother.

SCHWARZ: So, so—

LULU: You've either got it—

SCHWARZ: I learned it from you.

LULU:—or you don't.

SCHWARZ: How could I have learned it without you?

LULU: You can.

SCHWARZ: So what's the secret? What is it? Please.

LULU: It's nothing. Nothing at all.

SCHWARZ: I hate riddles. I only have to think about you—

LULU: *(Kissing him.)* Poor boy.

SCHWARZ:—your beauty—your limbs—the form of your body. *(Lifts her dress so that her light-green stockings are visible to above her knees.)* I see no voluptuousness here. *(LULU resists him. He is lost gazing at her.)* They're too spiritual—too chaste.

LULU: *(Covering her knees.)* Why break your head over it?

SCHWARZ: It has to be something.

LULU: *(Kissing him.)* Be still.

SCHWARZ: It has to be.

LULU: *(Closing his mouth.)* No! No!

SCHWARZ: Has to be.

LULU: *(Overwhelms him with kisses.)* There. There. There. There. There.

SCHWARZ: You know—

LULU: *(Straightening up, crossing her feet.)* Then it's out of my power and I can't change it.

SCHWARZ: *(Pressing her to him.)* You mustn't change it—child—you mustn't change it. You mustn't. It's everything you are. Your soul. Your everything.

LULU: (*Sinking back.*) You're making me crazy. (*Closing her eyes, parting her lips.*) I'm so hot. Oh, I'm so—

SCHWARZ: (*Raises her gently and lays her back in the armchair.*) Henriette's bound to be at the market.

LULU: (*Hands between her knees.*) Turn the key.

SCHWARZ: (*Goes upstage and locks the door. A bell rings in the corridor.*) Damn!

LULU: We're not in!

SCHWARZ: It could be the art dealer.

LULU: So let it be the Kaiser!

SCHWARZ: I'll only be a moment. (*Goes out.*)

LULU: (*Alone, stares motionless into space.*) You. You. You. You here! Ah. Ah. That's good.

SCHWARZ: (*Returning.*) A beggar. Says he fought in the war. Do you have any change? I'm all out. (*Bends down and kisses her.*)

LULU: Go. Please.

SCHWARZ: (*Picking up the brush and palette.*) Back to Iphigenia. The model sits waiting while we're out here flirting. (*Going off.*) Give him some change.

(*LULU gets up, slowly puts herself in order, strokes back her hair and goes to the door to let in SCHIGOLCH.*)

SCHIGOLCH: (*Entering.*) I imagined him a bit more solid. A bit chestier. He's awfully rattled. His knees sagged when he saw me.

LULU: (*Pushing a chair for him to sit in.*) You begged from him! How could you?

SCHIGOLCH: (*Sitting down.*) Why else drag my cadaver here? It's bad enough in weather like this. You told me he paints in the mornings.

LULU: He was exhausted. How much do you want?

SCHIGOLCH: Two hundred—if you have it. Or maybe three? My two best clients are traveling. Didn't even tell me.

LULU: (*Goes to her writing table and rifles through the drawers.*) I'm so tired.

SCHIGOLCH: (*Looking around.*) This got me going, too. I wondered what things looked like here.

LULU: And?

SCHIGOLCH: Overwhelming. (*Looking up.*) Like mine. Fifty years ago. Instead of Chinese whatnots we had rusty old sabers. Damn, you've come up in the world. (*Ruffling the carpet with his shoe.*) The carpets—

LULU: (*Giving him three bank notes.*) I'm always barefoot when no one's around.

SCHIGOLCH: *(Noticing LULU's Pierrot portrait.)* You?

LULU: Like it?

SCHIGOLCH: As long as it's the real thing.

LULU: Drink?

SCHIGOLCH: Such as?

LULU: *(Gets up.)* Elixir de Spaa.

SCHIGOLCH: Spaa or Timbuktu, makes no difference—it's all chamomile tea to me. He drink?

LULU: That's all I need. *(Coming downstage.)* Liqueur affects people differently.

SCHIGOLCH: Does he lash out?

LULU: *(Filling two glasses.)* He dozes off.

SCHIGOLCH: When he's drunk, you can see all the way down to his bowels.

LULU: I'd rather not. *(Sits opposite SCHIGOLCH.)* Tell me.

SCHIGOLCH: The streets get longer, my legs shorter.

LULU: And your harmonica?

SCHIGOLCH: It's short of breath. Short of breath like me and my asthma. Like I always say, it's not worth the trouble of patching the old tug up. *(Clinks glasses with her.)*

LULU: *(Empties her glass.)* I thought by now you'd have run the course.

SCHIGOLCH: You're not the only one. Just because the sun's set doesn't mean you sleep. I'm holding out for winter. By that time my— *(Coughing.)*—my—my precious asthma will have dug up a one-way ticket for me.

LULU: *(Refilling the glasses.)* What are you saying? They lost your paper work up there?

SCHIGOLCH: Looks like it. The order's all screwed up. *(Stroking her knee.)* So. Tell me all about it. Hm? Long time no see—my little Lulu.

LULU: *(Pulling back, smiling.)* Life is such a brain-tease!

SCHIGOLCH: But you're still so young.

LULU: You called me Lulu.

SCHIGOLCH: It's not Lulu? I never called you anything else.

LULU: Not for ages.

SCHIGOLCH: Another moniker, then?

LULU: Sounds downright antediluvian.

SCHIGOLCH: Mercy! Mercy!

LULU: Now they call me—

SCHIGOLCH: As if the honey pot held anything but honey!

LULU: Meaning?

SCHIGOLCH: What's it now?

LULU: Eve.

SCHIGOLCH: What's in a name?

LULU: I'm listening.

SCHIGOLCH: *(Looking around.)* This is exactly what I dreamt for you. It's what you set your mind on. What do you call *that?*

LULU: *(Spraying herself with a bottle of perfume.)* Heliotrope.

SCHIGOLCH: Can it smell better than you?

LULU: *(Spraying him.)* Sour grapes!

SCHIGOLCH: Ah, such palatial luxury!

LULU: Ugh! When I think back—

SCHIGOLCH: *(Stroking her knee.)* So how are things going? Still plugging away at the French?

LULU: I laze about and sleep.

SCHIGOLCH: Stylish. Impressive. Anything else?

LULU: I stretch. Till my bones crack.

SCHIGOLCH: And after they've cracked?

LULU: Why does it interest you?

SCHIGOLCH: Why does it interest me? Why does it interest me? Better live to Judgment Day and lose heaven than abandon my little Lulu to a life of struggle. Why does it interest me? Compassion. My better self has already been transfigured. But I still understand the ways of this world.

LULU: Not me.

SCHIGOLCH: You're too well off.

LULU: Almost to the point of losing my mind.

SCHIGOLCH: Better off than with the old dancing bear?

LULU: I don't dance anymore.

SCHIGOLCH: It was time to trade him in.

LULU: And now I'm—

SCHIGOLCH: Tell me, tell me, my dear, tell me how you really feel. At your heart's core! I had faith in you when you were nothing more than two large eyes and a large mouth.

LULU: An animal.

SCHIGOLCH: Damn—and what an animal!

LULU: I know. I'm stylish.

SCHIGOLCH: An elegant animal! A splendid animal!

LULU: You trained me.

SCHIGOLCH: Yes, well, they can cart off my carcass any time now. I'm rid of all my prejudices.

LULU: You were that from the start.

SCHIGOLCH: Even against washing the dead.

LULU: Afraid of a final wash?

SCHIGOLCH: You just get dirty again.

LULU: *(Spraying him.)* This will bring you back if anything will.

SCHIGOLCH: We're only decay.

LULU: I beg your pardon! Every evening I rub my body with oil and powder it till I look like a marble statue. It makes the skin like satin.

SCHIGOLCH: It's also worth the trouble, I take it—with all the swells you do business with.

LULU: Throw back the sheets and I'm like a peeled apple.

SCHIGOLCH: As if you weren't filth all along!

LULU: Me? Certainly not! I'm miserable if I'm not good to eat—all over.

SCHIGOLCH: So am I! I'm good to eat all over, too. I'm throwing a large dinner party soon. Open house!

LULU: You won't give the worms much to picnic on.

SCHIGOLCH: Patience, my girl! Your admirers won't preserve you in spirits. As long as the skin's tight, it's Helen of Troy. But afterwards? A cracked pair of boots! Not even the zoo'd give it a second look. The little beasties'd go around belching. *(Getting up.)* Maybe they'll turn you into artificial manure.

LULU: *(Getting up.)* Was it enough?

SCHIGOLCH: Enough will be left over to plant a terebinth tree on my grave.

LULU: I'll see to it.

SCHIGOLCH: I won't hold my breath. Do you remember how I dragged you naked out of the gutter?

LULU: How you tied my wrists and strung me up and thrashed my bottom with your belt—that I remember like it was yesterday.

SCHIGOLCH: Nothing else to do. Nothing else to do. *(Offers her his cheek.)* Bye.

LULU: *(Kissing his cheek.)* Bye. *(Leads him out and returns with SCHÖNING.)*

SCHÖNING: What was your father doing here, madam?

LULU: My father? Why the formality?

SCHÖNING: *(Faltering.)* I—I need a moment—to talk to you.

LULU: To me? Couldn't you have done that yesterday?

SCHÖNING: *(Taking a seat.)* If my name were Edward Schwarz, that antique would never cross my threshold.

LULU: *(Dropping into an armchair.)* What's the problem—for God's sake—

SCHÖNING: Please listen to me, madam.

LULU: Why are you being so formal? He's in the studio.

SCHÖNING: I was prepared to tell you yesterday. I've been prepared to tell you for some time now.

LULU: Believe me, he's in the studio!

SCHÖNING: Just don't work yourself up, for God's sake.

LULU: No? When you're so—weird?

SCHÖNING: Yes—well—I only ask that your visits to me—

LULU: My visits?

SCHÖNING: Your visits, yes. Come to an end.

LULU: You're insane!

SCHÖNING: I'm asking that your visits to me come to an end.

LULU: What can you be thinking of!

SCHÖNING: Do you understand?

LULU: No.

SCHÖNING: I've been thinking about it for months. My main thought is for you. You and your happiness. It's been that from the start.

LULU: May I get you an Elixir de Spaa?

SCHÖNING: Not just now. I beg of you. Promise me.

LULU: What's happened to you—since yesterday?

SCHÖNING: Nothing.

LULU: You're trying to make a fool of me.

SCHÖNING: I've asked you twice already.

LULU: You've caught a cold. Yesterday—

SCHÖNING: I feel quite well.

LULU: So do I.

SCHÖNING: If you refuse to listen to me—

LULU: I'm listening. All right?

SCHÖNING: If you refuse to listen, then—then you will simply not be given entry. You're forcing me—*(LULU gets up and paces.)* As far as I am concerned, I will do nothing to interfere with your position in society. You can at least be as proud of that as you can of my—my intimacy. I will not be paraded around town any longer.

LULU: Don't play these games with me! What crime have I been guilty of!

SCHÖNING: It's costing me more than it costs you.

(Pause.—LULU gracefully lets herself down into a chair beside him, her hand on the back.)

LULU: You're planning to—marry—

SCHÖNING: That, too.

LULU: Something Platonic, I take it?

SCHÖNING: Will you shut up!

LULU: Whatever you say.

SCHÖNING: I wouldn't want to fall between two stools.

LULU: May one ask—

SCHÖNING: Miss von Bergen. The Baron's daughter. *(LULU nods.)* That's all there is to it.

LULU: Do you know her, then?

SCHÖNING: When she was a child she sat on my knee.

LULU: Pretty?

SCHÖNING: Something like that.

LULU: She's still in the dark about it?

SCHÖNING: She's being prepared for it.

LULU: Still at boarding school?

SCHÖNING: Her first free step will be into my arms.

LULU: Poor child.

SCHÖNING: We paid her a visit last week. Her father and I. It's a bit too soon to make any predictions.

LULU: Is she sixteen yet?

SCHÖNING: Potentially, however, she could become anything.

LULU: And—the Baroness?

SCHÖNING: A painful, motherly nod.

LULU: How clever of you!

SCHÖNING: A signal of gratitude.

LULU: I know. You rescued her papa from prison.

SCHÖNING: He became a bit too friendly with the church coffers.

LULU: So first you reel in the mother.

SCHÖNING: For politeness' sake.

LULU: Yes, you—

SCHÖNING: As there is a God in heaven!

LULU: I'll be happy to look like that at thirty-seven.

SCHÖNING: She's brought six children into the world.

LULU: You'd never know it.

SCHÖNING: It doesn't show.

LULU: She wanted to reimburse you.

SCHÖNING: Her husband couldn't possibly have been taken in by the same infatuation. Besides, we saw each other only once. I asked her immediately to confess everything to her husband.

LULU: You were already thinking of the child?

SCHÖNING: That, too.

LULU: Why make the poor creature more happy than she is? My foot will never cross your threshold again.

SCHÖNING: Your word?

LULU: We can meet wherever you say.

SCHÖNING: We'll never meet again. Except in the company of your husband.

LULU: No one can ask that of me.

SCHÖNING: Your marriage has made him my friend.

LULU: Mine, too.

SCHÖNING: To go behind his back I find—most distasteful.

LULU: Good God!

SCHÖNING: I've grown used to him. If he were to find out tomorrow, I couldn't just say: "Go back to where you came from." I can't do that anymore. A man of my age doesn't easily make new friends. He's the only person in the world who's closer to me than—

LULU: You'll get friends enough. Once you're married again.

SCHÖNING: Thank you.

LULU: Just wait a while.

SCHÖNING: That's why I want to avoid quarreling with Schwarz.

LULU: There's no need.

SCHÖNING: Yes. He's too much of a child.

LULU: Too much of a sheep!

SCHÖNING: Too much of a baby. Otherwise he'd have caught your scent long ago.

LULU: It wouldn't have hurt him if he *had*. He might not be so insipid. He might even pull himself together.

SCHÖNING: Why did you marry him in the first place?

LULU: Because I'd never seen anyone be so foolish.

SCHÖNING: Poor man!

LULU: To hear him talk, he's in seventh heaven!

SCHÖNING: Imagine the day his eyes are opened!

LULU: He's banal. He's an innocent. He has no training. He has no idea how he compares with others. He sees nothing. Not himself, not me. He's blind. Blind. Blind as a stovepipe.

SCHÖNING: You need to take him in hand.

LULU: I'm not a governess.

SCHÖNING: He bores you.

LULU: I'm his wife.

SCHÖNING: Ninety percent of wives have no choice but to do so.

LULU: I didn't need to marry to do that.

SCHÖNING: What grand illusions you have about high society!

LULU: Illusions? No. None. But there are times—even now—when I dream
of—of Goll—

SCHÖNING: The old magician. He pampers you.

LULU: He wasn't banal.

SCHÖNING: That's for sure. With his dancing instruction.

LULU: There are times I see his thick red head floating above me.

SCHÖNING: You long to get back to his whip.

LULU: Every three or four nights I dream that his burial was a misunder-
standing. That he's here, as if he'd never left. Only now he walks very
softly, in stocking feet. The fact I married Schwarz doesn't anger him
in the least. Just a bit sad. But then he's easily frightened, shy, really.
As if he were here without permission. Otherwise he's quite comfortable with us. Except that he can't get over how much money I've
thrown out the window since he died.

SCHÖNING: Desecration of the dead.

LULU: He comes because he wants to.

SCHÖNING: You still don't have enough, do you?

LULU: What do you call enough?

SCHÖNING: Hm. I? You don't measure love by the yard. If he lacks education—initiate him into the sacred mysteries.

LULU: He loves me.

SCHÖNING: Fatal!

LULU: He wants me to produce children.

SCHÖNING: Love never conquers the animal.

LULU: I won't look at myself in the mirror anymore. I'm made a fool of.
He doesn't even know me. He calls me "little songbird," "little gazelle,"
and hasn't the faintest notion of what I am. He'd say the same thing to
any old maid. He doesn't see the difference. It's because he's never had
a girl. He admits it.

SCHÖNING: But he's an artist. He's been staring pop-eyed at artists' models since he was fifteen!

LULU: He even brags about it.

SCHÖNING: Hm.

LULU: He's afraid. He trembles for his life. At every full moon he fantasizes he's contracted some unspeakable disease.

SCHÖNING: He's a hypochondriac.

LULU: And all I am to him is his contraceptive.

SCHÖNING: Oho—

LULU: Why not just come out and say it. I'm not even a part of the picture. When I show disgust, he passes it off to childish modesty. But that never keeps him from getting rough. When everybody's happy, he's off howling like a drainpipe.

SCHÖNING: There's more than one unspoiled wife would feel lucky to be in your shoes.

LULU: Then let him go find one. He'll find enough. When I've perfumed my hair and slipped into my dark silk plissé chemise with the hand's breadth of lace ruffle and bangles at the knees—

SCHÖNING: I remember.

LULU:—so that only my arms are bare—he tears into me like an orangutan—ripping every which way. And all I get out of it are his grunts.

SCHÖNING: Unbelievable.

LULU: And when I put on my baby costume and dance my tah-rah-rah-*bum*-dee-ay number, he falls asleep.

SCHÖNING: But he's an artist.

LULU: At least *he* thinks so.

SCHÖNING: Which is all that matters.

LULU: He also thinks he's famous.

SCHÖNING: For which I am also responsible.

LULU: He'll swallow anything. Anything! He's as mistrusting as a thief but lets himself be lied to so shamelessly you lose all respect for him! When I married him I made him believe I was a virgin.

SCHÖNING: Sweet Jesus!

LULU: He'd have thought me immoral otherwise.

SCHÖNING: Can that be done? *(LULU is silent.)* That could be disagreeable.

LULU: I screamed.

SCHÖNING: Because—

LULU He misunderstood it.

SCHÖNING: And—wasn't disappointed?

LULU: He still boasts of it.

SCHÖNING: *(Rising.)* He's to be envied. I've always said so.

LULU: He learned self-respect at a single stroke. Since when he speaks of himself with a great deal of enthusiasm.

SCHÖNING: This changes nothing. *(Pacing the floor.)* I have to think of my future. This is no time for a scandal.

LULU: I'll do anything—anything—to make him happy.

SCHÖNING: That's not sufficient. I intend to take my wife into a respectable house.

LULU: What do you plan to do with the child?

SCHÖNING: That doesn't concern you.

LULU: She's too young for you.

SCHÖNING: That "child," as you call her, is three years younger than you. ·

LULU: You'll die of boredom. Take my word for it. Bored with her babble and bored with her silence.

SCHÖNING: I can whip her into shape, don't worry.

LULU: Good God! She'll crack like a china plate in your hands.

SCHÖNING: Just stay out of my way! Since you married Schwarz you've had no reason to take our relationship seriously.

LULU: Oh, God!

SCHÖNING: I've done for you everything you could want. You have a young husband who's healthy as a horse. I look out for his career. You have large amounts of money at your disposal. You have a place in society. So please leave me just a modicum of freedom. Whatever time I still have to live, I have every intention of living. When you come to me and toss your things in the corner before I know what is going on, not even you can ask me to respect you as a married woman.

LULU: You're fed up with me. Fed up. *(SCHÖNING bites his lips.)* That's about it.

SCHÖNING: I'd say so.

LULU: *(Getting up.)* But I will not allow myself to be pushed down.

SCHÖNING: Here it starts.

LULU: I'll stand my ground as long as I have the strength.

SCHÖNING: Quiet!

LULU: I'll stand my ground if the world collapses around me.

SCHÖNING: Mignon.

LULU: It's as if in one stroke you'd never laid eyes on me—from one day to the next!

SCHÖNING: This is the only way it could have ended.

LULU: I won't let you toss me aside. I'd go to pieces. The whole world can trample me under foot. Just not you. Not you. It would be terrible of you. Terrible! You're killing me!

SCHÖNING: Is it money you want?

LULU: If I belong to anyone in this world it's to you! You've done everything for me! Everything I have is from you! Take it! Take me as your servant if you want!

SCHÖNING: I educated you. I married you off. I married you off twice. All I want now is to see you a respectable woman.

LULU: What's that to me—a respectable woman!

SCHÖNING: If you feel you owe me any thanks, then show it.

LULU: Do whatever you want with me! Why else am I here? Just not that! Not that! Don't toss me away!

SCHWARZ: *(Enters from the right carrying his brush.)* What's going on here?

LULU: He's getting rid of me! He's said so a thousand times.

SCHÖNING: Be quiet! Be quiet! Be quiet!

LULU: Said so a thousand times—stammered—no one loves like me!

(SCHWARZ takes LULU by the arm and leads her off right.)

SCHÖNING: *(Alone.)* What a mess.

SCHWARZ: *(Returns still carrying his brush.)* Is this some sort of joke?

SCHÖNING: No.

SCHWARZ: Then please explain to me—

SCHÖNING: Yes.

SCHWARZ: Yes? Yes?

SCHÖNING: Let's sit down. I'm tired. *(Sits.)*

SCHWARZ: *(Hesitating.)* What's the meaning of this?

SCHÖNING: Sit down—please.

SCHWARZ: *(Sits.)* What—what is the meaning of this? Explain it, explain it!

SCHÖNING: But you've—already heard.

SCHWARZ: I heard nothing.

SCHÖNING: Wouldn't you *rather* hear nothing?

SCHWARZ: I don't understand.

SCHÖNING: You need to realize—how much you owe to her. And that—

SCHWARZ: I know that.

SCHÖNING:—you've married half a million.

SCHWARZ: So? And?

SCHÖNING: You're swimming in luck.

SCHWARZ: Yes.

SCHÖNING: That's what you owe to *her.*

SCHWARZ: Yes.

SCHÖNING: You were a beggar.

SCHWARZ: Yes. Yes. Has she complained about me?

SCHÖNING: That's not the issue.

SCHWARZ: She *has* complained!

SCHÖNING: Pull yourself together. Be serious for a change. We're not children.

SCHWARZ: What more does she want?

SCHÖNING: She wants the whip!

SCHWARZ: She has everything she wants.

SCHÖNING: You are—

SCHWARZ: Tell me what that was all about just now!

SCHÖNING: But she said it herself. Here. In front of you!

SCHWARZ: *(Growing pale.)* You don't mean she—

SCHÖNING: You've married half a million.

SCHWARZ: Has she tried to betray me?

SCHÖNING: Accept what's happened as happened.

SCHWARZ: Happened?

SCHÖNING: It's your own fault if you've been betrayed.

SCHWARZ: But what has happened?

SCHÖNING: For the last six months you've been in seventh heaven. That's something no one can take away. That's what you owe to her.

SCHWARZ: What has she done?

SCHÖNING: Something time can never change.

SCHWARZ: What has she done!

SCHÖNING: But she told you herself.

SCHWARZ: Just now?

SCHÖNING: Just now? No. I've known her for thirteen years.

SCHWARZ: You—?

SCHÖNING: You've made a name for yourself. You can work. That's impossible without money. You don't have to deny yourself anything. You're master of your fate.

SCHWARZ: You betrayed me.

SCHÖNING: Shall we shoot it out?

SCHWARZ: Shoot? Shoot?

SCHÖNING: I'm not going to hurt you.

SCHWARZ: Oh, God. Oh, God!

SCHÖNING: Don't you feel well?

SCHWARZ: Oh, God—

SCHÖNING: No one has betrayed you.

SCHWARZ: Then I don't understand.

SCHÖNING: You don't *want* to understand. I came here to put an end to it.

SCHWARZ: Yes. I know.

SCHÖNING: I came to deny her any further visits. I came for your sake.

SCHWARZ: It's true, then.

SCHÖNING: Help me bring her to a sense of duty. She doesn't know what she's doing. She knows nothing else.

SCHWARZ: You—you knew her—

SCHÖNING: Yes, I knew her. She was a flower girl. At seven she was running barefoot and without a petticoat from one café to another selling flowers.

SCHWARZ: She told me she'd grown up with an awful aunt.

SCHÖNING: The woman I boarded her with.

SCHWARZ: Flower girl. Without a petticoat.

SCHÖNING: She didn't tell you that?

SCHWARZ: No, no.

SCHÖNING: You can't blame her for that.

SCHWARZ: Flower girl.

SCHÖNING: Why am I telling you this? So that you don't think her depraved. In the time I've known her she's improved herself considerably. She was an excellent pupil.

SCHWARZ: How long did she go?

SCHÖNING: That's not the question. At final exams, mothers held her up to their daughters as an example. I still have her certificates.

SCHWARZ: As I was getting to know her, she told me she was—untouched.

SCHÖNING: A joke, I dare say.

SCHWARZ: She told me—she was still—untouched.

SCHÖNING: But she was a widow!

SCHWARZ: She swore to me—*(SCHÖNING gets up and walks left.)*—by her mother's grave.

SCHÖNING: She never knew her mother. Not to mention her grave. Her mother doesn't have a grave.

SCHWARZ: Oh, God.

SCHÖNING: *(Coming back.)* I'm not here to discuss your obsessions.

SCHWARZ: No, no. How long was she in school?

SCHÖNING: Five years. She behaved like a little goddess to the other girls. It was delightful. Seeing her cross the street with them at four on winter afternoons. The girls were coming home with her to do their homework. Later on she was in Lausanne for half a year.

SCHWARZ: At boarding school?

SCHÖNING: Yes. They were equally captivated with her there. She should have stayed longer, but I removed her. The head mistress had a crush on her.

SCHWARZ: Why didn't you tell me that before!

SCHÖNING: Why? Why? Why didn't I tell you that before? *(Sits opposite him.)* When Dr. Goll died she asserted greater claim on me than you.

SCHWARZ: Dr. Goll. She said he would let her dance.

SCHÖNING: You've married half a million!

SCHWARZ: Then where did he get her?

SCHÖNING: Directly from me.

SCHWARZ: She said he never touched her.

SCHÖNING: He married her. How she made you believe such things, I don't know.

SCHWARZ: I saw her as my salvation.

SCHÖNING: Well, surely you know by now.

SCHWARZ: I?—Yes.

SCHÖNING: Who knows? She might also have told him that *I* had never touched her.

SCHWARZ: My salvation. I said to myself that—that—that heaven made us for each other.

SCHÖNING: Yes. Dr. Goll said the same.

SCHWARZ: Because I was so miserable.

SCHÖNING: You can credit *her* with that. If she's not what you imagined her to be, then make her into it now. Assume responsibility for your mistake.

SCHWARZ: Oh, God.

SCHÖNING: Marrying you merely increased her reputation.

SCHWARZ: Really?

SCHÖNING: You made your life with her.

SCHWARZ: She said she was still—

SCHÖNING: You either make concessions, or you're nowhere. You're strange.

SCHWARZ:—she was still untouched—

SCHÖNING: Untouched—untouched or not—what on earth—

SCHWARZ: Without a petticoat. One café to another.

SCHÖNING:—would you have done with a virgin!

SCHWARZ: She was—or I don't want—

SCHÖNING: *(Gets up and walks upstage, then returns.)* Let me help you. I can't stand by and see you continue living this way. Nor her. That's not living. You can't even look anyone straight in the eye. Make her respect you. She's pitiable. She deserves a husband she can esteem. She deserves to be a respectable woman. After that, you can quietly slip away again behind your curtains.

SCHWARZ: After?

SCHÖNING: Considering Mignon's origins, you can't just make demands that—

SCHWARZ: What are you talking about?

SCHÖNING: Her youth.

SCHWARZ: I don't understand all this.

SCHÖNING: I mean the squalor I rescued her from.

SCHWARZ: Who?

SCHÖNING: Your wife.

SCHWARZ: Eve—

SCHÖNING: I called her Mignon.

SCHWARZ: I thought—her name was—Nelly—

SCHÖNING: Nelly—was what Goll called her.

SCHWARZ: I called her Eve.

SCHÖNING: What she was originally called—I don't know.

SCHWARZ: Dr. Goll called her Nelly.

SCHÖNING: Given the father she had, it was for you to keep things in order.

SCHWARZ: What did he—?

SCHÖNING: He follows me around even now.

SCHWARZ: He's still alive?

SCHÖNING: Who?

SCHWARZ: Her father?

SCHÖNING: But he was just here.

SCHWARZ: Where?

SCHÖNING: Here!

SCHWARZ: Here?

SCHÖNING: Here. In the salon.

SCHWARZ: Here.

SCHÖNING: He left just as I arrived. Look. Here are their two glasses.

SCHWARZ: She said—she said—he'd gone down in a typhoon in the Philippines.

SCHÖNING: Is something the matter?

SCHWARZ: *(Grasping his chest.)* A horrible pain.

SCHÖNING: Have you got—have you got any—any sodium bromide?

SCHWARZ: No.

SCHÖNING: Drink a glass of water.

SCHWARZ: You—you de—de—deflowered her—

SCHÖNING: Deflowered! There wasn't much to deflower.

SCHWARZ: *(Reels from the chair and staggers around the room.)* It's tearing at my heart. I can't breathe. If only I could cry. Oh—if only I could scream—

SCHÖNING: *(Supporting him.)* Be a man. You've married half a million. Who *doesn't* prostitute themselves! You've got her. The world's most beautiful creature.

SCHWARZ: *(Straightening up.)* Leave me alone.

SCHÖNING: *(Stepping back.)* Just don't turn this into some pathetic little song and dance number. It's absurd. Just don't lose her! Take care of her! She's your life.

SCHWARZ: You're—you're right. You're right.

SCHÖNING: Don't let the situation jump the tracks. It all depends on you. If you could be happy—you'll have lost nothing. She's your property. Let her know it. What do you want? A stainless reputation without a stitch to its name? You're a famous artist.

SCHWARZ: You—you're right. *(Wavers to the left.)*

SCHÖNING: Where are you going?

SCHWARZ: To—to—explain her position to her. *(Goes off left.)*

SCHÖNING: *(Alone.)* He's got to lighten up. Now for the trio. *(Pause. He looks right, then left, then right again.)* I could have sworn—he took her out in that direction. *(Terrible groans emerge from the left. SCHÖNING rushes to the door and finds it locked from the inside.)* Open up! Open up!

LULU: *(Enters from the right.)* What—?
(The groaning continues.)

SCHÖNING: Open!

LULU: *(Stepping closer.)* That sounds—gruesome.

SCHÖNING: Is there an axe in the kitchen?

LULU: He'll open up—once he's cried himself out.

SCHÖNING: *(Pounding his foot against the door.)* Open! *(To LULU.)* Get me an axe—if there is one.

LULU: Shall I send for a doctor?

SCHÖNING: Have you lost your mind! God knows what's—*(A bell rings in the corridor. SCHÖNING and LULU stare at one another.)* Let me—

let me see to it. *(Goes upstage and stops in the doorway.)* I can't let myself be seen here.

LULU: He's groaning. Like he had a knife stuck in him.

SCHÖNING: Quiet! *(Softly.)* There's no reason anyone should be home.

LULU: What if it's—the art dealer?

(The bell rings.)

SCHÖNING: Damn! Damn! If we don't answer—*(LULU creeps toward the door; he stops her.)* Stay! Stay! I mean, no one's always ready to—*(Goes out on tiptoe. LULU creeps to the locked door and listens. SCHÖNING returns leading in ALWA.)* I beg of you—be quiet.

ALWA: There's rioting in the Reichstag.

SCHÖNING: *(Hushed.)* I said be quiet!

ALWA: *(To LULU.)* You're pale as a corpse.

SCHÖNING: *(Rattling the door.)* Edward! Edward!

(A hoarse throaty rattle is heard from inside.)

LULU: Merciful heaven! Merciful—

SCHÖNING: *(To LULU.)* Where's the axe?

LULU: I don't know if there's one in the kitchen. *(Goes off uncertainly upstage left.)*

ALVA: Caught you *in flagrante,* did he?

SCHÖNING: An over-excited fool.

ALVA: A human soul in distress.

SCHÖNING: There's rioting in the Reichstag?

ALVA: The editorial room's a madhouse! No one knows what to write!

(A bell rings in the corridor.)

SCHÖNING: *(Stomping his feet.)* Damn! Damn! *(Exerting pressure on the door handle.)* Edward!

(Both listen.)

ALWA: Nothing! Should I break it in?

SCHÖNING: Anyone can do that. Even me. Who could that be! *(Straightening up.)* The beast! The fool! The idiot!

ALWA: Hm—he's certainly making fools of *us.*

SCHÖNING: He celebrates all day. Couldn't care less about anything. And leaves his dirty laundry for others to—

LULU: *(Enters carrying an axe.)* Henriette's come back.

ALWA: *(Seizing the axe from her.)* Give it to me, give it! *(Inserts it between the door frame and the lock.)*

LULU: *(Her hand at her breast.)* This might be—a surprise!

ALWA: *(Working at it.)* I'll base a tragedy on it.

SCHÖNING: Hold it farther back! Farther! It won't work that way.

ALWA: It's cracking. *(The door springs open. ALWA brings both hands to his head and reels back into the room.)* Oh! Oh! *(Pause.)*

LULU: *(Her whole body trembling, her hand raised toward the door, to SCHÖNING.)* This is your—

SCHÖNING: Will you shut up! *(Wipes his brow and enters the room.)*

ALWA: *(In an armchair downstage right.)* Monstrous! Monstrous! Monstrous!

LULU: *(Supports herself against the door frame with her left hand, while she excitedly puts her right hand to her mouth.)* I—I—I've never—seen anything—like this—

ALWA: My breakfast's turning somersaults in my stomach. I'm going to be sick. I'll never get over this.

LULU: *(Suddenly screaming.)* Oh! Oh, God! God, no! *(Rushes right and grabs ALWA by the shoulder.)* Let's go! He bent his head back and—! Oh! Let's go!

ALWA: *(Trying mightily to regain his self-possession.)* Horrible! Monstrous!

LULU: Let's go! I can't stay! I can't be alone here!

ALWA: I can't. I'm paralyzed.

LULU: I beg of you. *(Takes him by the hand and leads him off to the right. SCHÖNING enters left carrying a ring of keys. There is blood on his sleeve. He pulls the door shut behind him and walks unsteadily to the writing table, sits down, and writes two notes.)*

ALWA: *(Returns from stage right and sinks into an armchair.)* She's changing. She wanted to change.

SCHÖNING: *(Looking up.)* She left?

ALWA: To her room. She went to her room. Wants to change. *(SCHÖNING rings and goes upstage left. HENRIETTE enters.)*

SCHÖNING: Do you know where Dr. Bernstein lives?

HENRIETTE. Of course. Right next door.

SCHÖNING: Take him this note. But—be quick about it.

HENRIETTE. And if the doctor's not at home?

SCHÖNING: Just leave it, then. Take this one to the police station. Go on. *(HENRIETTE goes off. SCHÖNING goes to the broken door.)*

ALWA: *(Getting up.)* I have to see him once more.

SCHÖNING: *(Turning in the doorway.)* You disappoint me. Let yourself go all you want, just not—at an inopportune time.

ALWA: I'm not used to such jokes. I'm not that callous.

LULU: *(Enters in a gray dust coat and black gloves, a black lace hat on her head, and carrying a sunshade.)* I see it on all the walls.

SCHÖNING: Where does he keep his papers, his valuables?

LULU: I don't know. *(To ALWA.)* Let's go.

ALWA: You're very pretty.

(SCHÖNING goes to the writing table and opens the drawers.)

LULU: My heart's beating a mile a minute.

ALWA: I still feel it in my legs. I'm totally—

LULU: Take me away from here.

SCHÖNING: *(At the writing table.)* Goddamn this country!

LULU: You can thank yourself for all this!

SCHÖNING: Shut up—or—

LULU: You're the murderer!

SCHÖNING: How could I have been so good to the boy! What a fool I was!

(LULU begins to sob.)

ALWA: *(Staring straight ahead.)* Jesus! The poor man's not even cold yet!

LULU: *(Crying.)* He'll never be warm again.

ALWA: True. We're alone now. *(Sinks into a chair.)*

SCHÖNING: The only time I've ever admitted to a mistake!

LULU: What are you afraid of!

SCHÖNING: And a mere boy brings the house down around me!

ALWA: I'm trying to decide if this is play material.

LULU: *(To SCHÖNING.)* You can sweep this under the rug. Like so many other things.

SCHÖNING: How does that help me!

ALWA: Tomorrow you can write an obituary about him. You knew him better than any of us. Shed a tear or two and call him Raphael. That way no one will believe you're guilty.

LULU: *(To SCHÖNING.)* Write a charming little article about him.

SCHÖNING: *(Pacing back and forth.)* I can see the headlines now: "Don Juan's Victim!"

ALWA: His engagement's got him all in a tizzy.

LULU: He'll have to think of something.

SCHÖNING: *(To LULU.)* The police—what will you tell them?

ALWA: God knows, *I* have nothing to gain by another of your marriages.

SCHÖNING: I couldn't care less what you have to gain.

ALWA: Winter harvest! Another howling nursery to put up with!

SCHÖNING: You've learned twice already to "put up with" one half of my fortune!

ALWA: Marry your lover—

LULU: Everything's turning, turning—

ALWA: Fortunately she's back on the block.

SCHÖNING: *(Goes to the writing table.)* The boy lived alone for too long.

ALWA:—if marriage is an absolute necessity!

LULU: All I see is blood.

ALWA: She's my guard against a family population explosion.

LULU: Who says so!

ALWA: *(To SCHÖNING.)* Promise me.

SCHÖNING: *(Half turning away.)* A whore.

(LULU rushes at him with raised sunshade.)

ALWA: *(Interposing himself.)* People! People! Calm down! *(Leading LULU to the left.)* He's got to let off steam somehow. He's like a lovesick schoolboy.

SCHÖNING: You marry her. What could be better? Use her money to produce your plays. Pay your women with it.

ALWA: Thank you, dear father.

SCHÖNING: I've had it up to *here* with her!

ALWA: I haven't yet reached that tragic pass.

LULU: And I don't want *you* either. Not if I were on my deathbed.

ALWA: No danger of that, madam.

SCHÖNING: My hair's standing on end.

ALWA: I always love the start of a breakup.

SCHÖNING: A blow that would leave a hired thug speechless. At *least!* And this brutish mob—

LULU: You'll get used to it in time.

ALWA: I'm having trouble holding on to my objectivity.

SCHÖNING: I'm not master of my own yet.

ALWA: And to top it off, there's rioting in the Reichstag.

SCHÖNING: That, too! But that's hardly important now.

ALWA: The editorial room's in chaos! Babel couldn't have been much worse.

SCHÖNING: I'll wait for the police. Go on back. I'll follow in five minutes.

ALWA: I have to see him once more. *(Goes to the broken door and opens it.)*

LULU: *(To SCHÖNING.)* There blood on you.

SCHÖNING: Where?

LULU: Wait. I'll pat it off. *(Sprays her handkerchief with Heliotrope and cleans off the spot of blood on SCHÖNING's sleeve.)*

SCHÖNING: It's his.

LULU: It's not the first time I've seen it.

SCHÖNING: He's a bleeder?

LULU: *(Smiling.)* That should do it.

SCHÖNING: *(Through his teeth.)* Monster!

LULU: You'll marry me all the same.

ALWA: *(In the open doorway.)* Blood—blood—blood! It's horrible!

LULU: *(Approaching the door.)* He was always a bit frightening.

SCHÖNING: *(Approaching the door.)* For God's sake, just don't touch him!

LULU *and* ALWA: *(Together.)* God save us!

ALWA: Crazy bastard!

LULU: How could he!

ALWA: With a razor.

LULU: He's still holding it.

SCHÖNING: That's one good thing, at least.

ALWA: The feeling that must be—horrible—

LULU: To cut his throat with a razor—

ALWA: Look at the sheets—the floor—

LULU: Filthy business!

ALWA: Everything's dripping with it.

LULU: And his hands!

ALWA: Too high strung.

SCHÖNING: He's showing us the way.

LULU: He had no education!

ALWA: He was behind the times.

SCHÖNING: He lived on credit.

HENRIETTE: *(Enters with DR. BERNSTEIN.)* Dr. Bernstein.

BERNSTEIN: *(Going breathlessly to SCHÖNING.)* But how is this possible, Dr. Schöning!

SCHÖNING: Depression.

END OF ACT TWO

ACT THREE
BERLIN

A magnificent hall decorated in German Renaissance style with a heavy ceiling made of carved oak. The lower half of the walls are wainscoted in dark wood. Above and on both sides are hung faded Gobelins. The upper rear of the hall is closed off by a gallery hung with drapery, from the right of which a monumental staircase projects halfway downstage. Beneath the gallery is an entrance with a pediment supported by twisted columns. In the middle, opening to both right and left, is a closed portière made of heavy Genoese velvet. LULU's portrait as Pierrot sits on a decorative easel in front of the bottom pillar of the outer banister. The frame is antiqued so that the gold allows the red undercoat to show through. Downstage right a broad ottoman. In the middle of the hall a square oak table with two high-backed upholstered chairs. Old padded armchairs, antiques, oriental objets d'art, weapons, animal skins, etc. A porcelain vase painted with flamingoes and with a bouquet of white flowers sits on the table. COUNTESS MARTHA GESCHWITZ, her black-gloved hands clutched convulsively in a muff, sits on the ottoman. LULU, seated to the left of her in an armchair, is dressed in a low-cut morning dress decorated with large bright flowers; hair in a simple knot fastened with a gold clasp; white satin shoes; flesh-colored stockings. RODRIGO is at the left, unseen, behind the portière.

GESCHWITZ: *(To LULU.)* How delighted I am that you'll be at our Ladies' Arts Ball.

SCHÖNING: Let's hope my wife's costume doesn't offend against propriety.

GESCHWITZ: I wouldn't worry. My friend's taste is far too refined for that.

SCHÖNING: Your exclusion of men leaves us at some disadvantage. We'll never know the nature of your fantasies. Is there no possibility of smuggling us in?

GESCHWITZ: None, Dr. Schöning. Quite impossible. Just the suspicion would ruin the evening.

SCHÖNING: Ruin? Ruin?

GESCHWITZ: Freedom is everything to us, Doctor. The Ladies' Arts Ball is founded on its exclusivity. An intrigue of this sort would be nothing short of high treason. Our ladies have every opportunity they like to dance with men. At the Ladies' Arts Ball they belong to us.

SCHÖNING: If I came as an advertising pillar, say, would that count as unwanted competition?

GESCHWITZ: We are unrelenting.

SCHÖNING: I assure you, I offer no threat. *(Taking his cigarette case from his pocket, to himself.)* My self-control amazes me! *(Aloud.)* Will the ladies smoke?

GESCHWITZ: *(Helping herself.)* If I may.

SCHÖNING: *(To LULU.)* Mignon?

LULU: Thanks, no.

GESCHWITZ: *(To LULU.)* Don't you smoke?

LULU: I'm not fond of it.

SCHÖNING: *(Giving GESCHWITZ a light.)* My wife regards smoking from an exaggeratedly aesthetic point of view.

LULU: May I offer you a liqueur?

SCHÖNING: Thank you.

LULU: Countess?

GESCHWITZ: Don't trouble yourself on my account.

LULU: Not at all. It's right here. *(She goes to a small cabinet under the staircase.)*

SCHÖNING: *(Going to the table.)* Tuberoses. How magnificent. *(Taking a whiff.)* Ah.

LULU: Aren't they? The Countess brought them for me.

SCHÖNING: *(To GESCHWITZ.)* Don't bankrupt yourself. *(To LULU.)* I didn't know it was your birthday.

LULU: *(Brings forward a small Japanese table on which she has set the liqueur service and places it in front of the ottoman.)* That's just what I asked myself.

GESCHWITZ: *(To LULU.)* You're trying to hurt my feelings.

SCHÖNING: All white. Hm. What does it mean, I wonder?

LULU: *(Pouring another liqueur for GESCHWITZ and herself.)* Flowers are a language I don't understand.

GESCHWITZ: I'm sorry, Mrs. Schöning. They had nothing prettier.

SCHÖNING: *(Going left, to himself.)* What a coincidence.

LULU: *(Touching glasses with GESCHWITZ.)* Don't worry about it. *(She downs her glass in one.)*

GESCHWITZ: *(After a sip, looks around the hall; her eyes fix on Lulu's portrait.)* You're bewitching. You're ravishing. I wish I could see you like that just once. Is it by a local artist?

LULU: A man named Schwarz.

GESCHWITZ: Schwarz. I recall the name.

LULU: You'd hardly have known him.

GESCHWITZ: Is he dead?

LULU: Yes.

SCHÖNING: Cut his throat!

LULU: You're certainly in a snit.

GESCHWITZ: *(To LULU.)* If he was in love with you, I can understand.

LULU: He was a bit strange.

GESCHWITZ: Who isn't? *(Getting up.)* I really must go, Mrs. Schöning. I'm running out of time. There's a life class this evening, and still so much to do for the Ball.

LULU: *(Accompanying her to the door.)* Thank you, Countess, for your kindness and your visit.

SCHÖNING: *(Following them.)* Have a grand time—at the Ladies' Arts Ball. *(RODRIGO, left, sticks his head through the portière. Seeing the others, he pulls back frightened.)*

SCHÖNING: *(To GESCHWITZ.)* Is there no way—you might let us into the boxes?

GESCHWITZ: *(Taking her leave of him.)* Now-now, Dr. Schöning. *(LULU leads GESCHWITZ out.)*

SCHÖNING: *(Coming downstage, to himself.)* My own son! *(Goes to the table, looks at the flowers and goes right.)* He's here. *(Pulling himself together.)* Well. There's no doubt now. I don't care. *(Walks to the portière, left, and stands in front of it for a moment.)* He'll be here soon. *(Coming back.)* The scandal doesn't frighten me. He'll never get the upper hand on me. They'll accuse me of wanting the publicity. But my name, my honor, my respectable home! But first to the proof. And then—there's this feeling—something I've never felt before. I have to fight for my life. I'm no fool. It all depends on what's left of my strength. *(Looking at the liqueur service.)* Too bad the drink doesn't help her. That would be heavenly. But quick, otherwise—ah, she can put away unbelievable amounts.

LULU: *(Returning.)* She kissed my hand.

SCHÖNING: Will I at least see you in your costume?

LULU: No no.

SCHÖNING: And perfect strangers can?

LULU: You're no stranger.

SCHÖNING: I won't be critical.

LULU: It's not ready.

SCHÖNING: It's just that I'd like to see you beforehand.

LULU: You'd be angry with me.

SCHÖNING: You're not exactly obliging.

LULU: It's only for women.

SCHÖNING: Precisely.

LULU: Please.

SCHÖNING: Yes, all right. *(Goes left, to himself.)* It might have been a bit more romantic.

LULU: Where are you going?

SCHÖNING: I've reviewing the matinée.

LULU: You're never at home. Gone half the time.

SCHÖNING: Of course.

LULU: The least you could do is stay around a bit today.

SCHÖNING: I write to dress you in splendor, my dear. When one wears as little as you, the expense of maintaining your naked shoulders would bankrupt a prince.

LULU: Then why do you do it?

SCHÖNING: Because I admire you. You're quite right. One recognizes the artist by what he omits.

LULU: Rather death than a miserable life.

SCHÖNING: That has a real ring to it.

LULU: Dying is easy. It used to terrify me.

SCHÖNING: Those who live easy—

LULU: And I will, too! The least of my worries are my naked shoulders.

SCHÖNING: Those who live hard— Yes, well! That's why I married you.

LULU: You didn't marry me.

SCHÖNING: What, then?

LULU: I married *you.*

SCHÖNING: *(Kissing her on the forehead.)* A hazardous enterprise, to be sure.

LULU: You're going?

SCHÖNING: To have a good laugh.

LULU: Then do.

SCHÖNING: Later, later. *(Goes out right.)*

RODRIGO: *(Pokes his head through the portière.)* Madam—excuse me?

LULU: *(Finger at her lips.)* No, wait. One minute.

RODRIGO: This is no picnic. It's been almost an hour. How about a drink, at least.

LULU: For God's sake. *(RODRIGO comes out. He is dressed in a tight-fitting, tightly-buttoned up, bright chequered suit with sleeves too short, bell-*

bottom trousers, fiery red tie, and golden earrings. LULU gives him a small, filled glass.) Exhausted?

RODRIGO: *(Tossing down the drink in one.)* You get used to hardships. Thanks. But maybe madam doesn't have the time.

LULU: Yes, yes. Just a minute.

RODRIGO: *(Looking around.)* Some place you've got here. A real mean scene. Not the homiest place, maybe. If madam's busy—

LULU: Could you wait just a moment, please.

RODRIGO: Then at least let me ask for the fifty marks.

LULU: *(Looking at him.)* I like the muscles.

RODRIGO: The fifty marks? You know? For my poor hopeless wife.

LULU: Aha. So you're married.

RODRIGO: I can't just stand at her bedside empty-handed.

LULU: Wait a moment. Please. I have to wait, too.

RODRIGO: Madam isn't feeling well?

LULU: Very. Fresh as a daisy. I have too many things to think about.

RODRIGO: *(Shyly putting his arm around her waist.)* And my poor hopeless wife?

LULU: *(Pushing him away.)* Just one more minute. Please.

RODRIGO: Hm. Whatever. At least give me another drink.

LULU: *(Serving him.)* He could still come back. It would be the end of everything. And after we've waited so long.

RODRIGO: Then I suggest we meet at the Lorelei Hotel next time. At the Lorelei we won't be on constant alert. Some posh place you got here, and the drinks aren't half bad either; but a guarantee of survival is *de rigueur* for a happy relationship.

LULU: I get so anxious.

RODRIGO: Give me the fifty marks and write me.

LULU: One second more. It's so much nicer here. So cool.

RODRIGO: Then give me another drink.

LULU: *(Recoiling.)* Oh, God!

RODRIGO: Jesus! Another one?

LULU: *(Forcing him left.)* Behind the drape. I knew it!

RODRIGO: Give me the fifty marks and let me out of here!

LULU: *(Opening the portière.)* Come on! Come on!

RODRIGO: *(Stopping her.)* At least give me twenty.

LULU: Come on, for God's sake!

RODRIGO: Just tell me what to do!

LULU: You want to be shot dead? *(RODRIGO disappears behind the portière, LULU closes them.)* You've lost your mind!

SCHÖNING: *(Enters from the right; extremely pale.)* I forgot.

LULU: *(Motionless behind the table.)* Your opera glasses?

SCHÖNING: *(Goes upstage left, to himself, with a glance at LULU.)* He's here now. *(Opens an encrusted box, takes out two étuis, slips the larger one into his breast pocket, and comes downstage with the smaller one.)* What exactly did the Countess want?

LULU: I don't know. She wants to paint me.

SCHÖNING: *(To himself.)* I'm shaking like a leaf.

LULU: I think she's strange.

SCHÖNING: *(Downstage left, has opened the smaller étui and turns away to give himself an injection under his cuff.)* I think she's—strange, too.

LULU: You shouldn't do that.

SCHÖNING: She comes looking like misery personified—paying a formal call.

LULU: You promised me—you wouldn't do it anymore.

SCHÖNING: It's why I locked it away.

LULU: You're nothing to me anymore.

SCHÖNING: I've tried.

LULU: It'll kill you.

SCHÖNING: *(To himself.)* Thanks to you.

LULU: Drinking's better.

SCHÖNING: *(Shuts the étui and buttons his cuff, taking a deep breath.)* I'll probably be dining at Peter's. *(Puts on his hat. LULU puts her arms around his neck and kisses him. He gently disengaging himself.)* Yes, well. You're a well-behaved girl. As everyone knows. *(Squeezing her hand.)* I'll see you tonight.

(LULU accompanies him out, stands in the open doorway, and listens. RODRIGO sticks his head through the portière. LULU signals for him to get back. ALWA, in splendid evening attire, top hat in hand, appears in the open doorway and wraps LULU in his arms.)

ALWA: At last—at last!

(RODRIGO pulls back behind the portière.)

LULU: *(Her whole body shaking.)* Oh, God—

ALWA: *(Leading her downstage.)* I hid behind the door. The old bumbler can never get to the end.

LULU:—if only I was a hundred miles away.

ALWA: With me here?

LULU: Oh, if only you knew. I almost don't know anymore. I'm so unspeakably unhappy. If only you knew.

ALWA: You asked me to come! You promised me everything. You set my whole being on fire!

LULU: For God's sake! Stay! You're the only one I can talk to. You're so dear, so dear. He left here gnashing his teeth.

ALWA: Hemorrhoids! Hemorrhoids! Just don't talk about it. Please. His self-regard is almost monstrous. I can't be jealous. I assure you, I can't. He's nothing to me! I know who you belong to. And I feel you. When I'm out riding. When I'm at the Eden Café. When I'm lying on the sofa. I feel you! You! I feel your body!

LULU: It's yours. Or will be. But—make me calm—stun me—make me numb—please. Or I can't bear up. *(With a glance to the left.)* Did you hear?

ALWA: Quiet as death.

LULU: Shh! I think—we're being listened to.

ALWA: You aren't well.

LULU: I am, I am. Fresh as a daisy. I've been a virgin for two weeks now. I don't know what it is.

ALWA: Then why did you ask me here? You said we'd have a little orgy. I took extra care with my clothes.

LULU: *(Lost in her gaze.)* You're beautiful.

ALWA: A tuxedo!

LULU: I want to love you—and die.

ALWA: Ah!

LULU: It's all arranged. I've ordered a small supper. If—if only there wasn't all this commotion.

ALWA: Don't, Lulu, don't push me over the edge. This is me standing here, me! My nerves are so on edge I can barely breathe! From the time you first mentioned the possibility of this little orgy, I've imagined night after night that I'd already had you. And here I am. And here you are. I see your knees beneath the flowers of your dress, I see your movements, your fiery eyes, and if I didn't rave on like this you'd turn me into a sex murderer!

LULU: I have something important to ask you.

ALWA: Important?! What? Dear God! What else *could* be important? You're playing a deadly game, Lulu. Celebrating the dying spasms of a starving man!

LULU: I love hearing you talk like that.

ALWA: Yes, but what does it get me? *(Leading her to the ottoman.)* I may have been a bit blunt just now. I arrived in a horsecab.

LULU: I'd like falling into the hands of a sex murderer.

ALWA: Now what did you want to chatter on about?

LULU: The Ladies' Arts Ball. Oh, how I wish it were the *Men's* Arts Ball! I was invited three times. Countess Geschwitz just left. She wants to paint me. Finally I said to myself—you're not listening!—I said, it's best you go in something as simple as possible.

(SCHÖNING appears in the gallery at the top of the staircase, between the two columns, right, at the same time pulling the curtains slightly apart.)

ALWA: As simple as possible.

LULU: I tried something this morning when I'd finished bathing. My hair in a plain knot with a clasp in back.

ALWA: Like now?

LULU: Yes, exactly!

ALWA: It's charming.

LULU: I left it that way. I'd have gone down on myself this morning if I'd been able. When I looked at myself in the mirror, I suddenly understood her—Geschwitz. I wish I was a man, all for me, just once! If I could have myself on the cushions like this—

ALWA: Oh!

LULU: Otherwise I wouldn't like it. Never. No, it's much nicer this way— when you're open to being kissed all over, all over!

ALWA: *(Nestles his head in her lap.)* You're fantasizing. It's making the blood rush to my head! Katja! And your warm pliant flesh under the soft silk—I don't feel a slip—no bulky underclothes—just you—wherever I feel. You've become a woman. You were always a little slip of a thing. You're perfect now. But still with the ways of a child. How enticingly you've dressed yourself for me, Katya! I need that. You know your people. I'm spoiled. This slippery-smooth silk—that highlights every curve—

LULU: *(Digging her fingers into his curly hair.)* This is only my morning dress.

ALWA: God, no, I want to love you in it *now!* My fingers on the silk.

LULU: It's for my lord and master.

ALWA: The swine!

LULU: That's also why it's cut so low.

ALWA: But not too low.

LULU: They all want a peek at a little piece of heaven—

ALWA: It's not cut too low, Katya!

LULU: For astronomical sightings.

ALWA: I swear, it's not cut too—low. It—is—not—*(Begins unbuttoning her from the top. LULU extends her arms behind her while smiling into space. ALWA discovers an elf costume beneath the morning dress.)* What is this? Have I lost my mind? What is it? I'm hallucinating!

LULU: *(Gets up quickly; her dress remains on the ottoman.)* This is for you! *(She wears light-colored silk tights and an armless pale-red silk blouse split to the waist front and back that finishes in front high over her hips and in back is drawn down into a narrow strip fastened between her legs. White satin shoes. Dark roses at the breast. SCHÖNING, in the gallery, vanishes as he lets the curtain fall. ALWA has slid to the floor and presses his lips to LULU's feet.)*

ALWA: I'm afraid—it will dissolve—before my very eyes! I don't dare look up! I'm afraid—it will slip through my fingers! It's too much! How can you—how can you plumb so deep inside me, Katya—to my very core! I'm having a nervous breakdown! Oh, Katya! Katya!

LULU: *(Trying to break free.)* Ow, ow! You're biting me.

ALWA: No. I won't leave these feet! These slender ankles! This—this modest crescendo—every inch a—a—! These knees! Oh, merciful God! This childlike voluptuous capriccio—between the andante of lust—and the—the unspeakably tender cantabile of these calves! These calves! I hear it! Like children's voices! On every fingertip. Katya! I feel your embrace! I don't think—I don't think—I can get up.

LULU: *(Touching his shoulders.)* You don't have to. Not yet. *(Goes upstage and rings the bell.)* Come on now.

ALWA: *(Dragging himself wearily to the table.)* My head's an empty waste. I feel like I've finished off sixty bottles of champagne.

LULU: *(Sitting down opposite him.)* You're my good angel—you light up my life. *(ALWA sits left and LULU right of the table. RODRIGO, behind ALWA's back, sticks his head out through the portière. LULU throws him a furious glance. RODRIGO pulls back. FERDINAND enters through the middle entrance with a serving tray, covers the table with a tablecloth, sets two places, and serves a cold partridge pâté and a bottle of Pommery on ice. LULU rubs her hands.)* I've arranged everything to your taste.

ALWA: *(Taking possession of the bottle.)* I'm not sure I can manage a proper appetite. *(FERDINAND snaps the napkin under his arm, casts a look at the table, and withdraws through the middle door.)* But I'm parched with thirst.

LULU: He's discreet.

ALWA: *(Filling the glasses.)* I feel like a soul in heaven rubbing the sleep from its eyes.

LULU: *(Hands between her knees.)* I feel like a butterfly slipping from its cocoon.

ALWA: *(Clinking glasses with her.)* Your eyes are flickering like—like in a dark well—when you throw a stone down in.

LULU: *(The glass at her lips.)* You're training your mustache to turn up? *(ALWA nods and fills the glasses. They eat, lost in their own silence. LULU gives ALWA a truffle from her plate.)* I could never love a man who didn't take great pains with his dress.

ALWA: A man dressed like a hunter, for example?

LULU: I'd rather he strangle me than make love.

ALWA: Doesn't *he* still wear them?

LULU: How can you ask me such a thing?

ALWA: You should know!

LULU: How?

ALWA: My enchanting little whore!

LULU: You're everything I need to be happy!

ALWA: Oh, Katya! *(Rings. Pause. FERDINAND enters with a dish of asparagus, changes the plates.)* You're sweating?

FERDINAND: Certainly not, sir.

LULU: Leave him be.

FERDINAND: I'm only human.

ALWA: Bring us another bottle.

FERDINAND: Certainly, sir. *(Goes out.)*

(SCHÖNING, carefully parting the curtains, appears in the gallery between the two columns. He takes a place behind the banister and cleans his opera glasses.)

ALWA: I'm slowly coming out of my muddle. Your plate. *(LULU hands him her plate and fills the glasses; ALWA serves her.)* You're drowning my strength.

LULU: You gave me your word.

ALWA: If only I could get a word in edgewise.

LULU: Ah, yes!

ALWA: I'll give a rousing speech.

LULU: And I'll listen with lips a-tremble.

ALWA: You'll grab me by the hair. *(LULU laughs.)* I see you clearly now for

the first time. For the first time I see the details. Your delicate fingers—
how they manage the asparagus. I've never seen such fat asparagus spears.

LULU: I'm almost afraid to pick them up.

ALWA: And your precious little cupid head—between your naked shoulders.

LULU: Oh, to feel like this the rest of my life! My head and my legs feel so
free—

ALWA: And your tongue. The pleasure it gives you!

LULU: *(Taking the asparagus out of her mouth.)* And how it just hangs there.

ALWA: *(Sinking back.)* You're driving me insane.

LULU: Eat. Please.

ALWA: *(Getting up.)* One kiss.

LULU: *(Pushing him back.)* Shame on you!

ALWA: One kiss! Just one!

LULU: Can't even have supper with a lady!

ALWA: This is no supper. It's a condemned man's last meal!

LULU: *(Extending her hand to him across the table.)* You need a bit more
time on the vine, my dear. *(ALWA covers her hand with kisses, pulls her
middle and ring fingers apart, and kisses between them.)* There's still
some butter on them. *(ALWA sinks to his knees, lays her naked arm atop
her head, and kisses her armpit.)* Oh, how you excite me!

ALWA: Caviar! Caviar!

LULU: *(Pushing him back to his place.)* Be reasonable. *(Handing him her full
glass.)* Drink that down. *(Wiping her finger on a napkin.)* There's more
on the way. *(Rings.)*

ALWA: What are three dozen oysters compared to this!

> *(FERDINAND enters, changes the plates, serves roast quail on mushrooms
> with salad, arranges two fresh bottles of Pommery, one of which he uncorks.)*

LULU: Be sure the coffee's nice and hot.

FERDINAND: You may rely on me, madam.

LULU: *(To ALWA.)* Shall we have it in the conservatory?

ALWA: No.

LULU: *(To FERDINAND.)* In the bedroom.

FERDINAND: With rum, arrack, whiskey, curaçao?

LULU: Rum or whiskey?

ALWA: Both, please.

FERDINAND: You may rely on me completely, madam.

ALWA: *(To FERDINAND.)* You're trembling?

LULU: Leave him be.

FERDINAND: I'm new at the job.

ALWA: I'd never have guessed!

LULU: I said, leave him be.

FERDINAND: I'm usually the coachman. *(Goes off with the asparagus.)*

SCHÖNING: *(In the gallery, to himself.)* There's another!

ALWA: *(Dismembering a quail.)* You're feeding my greed for your body with these delicacies. These aromas! And this flesh! So Byzantine! So miraculous! But yours—

LULU: *(Placing her arms behind her head.)* But mine?

(RODRIGO sticks his head through the portière. When he discovers SCHÖNING sitting in the gallery he pulls back in horror.)

SCHÖNING: *(To himself.)* And another!

LULU: *(Serving ALWA salad.)* I wish you could come to the Ball with me. The women follow me around like foxhounds.

ALWA: What's that?

LULU: Celery.

ALWA: *(Collapsing helplessly.)* How much tighter can you pull the strings! Or don't you have a spark of decency left! God knows, you're destroying my health. You're ruining my life. *(Slides from the chair and embraces her knees.)* Let me die here! Let me die! I can't stare into your terrible eyes any longer! I'm barely human! I warn you, Katya! I warn you!

LULU: *(Lets his head slide between her knees.)* Your face is burning—

ALWA: *(Muttering.)* Let me relish the torment—to the limit of my moral strength! Save me before I've gone too far. Your body, your breath! So chaste! My lust is tearing itself to pieces! Shaking me! No woman! A warm knot of silk—let me up—

LULU: *(Holding him by the hair.)* No.

ALWA: Now.

LULU: Are you done?

ALWA: Oh, God!

LULU: Get up.

ALWA: I can't get up.

LULU: Let's finish eating.

ALWA: I can't eat.

LULU: Come on. Let's go to—

ALWA: Shut your hole.

LULU: —my room.

ALWA: You sewer! You meat grinder! You piss hole! You snotrag! You liquid shit! You crock of muck! You shit pit!

LULU: (Retreats trembling, sees SCHÖNING sitting in the gallery.) His father! He'll box his ears! (SCHÖNING has risen quickly and closed the curtains. ALWA lies still, hands folded over his head. LULU removes a rose from her breast and sticks it in her hair. She goes toward the stairs and, halfway up, leans back against the banister, feet crossed, her naked arms spread out along the velvet-upholstered rail. To herself.) This is the most beautiful moment of my life.

SCHÖNING: (Carrying a revolver, enters through the middle, sees ALWA lying on the carpet, and delivers him a kick to the posterior.) Get out!

ALWA: (Looking up.) You!

SCHÖNING: Out!

ALWA: What a joke!

SCHÖNING: I'll shoot! That what you want?

ALWA: (Grins at him.) The Idealists and Arbiters of Moral Order! The Knights of Impotence!

SCHÖNING: I could shoot you in cold blood!

LULU: (On the stairs, to herself.) He wouldn't dare!

ALWA: (Has risen.) That's one way to get revenge!

SCHÖNING: Get out!

ALWA: Congratulations!

SCHÖNING: Did I accuse you of anything?

ALWA: If you had, your books might be easier to swallow! Try writing something with blood in its veins!

SCHÖNING: Why are you here? One good reason!

ALWA: What a hack!

SCHÖNING: I'm throwing you out! That's all!

ALWA: (Retreating.) You and your weepy old German tragedies!

SCHÖNING: And your inept plagiarisms! (Grabbing him by the collar.) Let's be original for once. (Leads him out. The door closes behind them.) (RODRIGO propels himself through the portière, runs rapidly through the room, and stumbles up the stairs.)

LULU: (Obstructing his exit.) Going somewhere?

RODRIGO: Out!

LULU: Where?

RODRIGO: Let me out!

LULU: You can't leave me alone like this!

RODRIGO: I'll throw you over the banister!

LULU: This isn't the way. You'll run straight into his arms.

RODRIGO: (Sinks to his knees.) Please, madam, I beg of you, get me out of here! You invite me for a bottle of champagne, stuff me behind some ratty curtains, while that lunatic futzes with a pistol and you stuff your belly with partridge! And I can't even see which way he's shooting! Let me out of here, or—

LULU: He's coming.

RODRIGO: *(Staggers back down into the hall.)* Fucking shit! *(Looks around.)* How do I get out of this place! He'll put a bullet through my head! What have I done!
(SCHÖNING is heard approaching.)

LULU: He'll shoot you dead.
(RODRIGO disappears under the tablecloth. SCHÖNING returns with his gun cocked, goes to the portière, and throws back the curtains.)

SCHÖNING: Where's he gone?

LULU: Away.

SCHÖNING: Where?

LULU: Out the window.

SCHÖNING: Over the balcony?

LULU: He's an acrobat.

SCHÖNING: I didn't know. *(Goes upstage and locks the door. RODRIGO reaches for the plate of quails and disappears with it under the tablecloth. SCHÖNING comes downstage.)* Let's have look at you now. *LULU strokes the hair from her face as she descends.)* You're very tempting.

LULU: I know.

SCHÖNING: You're from a world apart. Beyond the sunset.

LULU: I thought it up myself.

SCHÖNING: A tightrope artist.

LULU: More an elf, I think.

SCHÖNING: Without those big round eyes of a child you'd scandalize people with the way you parade your hips.

LULU: It's smarter than hiding them under a pair of plush knickers.

SCHÖNING: Beauty conquers shamelessness. Your flesh triumphs over your body.

LULU: My flesh is Lulu.

SCHÖNING: Could it be your corset?

LULU: I'm not wearing one.

SCHÖNING: Excuse me?

LULU: I feel so good in this.

SCHÖNING: The only thing lacking is butterfly wings.

LULU: That would be awkward.

SCHÖNING: The swing of your legs isn't easily missed.

LULU: How's my hair?

SCHÖNING: You're going to the Ladies' Arts Ball like that?

LULU: Don't you like it?

SCHÖNING: Like that?

LULU: Like this.

SCHÖNING: And you're not ashamed?

LULU: They'll pull me apart and pass me around.

SCHÖNING: Don't you have any shame?

LULU: No.

SCHÖNING: What an old fool I am.

LULU: You are—*(As SCHÖNING leads her to the ottoman.)* What do you want?

SCHÖNING: *(Sitting.)* I want to feel myself against you one more time.

LULU: Just put the revolver away.

SCHÖNING: It's no bother.

LULU: *(On his knee.)* Give it here.

SCHÖNING: That's why I brought it. *(Places the revolver in her hand. LULU stretches her arm up high and fires a shot into the ceiling.)* Don't be foolish.

LULU: What a roar!

SCHÖNING: It's loaded.

LULU: *(Looking at him.)* It's pretty.

SCHÖNING: Not pretty enough for as bewitching devil as you.

LULU: What shall I do with it?

SCHÖNING: Kill yourself.

LULU: *(Rises and pulls her blouse straight over her tights.)* If only you'd brought your horsewhip with you.

SCHÖNING: Don't play games.

LULU: It could put other ideas in your head.

SCHÖNING: *(Holding her around the waist.)* One more kiss.

LULU: *(Sinks onto his knees, throws her arms around his neck, and kisses him.)* Just put down the revolver.

SCHÖNING: These lips! These lips! *(LULU kisses him.)* You grow more seductive every day.

LULU: *(Kissing him.)* Put it down.

SCHÖNING: You need it.

LULU: *(Kissing him.)* Please.

SCHÖNING: It's been this way since I first knew you.

LULU: Then why not do it yourself?

SCHÖNING: Because I'd end up in prison.

LULU: You love me too much for that.

SCHÖNING: It won't be difficult for you.

LULU: Don't say things like that. Please. Don't look at me that way!

SCHÖNING: Quiet, my dear.

LULU: It's all gone black in front of my eyes.

SCHÖNING: *(Stroking her.)* Do as I say. *(LULU yawns.)* Put it to your breast.

LULU: It's still warm.

SCHÖNING: Fire! *(LULU tries it several times.)* With the trigger finger. *(Attempts to guide her hand.)*

LULU: *(Lets the weapon sink.)* Ah.

SCHÖNING: I'm such a bungler. *(LULU lays back her head and rubs her knees together.)* Little goose. It would be over now.

LULU: *(Drawing a deep breath.)* And I'd be in the sauce.

SCHÖNING: *(Has recovered the revolver from her without her noticing.)* Your legs, your legs—

LULU: They've gone to sleep.

SCHÖNING: The two sweet rivals!

LULU: They all say that.

SCHÖNING: They snuggle so together, each one knowing itself the most beautiful.

LULU: Oh, God! *(Stretching her feet.)* Tie them for me.

SCHÖNING: So that when their devilish mistress is touched—

LULU: They fly wide open.

SCHÖNING: Like envious cavaliers!

LULU: Would you? Just once more?

SCHÖNING: What?

LULU: What else? Tie me. Whip me.

SCHÖNING: It makes no sense.

LULU: Till you draw blood. I won't scream. I'll bite on my hanky.

SCHÖNING: No use. I've lost my stuffing.

LULU: *(Lets her hand glide over his gray hair.)* Then why won't you forgive me?

SCHÖNING: It's the morphine. It's killing me. I forgave you a long time ago. I was always like a father to you. Now I'm *really* one.

LULU: I'm going to get dressed. Have the carriage come round. We'll go to the opera.

SCHÖNING: They're playing *Pagliacci*. You're wracking your brain trying to find some way out.

LULU: *(Pushing against his chest.)* Let me go. Let me go.

SCHÖNING: If only you were stronger.

LULU: Let me—I have to go to the bathroom!

SCHÖNING: It's not worth the effort now. *(LULU stares at the floor.)* You know perfectly well where you have to go.

LULU: I—I can't think of it.

SCHÖNING: Try thinking you're lying—*(While kissing her passionately.)* —in the arms of—

LULU: *(Checking his arm.)* Not yet! Not yet! I'm still so young!

SCHÖNING: Give me your hand. Stop it now! It doesn't hurt!

LULU: *(Holding the revolver.)* It'll kill me!

SCHÖNING: Quiet! Quiet!

LULU: Why should I have to die so soon?

SCHÖNING: Don't be childish!

LULU: Oh, God!

SCHÖNING: Ugh! How pitiful.

LULU: Even animals can still—afterwards I'll be nothing.

SCHÖNING: It'll make you drunk.

LULU: *(Breaks out in sobs.)* Why should I have to die so soon?

SCHÖNING: Quiet! Quiet!

LULU: *(Crying.)* I'm so—happy—so happy—why should I—even animals can—still live—the animals—can still—can still—I've done—what everyone does—I'm a woman—I'm a woman—I'm twenty years old—

SCHÖNING: Don't be childish.

LULU: Oh, God.

SCHÖNING: You won't feel a thing.

LULU: *(Putting the revolver to her breast.)* God save me.

SCHÖNING: *(Jolting her with his knee.)* You bore me.

LULU: Oh! It's all gone black in front of my eyes.

SCHÖNING: *(Directing the hand with the revolver under her left breast.)* There—there—just don't think about it.

LULU: *(Eyes wide open.)* Soon—

SCHÖNING: I've never seen you like this.

LULU: Stop—stop—

SCHÖNING: Ugh!

LULU: Soon—

SCHÖNING: Now.

LULU: Afterwards I'll be nothing—but a dead woman.

SCHÖNING: Damn! *(Yanks her from his knees and tosses her against the ottoman. Goes left, agitated. LULU lies in front of the ottoman, the revolver pressed against her breast, screaming and sobbing.)*

LULU: I can't. I can't. Not yet. Oh! My life! *(SCHÖNING comes back. LULU raises herself half way, the revolver still pointed at her breast, her face ravaged with terror.)* Be patient. I beg of you. Be patient. One minute more. Of life. Soon. *(Sliding toward him on her knees.)* I beg of you. I beg of you.

SCHÖNING: *(Stamping nervously.)* Now!

LULU: *(Hits her forehead on the floor.)* I can't. I can't. I can't. *(Doubling up.)* Can't think. Night. Night. Night. God! *(Thrashing about.)* Oh—oh—oh!

SCHÖNING: *(Suddenly pale, unsure.)* Have you no—no—

LULU: Everything is night. When it breaks—breaks—I'll shoot myself—in the heart!

SCHÖNING: *(At the left proscenium, stammering.)* Sha—al I—

LULU: No—no—no— *(SCHÖNING removes the étui and performs a morphine injection.)* I will—*(Lifts her head.)*

(ALWA emerges from the curtain and descends the gallery stairs, silently wringing his hands. RODRIGO hurls himself from under the table and grabs SCHÖNING by the arms.)

RODRIGO: Careful!

(Two shots resound. SCHÖNING tumbles forward.)

SCHÖNING: I—

RODRIGO: *(Catching hold of him.)* Don't say I didn't warn you.

SCHÖNING: *(Spurting blood.)* My number's up.

(LULU has jumped up, raced up the stairs, and clings to ALWA. RODRIGO leads SCHÖNING to the ottoman.)

RODRIGO: How the hell'd you—screw up like this? *(Showing his left hand, streaming with blood.)* I got my ass in a sling, too. *(Lays SCHÖNING on the ottoman.)* Hold on—I'll—run for the doctor—in a second.

SCHÖNING: *(Mouth hanging open.)* You—stay here.

(Pause.)

LULU: *(Tiptoes closer.)* Did I hurt you?

SCHÖNING: *(Catching sight of LULU.)* My—my murderess—it—it burns—get—to safety—to safety—the keys—take the keys—from my pocket—

LULU: You don't feel a thing.

SCHÖNING: In the safe—you'll find—sixty thousand—don't—don't lose
time—water—some water—a glass—water—please—

LULU: I can't go out like this.

SCHÖNING: Elf—my elf—

RODRIGO: Would the gentleman care for—champagne?

SCHÖNING: If you—happen—have any—*(RODRIGO has quickly filled
a goblet from the open bottle and takes it to the ottoman.)* Thirsty—I'm—
thirsty—

LULU: *(Taking the glass from RODRIGO.)* Let me. *(Kneels down and puts it
to SCHÖNING's lips.)*

SCHÖNING: My—little murderess—*(Drinking.)*—you—always stay—
the same—

LULU: It'll make you—drunk.

SCHÖNING: *(After emptying the glass.)* Oh! Oh! It burns. I'm drying up.
My tongue—my—my tongue—

RODRIGO: *(Uncorking the unopened bottle.)* Drink. That's only the first
glass. Go on, drink. As much as you can.
(ALWA has come near the ottoman.)

SCHÖNING: You, too—my son—

ALWA: Julius Caesar.

SCHÖNING: I understand—that you—intrigued—the next—the next—
you're—the next—you—

RODRIGO: *(Has refilled the glass and gives it to SCHÖNING to drink.)*
Keep it up! That's it! Keep it going!

SCHÖNING: Blood—there's blood—swimming in it—

RODRIGO: It's mine. Just mine.

SCHÖNING: I'm—dreaming—

RODRIGO: It's not poisoned. *(To LULU.)* If madam would be so good
as to—

LULU: *(Takes the bottle and glass from him.)* By everything that's holy, I didn't
see you.

RODRIGO: *(Binding his hand with his handkerchief.)* There's nothing to be
said.

SCHÖNING: You're—you're an—acrobat—

RODRIGO: Wrestling. Greco-Roman mostly. *(To LULU.)* Just keep filling
it up.

LULU: *(Continuing to pour.)* You mustn't think the worse of me.

SCHÖNING: My—elf—murderess—

RODRIGO: *(To himself.)* It only grazed me.

LULU: I might just as easily have—

SCHÖNING: Better—it's getting—better—

ALWA: Do you want me to send for a doctor?

SCHÖNING: Take—take—the keys—from my—pocket—I can't—can't—can't move—you know—the—papers—my mother—hid—hid—hid—she couldn't have known—merciful—a summer—month—summer—sum—on—

LULU: (Kissing him.) Look at us! Look at us! You can't see us!

SCHÖNING: Are you still—afraid—heartburn—morphine—morphine—mor—

RODRIGO: Give him more champagne.

LULU: (Does so.) I might just as easily have—

SCHÖNING: Get—get away—to safety—you're—you're lost—doctor—no doctor—I give you—money—money—with—bridges—build a—build a bridge—over—over—over—over—the isthmus—one is already—(Groaning.) Oh—

LULU: It curdles my blood.

SCHÖNING: Yes, yes—kiss me—once—more—

(LULU bends over and kisses him, while putting her right hand over his heart.)

RODRIGO: (To ALWA.) He looks like a clown with his chalk-white face. It makes you think. A color like that. I wouldn't want to look like that. God knows! All the same, maybe he's come up with the winning ticket after all. With kisses like that! Just before he goes down the tubes, I mean. Not a shabby sendoff! Our kind's lucky to get a filthy smoke stuck in our snout.

ALWA: Where the hell did you come from?

RODRIGO: The billiard hall, actually.

LULU: (Straightening up.) He's dead.

ALWA: My father.

RODRIGO: If the lady and gent don't mind, I'll be on my way. Otherwise I'll be left holding the bag here.

ALWA: We have to get the revolver in his hand—while there's still time.

RODRIGO: That won't do much good, sir. I don't know what your specialty is, but he could hardly have shot himself in the back.

LULU: I'm going to Paris. (To ALWA.) Get the keys. Hurry!

ALWA: (Emptying SCHÖNING's trouser pockets.) What will you do in Paris?

SCHÖNING: (Toneless.) A bridge—

ALWA: *(Stepping back.)* Oh! Oh!

LULU: Quiet!

RODRIGO: A voice from the tomb. He's far gone.

ALWA: *(Holding the keys.)* You've got to take me with you.

LULU: I have to change.

ALWA: Or I won't give you the money.

LULU: I can't keep you from going to Paris.

ALWA: You can't leave me behind penniless!

LULU: Hand me my dress.

ALWA: You're my destiny.

LULU: Hand me my dress.

ALWA: Yes.

LULU: He's lying on it.

ALWA: *(Pulling the morning dress from beneath SCHÖNING and throwing it over LULU.)* I can't imagine life without you anymore.

RODRIGO: Madam's soiling her tights.

ALWA: It's full of blood.

LULU: That hardly matters now. I'll be taking them off soon.

ALWA: I'll empty the safe. Then we can lock up.

LULU: *(In the doorway, right.)* The train leaves at eight.

ALWA: For Paris.

RODRIGO: I hear something.

SCHIGOLCH: *(Lifting the curtains in the middle of the gallery.)* It smells of gunpowder.

ALWA: *(Giving at the knees.)* Who's that?

LULU: My father.

END OF ACT THREE

ACT FOUR
PARIS

A spacious salon in white stucco. In the upstage wall, wide double-swing doors. A large mirror on either side of them. Two additional doors are situated in each of the side walls. Between them, right, is a rococo console topped in white marble, a large mirror above it; left, a fireplace of white marble, above it Lulu's portrait as Pierrot in a narrow gold frame set into the wall. In the middle of the salon, a delicate, brightly upholstered Louis XV sofa. Broad, brightly upholstered armchairs with thin legs and delicate armrests. Downstage left a small table. GESCHWITZ enters dressed in a light-blue, white fur-trimmed Hussar's jacket with silver braid, white bowtie, tight stand-up collar, and stiff cuffs with enormous ivory cufflinks. She appears nervous and listens with divided attention to the large-scale festivities in the gaming room. RODRIGO is heard delivering a toast.

RODRIGO: *(From the gaming room, a bit tipsy.)* Mesdames et Messieurs— excusez—Mesdames et Messieurs—vous me permettez—soyez tranquilles—c'est le—c'est le—how do you say birthday?

VOICES: *(Calling out, laughter.)* L'anniversaire! L'anniversaire!
(Laughter and merriment. GESCHWITZ turns away in scorn.)

RODRIGO: Thank you very much! C'est l'anniversaire de notre bien aimable—comtesse, qui nous a reunis ici—ce soir. *(GESCHWITZ, annoyed, takes a seat downstage. RODRIGO continues without interruption.)* Permettez, Mesdames et Messieurs—c'est à la santé de la comtesse Adélaïde d'Oubra—que je bois, à la santé de notre bien aimable hôtesse, la comtesse Adélaïde—dont c'est aujourd'hui l'anniversaire—*(Loud applause, laughter and conviviality off. RODRIGO, perspiring, enters immediately, grateful to be relieved of his task. He is in evening dress as are all the men in the scene. He goes to the console, scribbles a note, folds it, and continues holding it. Catching sight of GESCHWITZ.)* A la bonne heure! Hm. Your grace. *(GESCHWITZ starts at the sound.)* Do I look as dangerous as all that? *(GESCHWITZ stares absently at the floor.)* Your grace is searching for a topic of mutual concern. *(GESCHWITZ throws a despairing glance at the center doors. To himself.)* This calls for a bit more brio, I can see. Let's try a joke. *(To GESCHWITZ.)* May I make so bold as to—
(GESCHWITZ utters a small shriek. CASTI-PIANI leads LULU downstage from the gaming room. She is dressed in a white directoire gown with

large puff sleeves and white lace falling from the waist to the feet. Her arms are covered in white kid gloves, and her hair is piled high on her head with a small plume of white feathers.)

CASTI-PIANI: May I be allowed a few words?

LULU: Feel free.

(RODRIGO, unnoticed by CASTI-PIANI, slips the note into LULU's hand and goes off into the gaming room.)

CASTI-PIANI: Sit down. *(To GESCHWITZ.)* Leave us alone.

(GESCHWITZ doesn't move.)

LULU: *(Sitting on the sofa.)* Have I offended you?

CASTI-PIANI: *(To GESCHWITZ.)* Are you deaf?

(GESCHWITZ throws him a furious look and goes off into the gaming room.)

LULU: Have I offended you?

CASTI-PIANI: *(Sitting opposite her.)* How are your nerves doing?

LULU: Ask anything you want of me.

CASTI-PIANI: What do you have left?

LULU: You should be ashamed.

CASTI-PIANI: I even have your heart.

LULU: It's true. It's stronger than me. I'd be grateful if you showed a little consideration.

CASTI-PIANI: I envy you.

LULU: What more do you want?

CASTI-PIANI: You can consider yourself lucky.

LULU: To have met you? What can I say? You're right.

CASTI-PIANI: I don't even figure in this.

LULU: I could never have dreamt such a thing!

CASTI-PIANI: It's emotions—emotions that our kind should never allow ourselves.

LULU: You should thank God!

CASTI-PIANI: It's a bitter thing. Especially when you have a heart born for them.

LULU: I'd give up half my life not to have seen you!

CASTI-PIANI: Fighting for one's life makes for a hard heart.

LULU: You don't have one.

CASTI-PIANI: That's my sore point.

LULU: Hypocrite!

CASTI-PIANI: My Achilles heel. Especially since I lack power over women.

LULU: Merciful heaven.

CASTI-PIANI: Had you not thrown yourself at my feet—out of some pigheaded impulse of yours—I'd never have shared the joys of paradise with you.

LULU: Mock all you want.

CASTI-PIANI: And then the murderous torment of trying not to get hooked in the process. What a husband I'd have made! Too late now!

LULU: Why are you telling me this?

CASTI-PIANI: Because at this very moment I'm hanging naked again on a cross! Lord God, let this cup pass from my sight!

LULU: Cup? Cross?

CASTI-PIANI: It's murder pure and simple.

LULU: You're a—

CASTI-PIANI: Whatever you like.

LULU:—police spy.

CASTI-PIANI: Whatever you like. I began as an officer in the Hussars.

LULU: Jesus!

CASTI-PIANI: That didn't pan out either. I didn't enjoy being shot to death for other people's amusement.

LULU: Police spy?

CASTI-PIANI: Having resigned my sword, I founded an employment agency.

LULU: What has that to do with me?

CASTI-PIANI: I arranged for positions in Hungary, Siberia, India, Persia, and last but not least, America.

LULU: What sort of positions?

CASTI-PIANI: Profitable ones. At least for me. Until some hot little pesky pastor's wife crawled her way between my legs.

LULU: Oh, God, oh, God!

CASTI-PIANI: Little Hetty or Betty—or whatever she was called—was living high on the hog—but what good did that do me! I had been appointed to a government position.

LULU: In prison.

CASTI-PIANI: Yes, as a matter of fact! Six months later—thanks to my exemplary behavior and my extensive knowledge of languages—my cell door once again opened sesame. Given the opportunity, I allowed myself to be talked into settling here permanently to keep tabs on our fellow countrymen.

LULU: Police spy.

CASTI-PIANI: I could scarcely deny myself the satisfaction of breathing life back into my employment agency. I have the best of all possible connections, especially considering the territory is not exactly unprofitable. Parisian women love Paris, especially if they're hard-put. But the constant throng of foreigners offers me an enormous resource of materials.

LULU: I suspect you're—pulling my leg.

CASTI-PIANI: *(Taking an opened letter from his pocket.)* I have here an offer. From Epaminondas Oikonomopulos. A Cairo establishment. I sent them photographs of you.

LULU: The ones *I* gave you?

CASTI-PIANI: In your elf costume; as Pierrot; in your pleated chemise, and the one—with you as Eve in front of the mirror.

LULU: I should have known!

CASTI-PIANI: They weren't of any use to me. *(Giving her the letter.)* Here. Read.

LULU: It's English.

CASTI-PIANI: Six hundred pounds. That comes to—fifteen thousand francs. Twelve thousand marks.

LULU: I can't read it.

CASTI-PIANI: I have to guarantee that you speak French. English you'll learn quickly enough on the job.

LULU: I can't read it.

CASTI-PIANI: *(Taking the letter from her.)* All right—just so you don't accuse me of being a swindler.

LULU: You're a monster.

CASTI-PIANI: Not enough of one to suit me. Take my advice and accept. I've informed them that you're both versatile and experienced. You'll be absolutely safe there.

LULU: I'm not sure—I understand.

CASTI-PIANI: Then perhaps I can help you understand. If I were to grab you by the gullet and hold tight—till the police arrived—I'd have earned three thousand.

LULU: You wouldn't do that.

CASTI-PIANI: That's four thousand francs less than Epaminondas Oikonomopulos will pay for you.

LULU: Assure me—that you won't—turn me in—and then take from what I have left—more—than your Oi—Oi—Oi—

CASTI-PIANI: But you have nothing.

LULU: I told you so.

CASTI-PIANI: You gave it all to me.

LULU: It's not true.

CASTI-PIANI: Jungfrau shares are all you have left.

LULU: They're rising. You can sell them off.

CASTI-PIANI: I've never dabbled in shares. Epaminondas Oikonomopulos pays in pounds sterling and the relatives of your—suddenly deceased husband—pay in—

LULU: Give me—give me time to sell them.

CASTI-PIANI: I can't waste time.

LULU: Give me three days.

CASTI-PIANI: Not one night. So far I'm the only one privy to your estimable secret. I trust you won't blab it away.

LULU: How do you know? Prove it.

CASTI-PIANI: That's not my concern. I gave the Public Prosecutor's Office to believe that—I'd tracked you down—except that you'd most likely emigrated to—to America.

LULU: America.

CASTI-PIANI: Take my advice. Let yourself be shipped off to Cairo. The Epaminondas Oikonomopulos establishment will guard you against any trouble. You couldn't be safer in a nunnery.

LULU: A brothel!

CASTI-PIANI: When was the last time you heard of a girl being taken from a brothel—to cut off her head? If anything, they do that to the customers.

LULU: I'm not going to a brothel! I'd rather die.

CASTI-PIANI: Actually it's the only place that really suits you.

LULU: God help me!

CASTI-PIANI: What a pity. Don't do it now and you'll end up on the street.

LULU: That's not true.

CASTI-PIANI: Because they'd hack off your head.

LULU: Dear heaven. Dear heaven.

CASTI-PIANI: It's a house like no other in the world. With a trade more fashionable than you find in Paris. Scottish lords, Indian governors, high Russian officials, and our fat-cat industrialists from the Ruhr.

LULU: Dear God.

CASTI-PIANI: They'll dress you in the most exquisite taste. You'll wander about on fist-thick carpets. You'll have a room all to yourself, fitted out as if for a fairy tale princess, with the most magical view onto the minarets of the El Azher mosque. And you will remain completely your own mistress. A lady first and last. Supper in your own room. Nowhere in Europe will you find that. Not here, not London. And least of all in Germany.

LULU: Dear God. Dear God.

CASTI-PIANI: Four weeks ago I sent an eighteen-year-old Berlin girl there. A beauty from the most aristocratic of circles. Married for six months. If you'd care for proof—*(He hands her an opened letter.)* She did it out of the sheer desire to indulge herself. Her husband ended putting a bullet through his skull.

LULU: *(Unfolding the letter mechanically.)* I could never—not with a man who paid at a—

CASTI-PIANI. Have a look. Here's the postmark. In case you think I wrote it.

LULU: *(Holding the letter.)* Dear—Mr.—The lines are all—running together—I—can't—

CASTI-PIANI: She writes a bit unsteadily. *(Takes the letter from her and reads.)* "Dear Mr. Gross." That's the name I go by.

LULU: Dear God.

CASTI-PIANI: *(Reads.)* "The next time you visit Berlin, be certain to go to the Conservatory and ask for Miss von Falati, you'll be astounded, and give her the letter I'm enclosing here. As luck would have it, she's destitute and lives with her mother, though they are constantly at each other's throats. I've already discussed the matter with Madam Bertram. They're happy to take on another German as long as she is well bred. She promises to mention it to Mr. Leonidas. Describe the place to her, in any case be sure to get a definite address where I can write her. I've raved to her about the place, but I just don't have the right words. I'm too thoughtless. Get her stirred up and you'll see she's even more beautiful than me, especially her body, you may get even more for your troubles than you expect. She's often said to me, rather a week of pleasure than a life like hers. She may be afraid, she was still a virgin, but with a lot of spirit, don't let go of her, I feel sorry for her, and she will probably never marry even once. My life only began when I got here. Everything before that was stupidity and boredom. She also has a wonderful voice that will bring her a lot of pleasure. Time flies by so fast here, I feel like I arrived only yesterday."

LULU: I'd rather have my skin ripped off.

CASTI-PIANI: The choice is yours.

LULU: They're children. Hollow creatures. I'm no wild animal anymore.

CASTI-PIANI: It'll come back to you.

LULU: At fifteen I'd have jumped at the chance.

CASTI-PIANI: Love is love. Whether he's Chinese or Japanese. It's why your soul's never been soiled.

LULU: I'll go insane. All I have is myself. My body. And you want me to give myself to every piece of trash who—

CASTI-PIANI: Trash? Not there, my dear, not there.

LULU: Some hairy orangutan with breath like a cesspool. Dear God, dear God!

CASTI-PIANI: There's always consolation—when things take a turn for the worst—in booze.

LULU: You're a devil. No feeling, no heart.

CASTI-PIANI: Where would I be if I allowed my clients' righteous anger to get to me?

LULU: Why do you want to sell me? Why! Take me. Just as I am. Wherever you want. To love you. I'll do anything.

CASTI-PIANI: I have a wife and child.

LULU: You're married?!

CASTI-PIANI: Yesterday evening around ten I stepped into a tobacco shop on the boulevard. On the way out a girl spoke to me.

LULU: You call that being married?

CASTI-PIANI: It was my daughter. *(Pause. LULU stares at him.)* Sacrifice yourself on silk cushions.

LULU: To rot away in a hospital!

CASTI-PIANI: Or on the scaffold.

LULU: On the—

CASTI-PIANI: I'd prefer the cushions.

LULU: You can't do that.

CASTI-PIANI: I lose four thousand francs this way.

LULU: It's my head—they'd cut off, my body—they'd dissect, my flesh—they'd torture—

CASTI-PIANI: I can do anything.

LULU: You're not human! You're not human!

CASTI-PIANI: Thank God! *(Getting up.)* You have till the game in there is ended to think about it. There's still time today to get you to safety. The police are waiting outside. Think it over. *(Goes off into the gaming room, leaving the door behind him ajar.)*

(LULU stares, unmoving, into space, at the same time mechanically crumpling the note given her by RODRIGO which she has held between her fin-

gers during the preceding scene. ALWA enters from the gaming room with some securities in hand and comes downstage.)

ALWA: *(To LULU.)* It's going brilliantly! Brilliantly! Countess Geschwitz has bet her last chemise and I've just fleeced Puntschuh of the last of his shares! *(Goes off downstage left.)*

(LULU, alone, notices the note in her hand, flattens it out across her knee, reads it, and howls with laughter. ALWA enters with several bank notes in his hand.)

ALWA: *(To LULU.)* Aren't you playing?

LULU: Why not! *(LULU rises up and follows him into the gaming room. As she exits, GESCHWITZ meets her in the doorway.)*

GESCHWITZ: Am I chasing you away?

LULU: I'm sorry. I didn't see you coming.

GESCHWITZ: Ah—

LULU: I swear.

GESCHWITZ: *(Closing the middle door and coming downstage.)* I'm as lucky at gambling as I am at love.

LULU: You have your share of luck.

GESCHWITZ: You're making fun of me!

LULU: But you've just made a conquest.

GESCHWITZ: I'm at the point of shooting myself.

LULU: Enjoy the moment.

GESCHWITZ: You always find new torments.

LULU. He's deserting me for you.

GESCHWITZ: Have pity on me!

LULU: Have pity on yourself! The poor man's in a desperate way.

GESCHWITZ: So am I!

LULU: He's begged me to sing his praises to you.

GESCHWITZ: I have no idea who you're talking about.

LULU: He'll never leave your side.

GESCHWITZ: Rodrigo Quast?

LULU: He'll jump in the Seine.

GESCHWITZ: What misery! Dear God! Misery, misery!

LULU: He's an acrobat.

GESCHWITZ: But I'd never trade places with anyone as heartless as you!

LULU: Nor I with you! Not even if it cost me my life!

GESCHWITZ: You're murdering yourself! You always choose the most detestable, the most depraved.

LULU: *You* say that to *me?!*

GESCHWITZ: What's this between you and Casti-Piani?

LULU: Shut up!

GESCHWITZ: He's vile!

LULU: Shut up!

GESCHWITZ: It's written all over his face!

LULU: Shut up! Shut up!

GESCHWITZ: I've never seen such a bestial face!

LULU: *(Going at her with blazing eyes.)* Shut up or I'll—

GESCHWITZ: Hit me! *(As LULU retreats.)* You'd never do that—

LULU: Not to you.

GESCHWITZ: Listen to me—please—please—if you don't totally—I've sacrificed everything for you—everything—please—please—tell him—tell that monster—to go—

LULU: And turn myself over to *you?*

GESCHWITZ: *(Sinking to the floor.)* My love—my angel—

LULU: God help me! There are enough horrors in my life!

GESCHWITZ: Then stomp on me!

LULU: Get up—

GESCHWITZ: Stomp on me!

LULU: Get up—or I'll call—

GESCHWITZ: Stomp on me!

LULU: Get up!

GESCHWITZ: Stomp on me—and it's over.

LULU: I wouldn't mess my shoes on you!

GESCHWITZ: Stomp on me—out of compassion!

LULU: I'm opening the doors.

GESCHWITZ: Stomp on me! Strangle me!

LULU: Go to the Moulin Rouge! Go to the Café Americain!

GESCHWITZ: My love! My life!

LULU: You've got money! Buy yourself a whore!

GESCHWITZ: You! You!

LULU: Some women will do anything for money!

GESCHWITZ: One night!

LULU: We're all the same. Made the same. She'll have more—mm—you'll see.

GESCHWITZ: One night—and then—die.

LULU: What a fool you make of yourself—don't you have any shame—

GESCHWITZ: One—night.

LULU: Not for a million!

GESCHWITZ: Lulu!

LULU: Get up, for God's sake!

GESCHWITZ: *(Pulling herself to her feet.)* Ah—

RODRIGO: *(Enters and offers her his arm.)* Your Grace—

GESCHWITZ: Go to hell! *(Goes off into the gaming room.)*

RODRIGO: *(To GESCHWITZ.)* You'll pay for that! *(To LULU.)* So—read my little note?

LULU: Where do you come by such unheard of evil?

RODRIGO: Let me explain.

LULU: I don't have fifty thousand francs.

RODRIGO: Then I'll explain.

LULU: I have nothing, nothing.

RODRIGO: You've got three times that.

LULU: And what if—

RODRIGO: Don't brush me off!

LULU: Shameless!

RODRIGO: If my name was Casti-Piani—

LULU: Not even if it was Vasco da Gama!

RODRIGO. Why cram it down the throats of total strangers!

LULU: I told you, I have nothing left!

RODRIGO: You're swimming in gold.

LULU: God almighty!

RODRIGO: I just spoke to the Count.

LULU: The Count?

RODRIGO: Mr. Alwa.

LULU: Then go see *him!*

RODRIGO: He wouldn't give me a *button* if my life depended on it!

LULU: But he lets himself be made a fool of till you want to puke!

RODRIGO: Get the fifty thousand francs from him.

LULU: And you're just shameless enough to threaten me!

RODRIGO: He never refuses you.

LULU: You're tactless.

RODRIGO: He wants you so much he's gone goo-goo.

LULU: Betray me! Betray me!

RODRIGO: It'll cost you one night.

LULU: I said betray me!

RODRIGO: He's never loved you so much. He opened up to me.

LULU: You want him to love me—

RODRIGO: Offer him one night.

LULU:—so he can be robbed?

RODRIGO: He'd shoot his whole wad for it.

LULU: I can't.

RODRIGO: Not even if I ask?

LULU: He makes me sick.

RODRIGO: Jesus, he's your husband!

LULU: Turn me in! Betray me! If not you, someone else!

RODRIGO: Don't make such a tragedy. I only wrote that bit about informing on you to make a point. Now if you'd listen to my reasons.

LULU: I don't *have* fifty thousand francs anymore.

RODRIGO: But I need them! Not a cent less!

LULU: So betray me! Go on!

RODRIGO: Actually what I want it for is to—well—

LULU: Well what?

RODRIGO: You ready for this?

LULU: Shoot yourself?

RODRIGO: Get married.—Come on. Get a grip on yourself.

LULU: To Geschwitz?

RODRIGO: You lost your mind?

LULU: I couldn't care less.

RODRIGO: The toilet-mistress at the Folies-Bergère. Get a grip on yourself.

LULU: Marry the Queen of Spain for all I care!

RODRIGO: As you know, I did a turn at the Folies-Bergère. Offered me three thousand francs. But they don't know my worth, these Parisians. Fact is, I was a flop. If I'd been a kangaroo I'd've made the front pages! At least I got to know Celestine Rabeux—an angel no matter how you look at it. Thirty years in charge of the johns and she's squirreled away fifty thousand francs. She'd take me on tomorrow if I matched that amount. Told her I wasn't sure, but I could probably scrape it together. We're like two kids. Besides, she's hot to retire from the public view. If she told me to hatchet my old man, I'd do it.

LULU: Then why terrify poor Geschwitz with your billing and cooing?

RODRIGO: To prove to Paris I've got savoir-vivre.

LULU: You are—

RODRIGO: You have to when you move in good society.

LULU: You never do what you promise!

RODRIGO: I regret—

LULU: To get a knife in the back, all one needs is to meet you.

RODRIGO: And as a result my artistic career has suffered. My Strong Man number is a loser all around—with the weaker sex, I mean. First they tear the clothes off you and then they're wallowing around with the chamber maid—with me left to sort the dirty wash! But my Celestine loves me for myself.

LULU: Why should I stand between you and your demure little bride?

RODRIGO: Then sacrifice one night for us.

LULU: If I envy your intended anything, it's her cold-bloodedness.

RODRIGO: No girlish illusions for her.

LULU: Thank heaven for small favors.

RODRIGO: She knows you don't judge a marriage by the size of the bed.

LULU: All that matters is you love each other—hm?

RODRIGO: A little money helps.

LULU: I'm not sure I can get the fifty thousand.

RODRIGO: Try being nice—pleasure him instead of yourself for a change—

LULU: To please you?

RODRIGO: You'd never believe how grateful I'd be.

LULU: Please, please.

RODRIGO: Four people happy at a single blow.

LULU: Except for me.

RODRIGO: Two men, two women—not to mention a happy young couple. I know you—you still love me a little in spite of yourself.

LULU: Come have lunch with me tomorrow?

RODRIGO: Vous étes charmante! *(Offering her his arm.)* Permettez moi, Madame la Comtesse!

LULU: *(Taking his arm.)* Well, since you always manage your maneuvers so charmingly.
(They are both about to go off when CASTI-PIANI enters from the gaming room. LULU stops and RODRIGO goes off.)

CASTI-PIANI: Make up your mind before I bid you good night.

LULU: You can't do it.

CASTI-PIANI: What were you saying to him?

LULU: Who?

CASTI-PIANI: Your ex-lover! Your hotshot man about town!

LULU: Lovers' confidences.

CASTI-PIANI: It'll cost you your head.

LULU: You simply can't do it.

CASTI-PIANI: I can do anything. *(Goes off.)*

SCHIGOLCH: (*Enters through the gaming room, heads straight for an armchair and lowers himself exhaustedly into it.*) I need five hundred francs—to furnish an apartment—for my—mistress—elle veut se mettre dans ses meubles.

LULU: Good God! A mistress? You?

SCHIGOLCH: With God's good help.

LULU: But you're—eighty!

SCHIGOLCH: What else is Paris for?

LULU: My God!

SCHIGOLCH: She's no spring chicken, either.

LULU: Merciful heaven!

SCHIGOLCH: I've wasted too much of my life in Germany.

LULU: I—dear God—

SCHIGOLCH: You haven't laid eyes on me for six weeks.

LULU: I—I—I can't anymore—I can't anymore—it's too—too—

SCHIGOLCH: Too what?

LULU: Too—horrible! (*Breaks down, buries her head on his knees and shakes with convulsive sobs.*) It's—too—horrible!

SCHIGOLCH: I was in the clink the whole time. (*Stroking her hair.*) You drive yourself too hard. You need to let up for a few days.

LULU: Oh!—Oh!—How have I—deserved this! What have I—done! Oh— God in heaven!—Oh, God, oh, God—what will—become—of me!— Oh—the things I've suffered!—Merciful God! I can't take this anymore!—I can't go through it!—Oh—it's too—horrible!

SCHIGOLCH: They let me out only yesterday. (*Stroking her.*) You should wash yourself in snow. Cry it out—if it helps you any—go on.

LULU: (*Groaning.*) Oh!—Oh!—Oh, God—oh, God!

SCHIGOLCH: I learned a little French in the clink. You should take salt baths. Cry it out. Go on. Spend one day a week in bed with a novel.

LULU: What will become of me! Oh! What will become of me!

SCHIGOLCH: It'll be over soon. Just cry it out. I haven't had you on my knee like this for—good lord!—twenty years. How time flies! How you've grown! You cried the same way then. I had you here. I stroked your hair and rubbed your knees warm. Of course you had no white satin dress then, no feathers in your hair, no see-through stockings. You had no stockings at all. Scarcely a shirt to your name. But crying—that was something you knew how to do.

LULU: Please! Please take me with you! Take me! Take me with you! Please!

Have pity on me! Take me with you! Now! Take me—back to your attic!

SCHIGOLCH: Me? Take you with me?

LULU: To your attic! To your attic!

SCHIGOLCH: And my—my five hundred francs?

LULU: Oh, God!

SCHIGOLCH: You live too much for pleasure. More than you can endure. You need to allow your body time to—to find peace again.

LULU: They want my life.

SCHIGOLCH: Who wants your life? Who? Who?

LULU: They're going to betray me.

SCHIGOLCH: Who's going to betray you? Tell me.

LULU: They're going to—oh!

SCHIGOLCH: What?

LULU: Cut off my head! Cut off my head!

SCHIGOLCH: Who's going to cut off your head? I may be eighty years old, but—

LULU: I can see myself tied in their ropes!

SCHIGOLCH: Who wants to cut off your head?

LULU: Rodrigo! Rodrigo Quast!

SCHIGOLCH: Him?

LULU: He told me so just now.

SCHIGOLCH: Don't lose sleep over that. I'll take him out to a bar.

LULU: Kill him! Oh, please! Kill him! Kill him! You can do it—if you want to!

SCHIGOLCH: He's a gigolo. He says all kinds of things he doesn't mean.

LULU: Kill him! Kill him!

SCHIGOLCH: He tries to look important.

LULU: For your child's sake! Kill him!

SCHIGOLCH: I don't know—whose child you are.

LULU: I won't get up till you've given me your word.

SCHIGOLCH: The poor devil.

LULU: Kill him!

SCHIGOLCH: Once he's gone—you can't bring him back. I could throw him out my window into the Seine.

LULU: Please!

SCHIGOLCH: And what do I get out of it?

LULU: Do it! Do it!

SCHIGOLCH: What do I get out of it?

LULU: Five hundred francs.

SCHIGOLCH: Five hundred francs. Five hundred francs.

LULU: A thousand.

SCHIGOLCH: If I really wanted to put my hand to this—here in Paris— I could be rich again.

LULU: How much do you want?

SCHIGOLCH: I could drive around in style again, no matter what my age.

LULU: How much? How much?

SCHIGOLCH: If you could manage to—

LULU: Me?

SCHIGOLCH:—lower yourself to—

LULU: God have pity on me!

SCHIGOLCH:—like you used to—

LULU: With—you?

SCHIGOLCH: Now, of course, you have beautiful clothes.

LULU: What do you want—with me!

SCHIGOLCH: You'll see.

LULU: I'm not—like—I was then.

SCHIGOLCH: You think I'm an antique?

LULU: But you've got someone.

SCHIGOLCH: The little lady's sixty-five years old.

LULU: What do you do, then?

SCHIGOLCH: Play patience.

LULU: And—with me?

SCHIGOLCH: You'll see.

LULU: You're a brute.

SCHIGOLCH: It's been so long since we've known each other.

LULU: For—God's—sake.

SCHIGOLCH: We'll renew old memories.

LULU: *(Getting up.)* But you swear to me that—

SCHIGOLCH: When will you come?

LULU: Merciful heaven!

SCHIGOLCH: Just so I'm alone.

LULU: Whenever you want.

SCHIGOLCH: Day after tomorrow.

LULU: If I have to.

SCHIGOLCH: In white satin.

LULU: But you *will* throw him in?

SCHIGOLCH: With diamonds and pearls.

LULU: Just as I am now.

SCHIGOLCH: Just once more—to make the earth shake.

LULU: You swear.

SCHIGOLCH: Just send him.

LULU: You swear, you swear.

SCHIGOLCH: By all things holy.

LULU: You'll throw him in.

SCHIGOLCH: I swear.

LULU: By all things holy.

SCHIGOLCH: *(Feeling around under her dress.)* What more do you want?

LULU: *(Trembling.)* By all things—holy.

SCHIGOLCH: By all things holy.

LULU: How that cools me!

SCHIGOLCH: *(Letting go of the dress.)* You're blazing with hate.

> *(Pause. LULU goes stage left, puts her dress in order, straightens her hair at the mirror, and dries her eyes.)*

LULU: Go now—right now—go.

SCHIGOLCH: Today?

LULU: Just be sure you're home when he comes with her.

SCHIGOLCH: With who?

LULU: *(Feeling her cheeks and powdering them.)* He's coming with the Countess.

SCHIGOLCH: A Countess?

LULU: Get them to drink. Tell him it's the Countess' room—that you live next door. The Countess will get drunk. Put something into his drink. Whatever you've got.

SCHIGOLCH: It'll turn the trick.

LULU: I only hope you can lift him. God—oh, God.

SCHIGOLCH: Three steps to the window.

LULU: In the morning the Countess will silently steal away.

SCHIGOLCH: What if I have to roll him?

LULU: She'll never recognize the house again.

SCHIGOLCH: My window goes clear to the floor.

LULU: Don't forget. Bring me his earrings.

SCHIGOLCH: Once he's overboard, I'll bid a fond farewell to the old hole in the wall.

LULU: You hear? His golden ear—rings.

SCHIGOLCH: What is it?

LULU: I think —

SCHIGOLCH: What in the name of—

LULU: I think—my garter—

SCHIGOLCH: Why are you staring at me?

LULU: My garter—broke.

SCHIGOLCH: So then I'll look for a place behind the Bastille. *(LULU has pulled up her dress and is tying her garter.)* Or else behind the Buttes-Chaumont. Yellow stockings.

LULU: Orange.

SCHIGOLCH: What a lovely smell!

LULU: Everything orange—to white satin. *(Straightening up.)* Go—go on now.

SCHIGOLCH: Orange. Hm! Who's this Countess of yours?

LULU: The crazy woman. You know her. You need to take a cab.

SCHIGOLCH: Of course I do. Of course! *(Getting up.)* What crazy woman?

LULU: The one who kisses my feet. Please, go.

SCHIGOLCH: *(As he goes off.)* His golden earrings.

> *(LULU leads him off upstage left. CASTI-PIANI shoves RODRIGO into the salon through the middle door.)*

RODRIGO: Have a little respect!

CASTI-PIANI: *(Shaking him.)* I want to know what she told you!

RODRIGO: Nothing—nothing!

CASTI-PIANI: *(Knees him in the groin.)* Bastard!

RODRIGO: Oh, God!

CASTI-PIANI: You're planning to meet her!

RODRIGO: All I can say is—what's true.

CASTI-PIANI: Confess! *(Punches him.)*

RODRIGO: I'm getting married—please—spare me—I'm getting married—oh, God—I'm getting married—I mean it!

CASTI-PIANI: A meeting! A meeting!

RODRIGO: A local girl! Jesus—a local girl—spare me—it's all about—money—she's got to give me—the money—

CASTI-PIANI: *(Pulling a revolver.)* Liar!

RODRIGO: Stop—stop—ask her—it's all about—about money—just money—she—she shot someone.

CASTI-PIANI: *(Lets loose of him and goes right.)* Forgive me, then. As you can see, I'm in love—and when I'm in love, I'm a—

RODRIGO: Filthy bastard!

CASTI-PIANI: *(Going off into the gaming room.)* Good evening.

RODRIGO: *(Alone.)* Mad dog! God save me! Bastard! A bastard I could toss up to the ceiling with one hand! *(LULU enters. RODRIGO looks around with alarm.)* What—? Oh, you!—Bless you!

LULU: Yes, me. I've come—

RODRIGO: Bless you!

LULU: I've come from Countess Geschwitz.

RODRIGO: Ah, so. Yes. Yes, yes—I was just telling her—

LULU: She told me. Just now.

RODRIGO: What I said was—I said to her—

LULU: That she was the first girl—

RODRIGO: More or less. Yes.

LULU: That you ever wanted to make love to.

RODRIGO: That I'd like to fool around with is more like it. Of course she immediately—haha!

LULU: You've driven her half mad.

RODRIGO: I couldn't care less.

LULU: She's never heard anything like that before.

RODRIGO: If only Celestine was as easy!

LULU: Made no headway, have you?

RODRIGO: I still don't have your fifty thousand francs.

LULU: But I promised.

RODRIGO: Oh—lady!

LULU: On one condition—

RODRIGO: When do you want me to—

LULU: —that you'll make Countess Geschwitz happy tonight.

RODRIGO: I'm afraid I can't do that.

LULU: As you wish.

RODRIGO: I can't.

LULU: As you wish.

RODRIGO: I don't think it'd work.

LULU: As you wish.

RODRIGO: As you wish? Wishing has nothing to do with it! As I see it, all she has going for her is that she's an aristocrat.

LULU: That's nothing to sneeze at. Ever had an aristocrat?

RODRIGO: By the dozens! They drop around me like flies! Baronesses! Princesses! But they had legs!—good God!—asses and—

LULU: But you haven't *seen* her legs.

RODRIGO: Nor do I want to!

LULU: As you wish.

RODRIGO: It won't work. You can bet your boots on that.

LULU: But you're the Strong Man!

RODRIGO: It's my arms that are strong. Take a look at these biceps!

LULU: Spare me your biceps. If you can't see your way to—well, you can understand. She and I are friends.

RODRIGO: I didn't mean it that way! Our relationship was platonic. Educated classes do that. Not everybody is like you—ready to jump in the sack at first meeting.

LULU: Me?

RODRIGO: Who do you think! Were you ever any different? Have you ever loved a person for his own sake?

LULU: I'm no—latrine pick-up.

RODRIGO: Latrine yourself!

LULU: *(Biting her lip.)* What shall I tell the Countess?

RODRIGO: Tell her I'm a castrato.

LULU: As you wish. *(Goes upstage.)*

RODRIGO: *(Turning toward her.)* What—what does she want?

LULU: Love.

RODRIGO: That's hard to believe.

LULU: Blame it on your belly muscles.

RODRIGO: If I'd ever imagined—

LULU: Why did you make her drool?

RODRIGO: That hat rack!

LULU: She's still a virgin.

RODRIGO: You're a—! If you saw a man hanging from the gallows, you'd stick out your tongue and wiggle it at him!

LULU: I don't do that anymore.

RODRIGO: I know!

LULU: And you thought I was—ungrateful.

RODRIGO: All right, I'll do it. I'll show it to her. The things people do when they're in love! *(Goes upstage right.)*

LULU: Where are you going?

RODRIGO: To get another caviar sandwich. *(Goes off upstage right.)*

LULU: *(Opens the middle door and calls into the gaming room.)* Martha—

GESCHWITZ: *(Entering with downcast eyes.)* Lulu—

LULU: *(Leading her downstage.)* If you do as I say—tonight—you hear—?

GESCHWITZ: Yes.

LULU: You hear me? Then tomorrow night you can—

GESCHWITZ: What?—What?

LULU: Sleep with me.

GESCHWITZ: *(Grasping LULU's hand and covering it with kisses.)* Oh—!

LULU: And undress me.

GESCHWITZ: Oh!—Oh!

LULU: And do my hair.

GESCHWITZ: Oh—Lulu!

LULU: *(Freeing her hand.)* But just now—

GESCHWITZ: Say it!

LULU: Just now—you have to go with Rodrigo.

GESCHWITZ: Why?

LULU: Why? Why?

GESCHWITZ: Why—for God's sake—!

LULU: That much, at least, you know.

GESCHWITZ: With a man?

LULU: Yes! Yes! You should be glad!

GESCHWITZ: For God's sake!

LULU: With a man! It's why you're a girl!

GESCHWITZ: Ask—ask anything of me—anything—ask—every—
hideous thing of me—anything—anything—

LULU: I was forced into it, too—before I could even count to three. That
was no picnic, either.

GESCHWITZ: My life—whatever you want—ask me—I beg of you—

LULU: Who knows, you might even be cured.

GESCHWITZ: I can't—I can't—not—not a man.

LULU: And I can't either—not a woman!

*(GESCHWITZ turns away, reels, straightens up, clenches her fists, breaks
into hysterical sobs, and cries—supported on the mantelpiece—into her
handkerchief.)*

LULU: Can you believe—believe—I'd let you—you!—come to me—if this
man wasn't after my head—didn't threaten to—sell me—if I didn't
have to—to save my head—with my body!

GESCHWITZ: *(Straightening herself.)* What do you—want me to do?

LULU: He'll be here soon.

GESCHWITZ: And—then—

LULU: You need to overwhelm him—implore him—

GESCHWITZ: To do what?

LULU: To do what? Don't play so dumb.

GESCHWITZ: No, no—but—I don't know—it's the—the first—the first
time—

LULU: Act as if you've fallen for him—hook, line, and sinker.

GESCHWITZ: Oh, God!

LULU: He demands it. Otherwise he flies into a rage.

GESCHWITZ: I'll do—what I can.

LULU: He's a circus Strong Man—and you've offended him.

GESCHWITZ: I just hope he believes me.

LULU: Get a cab downstairs and tell the driver soixante-quinze Quai de la Gare.

GESCHWITZ: Yes.

LULU: Soixante-quinze Quai de la Gare.

GESCHWITZ: Yes.

LULU: Should I write it for you?

GESCHWITZ: Yes.

LULU: *(Writes on the mantelpiece and hands the card to GESCHWITZ.)* Soixante-quinze Quai de la Gare. On leaving the cab, you pay the driver.

GESCHWITZ: *(Taking the card.)* Yes.

LULU: It's a hotel. Tell him you live there.

GESCHWITZ: Yes.

LULU: Otherwise you have nothing to worry about. *(GESCHWITZ shudders.)* He can't take you to his room because—he doesn't have one. He hasn't a sou to his name. *(Opens the door upstage right and calls.)* Monsieur—s'il vous plaît. *(RODRIGO enters upstage right with a full mouth. She whispers to GESCHWITZ as she passes her.)* Throw your arms around his neck.

RODRIGO: *(Chewing.)* Excuse me? *(GESCHWITZ goes to RODRIGO with downcast eyes and throws herself around his neck.)* Let's get started, then.

LULU: Would you like a cab? You'll find some in the street downstairs.

RODRIGO: *(Groaning; to GESCHWITZ.)* Will you get off me, for Chrissake!

GESCHWITZ: *(Not looking at him.)* I love you.

RODRIGO: Jesus!

GESCHWITZ: *(Trying to pull him along.)* Please.

RODRIGO: Surprise, surprise!

GESCHWITZ: *(Covering her face with her hands.)* I can't do this!

RODRIGO: *(Wringing his hands.)* Give it another try?

LULU: *(Icy, beside GESCHWITZ.)* You know what depends on this.

GESCHWITZ: *(Hands at her temples.)* Oh, God, oh, God, oh, God, oh, God, oh, God!

RODRIGO: Have I ever told you a filthy joke? Ever taken "liberties" in your presence? Ever pinched you on the fanny even once, for God's

sake! If you can't handle it, I'll lend you a contraption you can wind
up ten times a night—something you can't do with me!

LULU: *(Close beside him.)* Don't forget the fifty thousand francs—

GESCHWITZ: *(With haggard face, pulling violently at his coat.)* Please—do
it—now—on top of me—hurry! I'm going to faint!

RODRIGO: *(Getting a grip on himself.)* Jesus, man! What've you got to
lose! Some damage compensation! *(Offering her his arm.)* Let us mount
the scaffold! *(Leads her upstage left.)*

LULU: *(Near GESCHWITZ.)* Have you got the card?

GESCHWITZ: This will kill me! Kill me!

LULU: *(Opening the door.)* Bonne nuit, chers enfants.

*(Sounds of a rising commotion have been coming from the gaming room dur-
ing the end of the previous scene. PUNTSCHUH, a banker, rushes in.)*

LULU: What's going on in there?

PUNTSCHUH: It's over! A disaster! It's—

LULU: What—?

PUNTSCHUH: It's the end, madam!

LULU: *(To PUNTSCHUH, leading him downstage.)* Would you kindly
explain!

PUNTSCHUH: *(Almost unable to speak.)* Oh, God—

LULU: What *is* all this!

ALWA: *(Rushing in from a side door.)* What is—?

PUNTSCHUH: The Jungfrau shares, madam—fallen—fallen—

LULU: *(Stunned.)* I don't—

ALWA: Are you insane?

PUNTSCHUH: A total disaster! A monstrosity! I received this telegram—
(Takes the telegram from his breast pocket.)

ALWA: *(Pale as a ghost.)* Is this possible? *(Runs off into the gaming room.)*

LULU: *(Taking the telegram and reading it.)*—Then we're out on the street
again—

PUNTSCHUH: And I've lost a fortune! Again—

LULU: *(To herself.)* To Cairo—hurry—to Cairo—*(About to run off, turning
to PUNTSCHUH.)* Have you seen Casti-Piani anywhere?

PUNTSCHUH: The Marquis Casti-Piani left with his hat and coat immediately upon hearing the news. *(Goes out.)*

LULU: *(Calling at the door into the gaming room.)* Alwa!

ALWA: *(Enters almost immediately with a large wad of Jungfrau shares in his
fists.)* Nothing! Not worth a sou!

LULU: We haven't a moment to lose!

ALWA: What are you—? We'll make a comeback—we'll—

LULU: We've been betrayed! Turned in! Do you understand!

ALWA: Wha—wha—wha—

LULU: You'll go to prison and they'll cut off my head—

ALWA: *(Weak in the knees.)* Lulu—

LULU: Get the cash box—wrap your coat around it—

ALWA: I've got—the key.

LULU: Hurry! Every minute counts!

ALWA: *(Stunned.)* Who—

LULU: It doesn't matter! Come on!

ALWA: You've let this throw you into a panic!

LULU: Casti-Piani!

ALWA: Your sweetheart!

LULU: Hurry!

> *(They both rush off stage left. In his haste ALWA drops the crumpled shares in his fists as he runs. As they go off, PUNTSCHUH enters from the gaming room, sees the scattered shares, picks up a few, and shakes his head in despair. At the same time a GENDARME enters and strides to the middle of the floor.)*

GENDARME: Au nom de la loi—vous êtes arrêté!

PUNTSCHUH: Moi?

> *(Slightly behind the GENDARME, CASTI-PIANI enters in hat and overcoat.)*

CASTI-PIANI: Mais non!—Mais non!

END OF ACT FOUR

ACT FIVE
LONDON

An attic room without mansards. Two large panes of glass in the slope of the roof open outward. Downstage right and left is a door that closes badly, made out of rough wood and with a primitive lock. At the right proscenium, a tattered gray mattress. Downstage left, a red-painted flower stand with a bottle of whiskey on it. Beside the whiskey bottle stands a small, smoking kerosene lamp. In the upstage left corner an old green chaise longue. Right, next to the center door, a wicker chair with a hole in its seat. The walls have a reddish tinge. Rain can be heard pounding on the roof. Downstage left, a drip through the overhead window. The wooden floor is covered with water. SCHIGOLCH, in a long gray tight-waisted overcoat with tails all the way to the feet, lies on a mattress stage right. Upstage left, ALWA SCHÖNING lies on the chaise longue, hands locked behind his head and wrapped in a red rug the straps of which hang above him on the wall. LULU, hair cut half-length so that it falls freely onto her shoulders, enters barefoot down left carrying a wash basin and dressed in torn, shabby black clothes.

SCHIGOLCH: Where've you been!

ALWA: She had to wash first, didn't she?

SCHIGOLCH: They don't do that here.

ALWA: So she's a dreamer!

LULU: *(Placing the wash basin beneath the drip.)* Why don't you just die!

ALWA: It's what she's waiting for!

LULU: *(Straightening up and throwing back her hair.)* God knows!

SCHIGOLCH: Go now, child.

ALWA: *(Tossing on his back.)* My wife! My wife! My wife!

LULU: You're not worth getting my hands dirty!

SCHIGOLCH: Starting out is never easy. It's the same no matter what the business.

ALWA: The basin's already overflowing.

LULU: So what should I do with it?

ALWA: The rain's beating a tattoo. Setting the stage for your debut.

LULU: *(Shaking.)* I wish I was dead.

SCHIGOLCH: Three days and we won't be able to keep her down. They need to learn to enjoy it first. I've seen it oftener than I have fingers to count on. It's always hell at first. Later you can't tie them down.

ALWA: Are you planning a pilgrimage in bare feet?

LULU: My shoes are wet.

SCHIGOLCH: These English couldn't care less.

LULU: Why doesn't the old man go?

SCHIGOLCH: This beastly weather's not fit for a dog!

LULU: Only for me!

SCHIGOLCH: She'd rather we starved than go out and have a little fun.

ALWA: Can you blame her? Who likes prostituting their most sacred feelings!

SCHIGOLCH: Fucking bastard!

LULU: *(Back to the wall, she sits on the floor and wraps her arms around her knees.)* Whhhh! It's cold!

ALWA: I dreamt we were dining chez Sylvain.

SCHIGOLCH: With her talent for languages, she has a great future here.

ALWA: I ordered fers de cheval.

LULU: If only I could warm myself against one of you.

ALWA: I actually felt them in my belly. I could have cried with happiness! The plates clattered. My shirt dripped with champagne. I was soused. It ran out of my mouth.

SCHIGOLCH: Yes, yes.

LULU: My hands and feet are frozen solid.

SCHIGOLCH: She's wasting valuable time. People are leaving restaurants about now.

LULU: I'd rather freeze to death!

ALWA: Me, too. Why drag out this dog's life? We've had it.

LULU: Stuffing other people's craws with the little life I've got left! Shit!

SCHIGOLCH: Go on, get your shoes on!

ALWA: I won't touch a penny of her money!

SCHIGOLCH: She was doing it before she even knew what it was.

LULU: *(Looking at the bottle of whiskey.)* You drank it!

SCHIGOLCH: She could have kept her father and mother in style when she was ten.

ALWA: *(Shifting from side to side.)* A beefsteak, Katya! A beefsteak! My kingdom for a—a—a—

SCHIGOLCH: Give her ass a good boot down the stairs. I can't keep this up! I'm too old and weak.

LULU: You want me out on the streets so I can never go anywhere again. I could have found work here earlier. One ride through Hyde Park would have done it. Now all I have is rags. I was your gold mine once—till I went to the dogs!

SCHIGOLCH: You'll be punished according to your sins. *(Coughs from his hollow chest, slowly lifts himself, coughs again, and spits on the floor.)*

LULU: *(Empties the full wash basin through the window into the rain gutter.)* You let them spit in my face! You let them kick me!

ALWA: If only I had a smoke. I dream of a smoke—a smoke—a smoke that outdoes anything ever smoked. The ideal of a smoke—

LULU: Men! Men you can't even see! Hats pulled down, ears in their collars, hands in their pockets! They'd sooner leave their jackets and coats than go without the thing they came for! And that's what you expect me to—

SCHIGOLCH: Yes—

LULU: Why *should* I go down? I haven't cost you a penny. And behold our invalid writer! Let him get off his ass and start using some of that Goddamn talent!

ALWA: Monster! Who dragged me through the muck? Who stole my ideals? Who strangled the last spark of humanity in me?

LULU: Bastard!

ALWA: Who made me into my father's murderer!

LULU: You? You? Did *you* shoot him?

ALWA: *Still* trying to take credit!

LULU: Lazy lout! Looking at you, I wish I had cut off the hands that did it. Not to save him—he lost nothing—he had nothing to lose. But just to spite you—merciful God!

ALWA: Do you see what she's made of me?

LULU: Did I chase after you?

ALWA: *(Laughs.)* Do you see what she's made of me?

LULU: Have you forgotten how you pleaded with me on bended knee?

ALWA: My little Marie! When I think back—life was so good, so happy— as a child! How cheerful my life was then! And success—success—success all before me! The most brilliant future a man could hope to achieve—on the way to being one of the important men of the time— all wasted—all squandered—thrown away—spent! Oh, God, what have I done!

SCHIGOLCH: He's having spasms again.

ALWA: I'll stick it out to the end. I've searched life's highways for everything human! So why not starve now! Why not starve!

LULU: What he needs to search for is a good nurse.

ALWA: For what's left of me—what you left behind? For the rotted marrow of my bones—my revolting lust?

LULU: Weakling!

ALWA: Wolf-bitch! Hyena!

SCHIGOLCH: Don't wait on ceremony. You've got everything you need.

LULU: Once I get out there, it'll be *me* I'm working for—to get myself out of this fucking hole—back up on top. I can do anything on my own.

SCHIGOLCH: All I want is a slice of Christmas pudding. It's all I really need.

LULU: I'm not about to be your banker!

ALWA: What haven't I done to prostitute myself!

SCHIGOLCH: Yes, yes.

ALWA: I dreamed charts—spent nights brooding over them—calculations for gambling founded on eternal laws. But I lost money faster than if I'd thrown it out the window with both hands!

SCHIGOLCH: Oh, yes.

LULU: He let himself be rooked by every man and women he ran into!

SCHIGOLCH: I don't understand women.

ALWA: I've never understood them.

LULU: I understand them.

SCHIGOLCH: His body is smooth as porcelain. Not a hair on him—

ALWA: I offered myself up to them—

SCHIGOLCH: Tiny ears like mother-of-pearl. If only I had some pudding—a slice of pudding, child.

ALWA: Each woman threw me into the arms of the next. Oh, these English women's feet! The men all have their women, but then compensate themselves in the orgies they have with ours.

LULU: He's too dumb to tame a dog!

ALWA: What haven't I tried! In Paris that speaks straight to the heart. I saw the longing in their eyes. God save me! One woman—and she even wanted money for it afterward!—broke my umbrella in two! I yelled for the police and she grabbed up a handful of fresh horse shit and threw it in my face! That's what they call their daughters of joy! I spared myself no disappointment! Better to starve to death, to freeze, than go to one of their High Priestesses in search of human kindness!

SCHIGOLCH: Talking of death is easy when you're young.

ALWA: I haven't sniffed at a woman since we arrived in this hellhole! Who'd have thought it! When I make jokes, they laugh at me! When I have the balls to be natural, they box my ears! When I'm common as a guttersnipe, they go chaste as driven snow, the pigs—and take a seat at the next table and listen to me mechanically rattle off my repertoire to the empty chairs! And the less you get to eat, the worse love tears at your guts!—Katya!—You're a monster!—but if it's a choice between you and madness—*(Rises and totters in torn trousers toward LULU, who grabs his extended hands, wrestles him to the floor, and tosses him on his back.)*

LULU: First get yourself to a hospital!

ALWA: Who made me sick?

LULU: Am *I* sick?

ALWA: *(On all fours, with head extended forward.)* No—no—you're not sick—you're healthy—you'll be making lots of men happy!

SCHIGOLCH: Your dependents are crying for bread—

ALWA: You're not sick!—You're not sick!

LULU: I kept myself clean all my life, only to drown in filth! *(Sits at the foot of SCHIGOLCH's mattress and props her elbows on her knees.)*

SCHIGOLCH: She wants to see us with our tongues hanging out.

LULU: Warm me up—

SCHIGOLCH: Children, children—this is my reward for nights of sleeplessness and worry!

LULU: I'll get the blanket—

ALWA: So what do *you* have to worry about—*you*—*you* with your—*health!* *(Struggling to his feet.)* You'll make me the death of you yet! I'll kill you, you bloodhound! Kill you! I'll drink your blood! *(Drags himself back to his bed.)*

LULU: *(To SCHIGOLCH.)* Unbutton your coat.—I'll put my feet inside.

SCHIGOLCH: I wish you still wore silk undies and garters—

LULU: Please—

SCHIGOLCH: Be sure they pay.—I'd prefer a slice of Christmas pudding.

LULU: It's me all the same.

SCHIGOLCH: Yes, yes.

LULU: Unbutton it. Please, please. I'm dying of cold.

SCHIGOLCH: I could kick the bucket anytime. My fingertips have been numb since Paris. They get bluer every day.—I'd just like one last Christmas pudding.—Around midnight I'll drop into the club downstairs.—I always liked traveling.—There may be gambling.—I don't go in for that.—But there's a really beautiful blonde young miss hovering behind the bar—

LULU: Jesus! *(Goes to the flower stand and puts the whiskey bottle to her mouth.)*

SCHIGOLCH: So they can smell her coming a block off—before she even opens her mouth!

LULU: *(With a poisonous look at SCHIGOLCH, as she puts down the bottle.)* I won't drink it all. *(Goes out left.)*

ALWA: *(Wrapping himself in his rug.)* She could have become Empress of Russia. A second Catherine the Great.

(Pause. LULU enters from the left carrying a pair of worn lace-up boots and sits on the chair beside the door.)

LULU: *(Stuttering with cold.)* I already feel—the—the—the—the—if only I—didn't—didn't have to—go—down—it makes me laugh—je jouirai—ah—je jouirai—*(Stamping her feet securely into the boots.)* Whhh—but it's—cold! *(Goes to the flower stand and drinks from the bottle.)*

SCHIGOLCH: A dog wouldn't piss on her.

LULU: *(Putting the bottle down.)* Ça m'excite! *(Takes another swallow and weaves out through the middle door.)*

ALWA: It's a pity about her—when I think back.

(Pause.)

SCHIGOLCH: When we hear her come back, we'll have to creep into my hole—till it's over.

ALWA: You might just say I grew up with her—

(Long pause.)

SCHIGOLCH:—She'll last as long as I do.

ALWA:—The first time—I met her—she was—was dressing.—But we were like brother and sister from the start. She was dressed in her chemise and lying in the rocking chair—Turkish pompon slippers on her tiny feet—having her hair done. Dr. Goll had been called to an operation.—Mama was still alive. We talked about my first poem that had been published in *Vienna Mode*. The hairdresser had read it, too. "Chase your hounds far across the mountains—they will return covered with sweat and dust—"

SCHIGOLCH: Yes, yes.

(Pause.)

ALWA: And then there was the Museum Ball. She was in rose-colored tulle—a white bodice underneath. Father had arranged it. She came with Dr. Goll. They weren't married yet. At the last moment mama went, too. She'd had a headache all day.—Papa didn't want to talk to her. So I had to go and dance with her.—Papa never took his eyes off me all night.—Afterwards she shot him.—It's monstrous—

SCHIGOLCH: I doubt anyone will bite.

ALWA: I was there.—I wouldn't recommend it to anyone.

SCHIGOLCH: What an ass!

(Pause.)

ALWA: At the time she was still three years younger than me. But she was already treating me like a mother.—She mothered me despite her tender years.—She was actually my stepmother in those days—my little sister. Papa sent her off to boarding school.—My wife.—Hm—

SCHIGOLCH: I hope she doesn't bolt on us.

ALWA: Later—during the few months she was married to the painter—she saw me in a better light—saw something superior in me.—From time to time she discussed my spiritual problems with me.—It didn't last long.—The first time I made love to her was in her rustling wedding dress—the day she married papa.—She mixed us up.

SCHIGOLCH: There they are—

(Heavy footsteps are heard ascending the stairs.)

ALWA: (Jumping up.) I won't let her—

SCHIGOLCH: (Pulling himself with difficulty from the mattress.) Forwards!

ALWA: (Standing in front of his chaise longue, throwing the rug around his waist.) I'll beat the bastard to a pulp!

SCHIGOLCH: (Dragging himself across the room and taking ALWA's arm.) Forwards!—He can hardly unburden himself of his troubles with us bumbling all over the place.

ALWA: Let me go! I'd sooner be beaten to death!

SCHIGOLCH: What a little coward—little dandy—little rascal! You want your family to go hungry? (Pushes him down right.)

ALWA: (Threatening.) What if he forces her to do something dirty!

SCHIGOLCH: So?

ALWA: God help him if he does!

SCHIGOLCH: Forwards! (Pushes ALWA into the cubbyhole.)

ALWA: Leave the door open.

SCHIGOLCH: (Following ALWA into the cubbyhole.) You won't hear a thing.

ALWA: I will—I'll hear—

SCHIGOLCH: Shut your trap!

ALWA: Heaven help him if he—!

(LULU opens the door and allows MR. HOPKINS to enter. He is a colossus of a man, with a rosy, smooth-shaven face, bright blue eyes, and a friendly smile on his mouth. He wears a top hat and a long Havelock and holds a dripping umbrella in his hand. He places his index finger to his mouth and regards LULU meaningfully.)

LULU: I'm afraid it's not terribly comfortable—(He puts his hand over her mouth.) What do you mean? (He puts his hand over her mouth and places his index finger against his lips.) I don't understand you. (He holds her mouth shut. LULU breaks free.) We're alone. There's nobody here. (He places his index finger against his lips, waves his hand in a negative sign, points to LULU, opens his mouth as if to speak, points at himself and then at the door.) Mon Dieu, mon Dieu—(He holds her mouth shut. Then goes upstage, carefully folds his Havelock, places it on the chair beside the door, opens his umbrella and sets it on the floor to dry.)

SCHIGOLCH: (From behind the half-open door down right, to ALWA.) This one's got a bee in his bonnet.

ALWA: One false move and he's—

SCHIGOLCH: Could she have sunk much lower?

(HOPKINS comes downstage with a broad grinning smile, takes LULU's head in both hands, and kisses her on the forehead.)

LULU: (Stepping back.) I hope you'll give me some money. (He holds her mouth shut and presses a ten-shilling piece into her hand. LULU inspects it and tosses it from one hand to the other. He regards her with questioning uncertainty. LULU pockets the ten-shilling piece.) All right. (He rapidly holds her mouth shut, gives her a five-shilling piece and tosses her a threatening glance.) You're generous. (He jumps madly around the room, flailing the air with his arms, and stares despondently up to heaven. LULU draws closer to him, slings her arm around his waist, places her index finger to his lips, and shakes her head No. He takes her head in both his hands and kisses her on the mouth. LULU tosses her arms around his neck, presses close to him, and plants a long kiss on his mouth. He frees himself from her with a soundless laugh and looks questioningly at the mattress down right and at the chaise longue up left. LULU takes up the lamp from the flower stand, tosses him an enticing look, and opens the door down left. HOPKINS nods and enters smiling, removing his hat as he walks through the doorway. LULU follows him. The stage is dark except for a single ray of light that emerges down left through the space beneath the door.)

ALWA: (On all fours in the half-open door.) They're inside.

SCHIGOLCH: (Behind him.) Wait.

ALWA: You can't hear from here.

SCHIGOLCH: Stupid ass.

ALWA: I'll go to the door.

(LULU, carrying a lamp, comes from the left. She smiles and shakes her head. She takes the rug from the chaise longue and is about to pick up the wash basin from the floor. Catching sight of SCHIGOLCH and ALWA, she jumps with alarm and directs them to remain inside.)

SCHIGOLCH: *(Sharply.)* Was the money real?

(LULU places her index finger to her lips and wrinkles her forehead pleadingly, removes the wash basin from under the drip, goes out stage left, closing the door after her.)

ALWA: Now.

SCHIGOLCH: Stupid fuck. *(Squeezes past ALWA, gropes his way across the stage, takes the Havelock from the chair, and looks through the pockets. ALWA has crept to LULU's door.)* Gloves.—That's it. *(Turns the Havelock inside out in order to look through the inner pockets. Pulls out a book, holds it so the ray of light hits it, and deciphers the title page with some difficulty.)* Primer for Pious Pilgrims and Those Who Aspire Thereto— with a preface—by Rev. W. Hay, M.H.—Very helpful.—Price three shillings six. *(Putting the book back into the coat.)* This man is in a bad way.

ALWA: Now—

SCHIGOLCH: *(Feeling his way back to down right.)* London's had its day. England's greatness is a thing of the past. *(Whispering across to ALWA from the doorway down right.)* What's happening?

ALWA: *(After a pause.)* Il fait sa toilette—

SCHIGOLCH: The world is never as bad as we imagine.

ALWA: My wife! My wife! *(Creeps back right, pulling SCHIGOLCH with him into the cubbyhole.)*

SCHIGOLCH: The bastard didn't even wear a silk scarf.

ALWA: Just be quiet!

SCHIGOLCH: And in Germany we grovel on our bellies in front of these people!

ALWA: He's got a repeating rifle.

SCHIGOLCH: For his measly handful of coppers!

ALWA: I envy him his luck.

SCHIGOLCH: Me, too. Me, too.

(HOPKINS reenters from the left. LULU follows him with the lamp. They look at each other.)

LULU: Do you think you'll come again? *(HOPKINS holds her mouth shut. LULU, somewhat radiant, looks in consternation at heaven and shakes her head nervously. HOPKINS has put on his Havelock and approaches her grinning. She throws her arms around his neck. He gently frees himself, kisses her hand, and turns to the door. She is about to go with him; he makes a sign for her to stay. He goes out through the middle door. LULU comes downstage.)* God, he wore me out! Jesus!

SCHIGOLCH: How much?

LULU: He wore me out! *(Putting the lamp on the flower stand.)* I—I've got to go back down—

ALWA: *(Blocking her way.)* You're not going out there again!

LULU: Shut your—! Oh, God, oh, God!

SCHIGOLCH: She's far gone. The spirit's come over her. Just as I prophesied!

LULU: *(Throwing her arms back.)* I can't stand this!

SCHIGOLCH: All the better. It's all beginning to come together. How much?

LULU: *(Pushing ALWA aside.)* I have to. I can't help it. *(Stops as though suddenly rooted.)*

ALWA: What is it—?

LULU: He's coming back—

SCHIGOLCH: *(Taking ALWA by the sleeve.)* Come on!

LULU: It's someone else—

ALWA: Who—who could it—be?

SCHIGOLCH: Come on!

LULU: God knows.

ALWA: It's coming!

> *(A knock at the door. LULU, ALWA, and SCHIGOLCH look silently at one another. The door is opened from outside. GESCHWITZ enters with a pale, sunken face, in poor clothes and carrying a rolled canvas.)*

LULU: You—!

GESCHWITZ: If I've come at a bad time—

LULU: Where have you—?

GESCHWITZ: I haven't spoken to anyone for nine days—

LULU: But did you—?

GESCHWITZ: *(With downcast eyes.)* No—nothing—

LULU: *(Goes downstage left with her chin stuck out.)* I can't stand this—

SCHIGOLCH: Would Her Grace care to inquire about our health?

GESCHWITZ: I wrote to my brother. He sent me nothing.

LULU: In a barracks—

GESCHWITZ: I had no money today to buy food.

SCHIGOLCH: Her Grace would just love to settle her feet under our table. *(Goes to GESCHWITZ and touches the rolled canvas.)*

GESCHWITZ: Lulu—

LULU: I have to go down. I'm in a hurry.

GESCHWITZ: Lulu—

LULU: I'll be right back.

SCHIGOLCH: What's this?

GESCHWITZ: *(To LULU.)* I've got it—

LULU: I'm going out of my mind!

GESCHWITZ: The picture—

ALWA: What? You've got the portrait?

LULU: *(At the door.)* I'll jump in the Thames if no one takes pity—

ALWA: *(Has taken the picture from GESCHWITZ and unrolled it.)* There! She's back with us again!

LULU: *(Coming downstage.)* What's that?

GESCHWITZ: Your picture.

ALWA: It looks darker to me.

LULU: *(Crying out.)* Oh—oh, God in heaven!

SCHIGOLCH: We'll have to nail it up.

ALWA: *(To GESCHWITZ.)* How did you come by this?

SCHIGOLCH: Quite an impression it'll make on our clientele.

GESCHWITZ: I cut it out.—I crept back quietly the next day.

ALWA: There's a nail. *(Goes right and secures the picture on a nail sticking from the wall.)*

GESCHWITZ: It's quite cracked. I carried it the best I could.

SCHIGOLCH: It'll need another at the bottom.

ALWA: I know what I'm doing! *(Removes a nail from the wall, takes off one of his boots, and hammers it into the bottom of the canvas with the heel.)*

SCHIGOLCH: It'll hang itself straight. It was rolled up too long.

GESCHWITZ: A junk shop dealer in Drury Lane offered me half a crown for it when he saw it. I didn't want to part with it.

ALWA: *(Putting on his boot.)* Hanging there awhile will do the trick.

SCHIGOLCH: It gives the old place a touch of class.

ALWA: *(Stepping back, to LULU.)* The lamp, dear heart—
(LULU approaches with the lamp.)

SCHIGOLCH: They'll be flattered to have seen it!

ALWA: She had all it takes to make a man happy.
(LULU laughs.)

SCHIGOLCH: What's gone is gone; they'll just have to imagine it.
(LULU laughs.)

ALWA: She's lost a lot of flesh—

SCHIGOLCH: Can't be helped. I've lost, too.

ALWA: The eyes are still the same—exactly.

SCHIGOLCH: In those days she gorged herself on pâté de fois gras. You only have to look at her arms.

ALWA: What splendid breasts!—It was shortly before she reached her peak.

SCHIGOLCH: At any rate she can say: That was me.

(LULU laughs.)

ALWA: The resemblance was beguiling. The bearing—the line—the dew-fresh skin—

GESCHWITZ: He must have been a highly gifted artist!

(LULU laughs.)

ALWA: *(To GESCHWITZ.)* Didn't you know him?

GESCHWITZ: No. He was before my time.

SCHIGOLCH: Ah, look at the legs! They don't make 'em like that anymore.

(LULU laughs.)

ALWA: The delicate smile that suffuses her face. Enough to knock the world off its course.

SCHIGOLCH: Whoever gets his hands on her today would never guess.

ALWA: This rosy whiteness—angelic light—as if air had settled in drops on her skin—

SCHIGOLCH: Her whole body radiates light.

(LULU laughs.)

ALWA: She feels happiness in every part of her. Below desire, above the dawn. She has no lips—only kisses.

SCHIGOLCH: Yes. By divine fiat. Woman is transitory.

ALWA: The old excitement comes flooding back. *(LULU laughs.)* This picture explains everything that's happened to me.

SCHIGOLCH: I knew that mouth when it lost its milk teeth.

ALWA: When you live with a person for years, you don't notice the ravages of time.

SCHIGOLCH: In those days I'd still appear in broad daylight. I had an affair of the heart in every second street.

ALWA: I'm getting back my self-respect.

SCHIGOLCH: It's all been swept into the dustbin. It's the times.

ALWA: Nature's trick to entrap us. Woman blossoms for the few seconds we need to deceive ourselves for all time.

SCHIGOLCH: Trick? She doesn't need tricks. Not now. Not anymore.

Under a street lamp she's a match for any dozen of these chattering English chippies.

ALWA: Providence strings up the noose—you put your own head in. What's to complain?

SCHIGOLCH: Anyone still needs it this time of night won't be too picky.

ALWA: And in what woman has nature ever fought with more powerful means!

SCHIGOLCH: He's out for soul, not flesh. He picks a pair of eyes with the least hint of thievery in them.

ALWA: Other men may have been spared my misery, but they'll never know my joy.

SCHIGOLCH: We don't count—not anymore. A man handing out money usually has a reason for it. Once you're a survivor, you're too sly to pay. She's not as dumb as she wants us to think. That right, girl?

LULU: *(Setting the lamp on the flower stand.)* I'll be back soon.

ALWA: You're not going!

GESCHWITZ: Where are you—?

LULU: Out! Out!

ALWA: To prostitute herself!

GESCHWITZ: *(Crying out.)* Lulu!

LULU: *(Tears in her eyes.)* Don't make it worse than it is—

GESCHWITZ: Lulu, Lulu, I'm going with you, no matter where?

SCHIGOLCH: That's all we need!

GESCHWITZ: *(Falling at LULU's feet.)* Come with me—I'll work for you.

LULU: Get away! Monster!

GESCHWITZ: I—I'll go out there *for* you.

SCHIGOLCH: *(Walking on GESCHWITZ's fingers.)* With that bag of bones you call a body?! *(Sententiously.)* Bless you, child! Go forth and appease your thirst! It's lasted a century—

GESCHWITZ: Lulu! Lulu!

SCHIGOLCH: Just don't chase off our noble sons of Albion! Find your own beat! And fish with your own bait!
(LULU has rushed down the stairs.)

GESCHWITZ: *(Struggling to her feet.)* I won't leave her side. I have weapons. *(Runs after her.)*

SCHIGOLCH: Shit!—Shit!—Shit!—Shit!—

ALWA: *(Tossing and turning on his chaise longue.)* I think I've reached the end of my rope.

SCHIGOLCH: Why didn't you grab her by the throat!

ALWA: Passion has burned me out—body and soul.

SCHIGOLCH: She'll scare off anything that breathes—like rat poison—with that death's head she calls a face.

ALWA: She tied me to the post and regaled my body with thorns.

SCHIGOLCH: Providence provides—man accepts.

ALWA: She's eaten me out like a pest of boils.

SCHIGOLCH: *(Stretching out on his mattress.)* Fate doesn't come any better than her. She lured that bastard back to my hole.

ALWA: Ah, for the coup de grâce! How grateful I'd be.

SCHIGOLCH: The toilet-bridegroom!

ALWA: I envy him.

SCHIGOLCH: He robbed her of her ossified virginity. With her permission.

ALWA: My house became the campground for all the poisons and parasites that flocked to her Babylonian orgies.

(Pause.)

SCHIGOLCH: You might turn up the lamp a bit.

ALWA: I dread thinking about the end of it all.

SCHIGOLCH: At twenty-three I knew how to take care of myself—

ALWA: I wonder—does a child of nature suffer the same as us?

SCHIGOLCH:—even if all I had was a necktie to hide my nakedness.

ALWA: Not many enjoyed a youth like mine. It was glorious—

SCHIGOLCH: Once I owned three houses on the edge of town. You learn to break such habits.

ALWA: What have I made of my life!

SCHIGOLCH: It'll soon be pitch black in here. When's she coming?

ALWA: The years go by—how hard it is to remember—

SCHIGOLCH: What has this shitty weather done to my fool's cap!

ALWA: You don't hear the rain anymore.

SCHIGOLCH: I hope they didn't stay together.

ALWA: It looks to be nice by morning.

SCHIGOLCH: It never works in pairs.

ALWA: They didn't stay together.

SCHIGOLCH: She'll fight her off with her fists if she has to.

ALWA: One man wins the respect of his nation—

SCHIGOLCH: I think I—hear something—

ALWA:—the other's down and out in London, on a pile of garbage, unable to die.

SCHIGOLCH: Don't you hear it?

ALWA: Where?—The happy hours we spent together—hours of creative inspiration—doting on the future.

SCHIGOLCH: They're coming! They're coming!

ALWA: Who?

SCHIGOLCH: *(Pulling himself up.)* Madame la Comtesse!

ALWA: I'm not moving.

SCHIGOLCH: Blockhead!

ALWA: I'm not moving. I'll creep under the rug. At least I won't miss it.

SCHIGOLCH: Mama's baby! *(Creeps into his cubbyhole down right and closes the door behind him. ALWA creeps under his rug.)*

LULU: *(Opening the door.)* Come in, come in—

KUNGU POTI: *(In a light top hat, light overcoat, and light trousers is heard stumbling up the stairs.)* Is dark out here.

LULU: Come in, darling. There's more light in here.

KUNGU POTI: Is your sitting room?

LULU: *(Closing the door.)* Yes.—Why so serious?

KUNGU POTI: It cold here.

LULU: You'll have a drink?

KUNGU POTI: Well. If brandy.

LULU: Yes. Come on. *(Taking the bottle.)* I don't know where the glass is.

KUNGU POTI: That not matter. *(Putting the bottle to his lips.)* Well—well—

LULU: He looks like a burned pancake.

KUNGU POTI: What that?

LULU: I said you're a very nice young man.

KUNGU POTI: Well. Do you think so?

LULU: Oh, yes.—In the street he didn't look so black.

KUNGU POTI: My father Sultan of Ouaoubée.

LULU: Is he? How many women does he keep?

KUNGU POTI: Only four. I six here London. Three English, three French. Well. I don't like see them.

LULU: You're not on good terms with them?

KUNGU POTI: Well. They too stylish for me.

LULU: You prefer to come with me?

KUNGU POTI: Yes, I do.

LULU: He reeks like a menagerie!

KUNGU POTI: What you say?

LULU: Will you stay in London long?

KUNGU POTI: Well. When father dead, I must go Ouaoubée.

LULU: What will you do there?

KUNGU POTI: I be king my country. Kingdom twice size England. Well, I rather stay London.

LULU: I believe that.—How much will you give me?

KUNGU POTI: What your name?

LULU: Daisy.

KUNGU POTI: *(Sings and does a fidgety movement with his feet.)*
> Daisy, Daisy,
>
> Give me your answer, do!

LULU: Tell me—what do you want to give me?

KUNGU POTI: Daisy, I give sovereign.

LULU: Well.

KUNGU POTI: *(Sings and does a fidgety movement with his feet.)*
> I'm half crazy
>
> All for the love of you!
>
> *(Tries to kiss her.)*

LULU: *(Resisting him.)* Let me see the money first.

KUNGU POTI: Yes. I give one pound. I always give sovereign.

LULU: You can give it afterwards, but you must show it to me first.

KUNGU POTI: Never I pay beforehand!

LULU: All right, but show me your money.

KUNGU POTI: No, Daisy. Come—

LULU: Go away, please!

KUNGU POTI: *(Grabbing her by the waist.)* Come, come—

LULU: Let me go! Let me—

KUNGU POTI: *(Grabbing her by the hair.)* Come, Daisy—where is bed—

LULU: *(Screaming.)* No!—No!—Don't do that!—Oh!

KUNGU POTI: Well. *(Throws her to the floor.)*
> *(ALWA has unwrapped himself from his rug, comes downstage with long strides, and lets fly at KUNGU POTI's throat.)*

LULU: *(Crying out.)* Jesus God!
> *(KUNGU POTI reaches into his pocket and lands ALWA a blow to the head.)*

ALWA: *(Collapsing.)* Mama—

KUNGU POTI: Well—that a den! That a murder hole! I go. *(Goes out through the middle door.)*

LULU: *(Getting up.)* There he lies!—Alwa!—I won't stay here. Why did I pick the black? Hordes of men pass by every minute. You have to ask for the time—what time is it, please? What're you doing out so late?

Get a conversation going: Why so sad? Show understanding for everything. *(Goes out through the middle door.)*

SCHIGOLCH: *(Groping his way in from down right, bends over ALWA.)*
C'est la vie! Never mess in other people's love affairs! *(Touching ALWA's
head.)* Blood—blood—*(Goes to the table and returns with the lamp.)*
Nothing to see.—Alwa!—Dear boy!—His ears must be stopped. *(Sets
the lamp on the floor and puts his ear to ALWA's back.)* Something's kick-
ing up a row in there. *(Turns him over and feels his forehead.)* There's no
fever. He's cool. *(Yelling into ALWA's ear.)* Alwa!—Alwa! *(Opens the left
eyelid with his thumb.)* I know that. I know that. I know that. *(Takes
his head in both hands and feels it.)* The cannibal!—Deep—deep. *(Lets
it fall. The head strikes the floor.)* Oops!—He has to get to bed. *(Takes
hold of ALWA under the shoulders and under the knees, tries to lift him,
and lets him fall. Straightens up.)* The youngster doesn't weigh much
these days. If only there was someone here. *(Bending over him.)* Say
something, for God's sake! You didn't take a spill on your tongue!
Don't be such a sleepyhead! You've got the whole world ahead of you!
(Shaking him.) There, there. Don't take it so to heart. He didn't really
mean it. You can still—a hundred times—don't be stupid. It's not
worth the effort. You're still too young for this life. Come on, now. Be
reasonable. *(Straightens up.)* Can't be reasoned with, you can't be
helped.—Give him time to think it over.—He's smiling like he'd put a
lump of sugar in his mouth. *(He again takes hold of him, one arm under
the shoulders, the other under the knees, and drags him a few steps left,
then sets him down.)* In cases like this it's either/or—except when they
don't know their own mind. *(Shaking ALWA.)* You can still dote on the
future.—Are you deaf? *(Boxes his ears.)* I'll knock the silliness out of
you yet! *(Picking him up again.)* He wants a little peace—*(Drags ALWA
into LULU's room. Pause. SCHIGOLCH returns, picks the lamp off the
floor, and places it on the flower stand. Speaking to the lamp.)* You're on
the way out, too. *(Turning it up and staring at LULU's picture.)* Still not
hanging right, are you? There's something—something—the white
legs—the arm lifted in the air—something of—of—death about it. It
comes like in a dream.—Time comes for each of us by and by. God
knows when she'll come back from her little jaunt. Once she's lived to
our ripe age—seen so much flame into life—and die down again to
nothing—there'll be no more baying the moon—no more thoughts of
jumping in the Thames. *(Goes into his cubbyhole and returns with a
bristly, dented-in top hat.)* But now we're off for a scotch whiskey and a

slice of Christmas pudding. *(Suddenly startled.)* Jesus!—Someone's there! *(GESCHWITZ opens the door silently.)* You—

GESCHWITZ: Me—

SCHIGOLCH: I thought—maybe—it was the—

GESCHWITZ: He'll be here soon.

SCHIGOLCH: *(Going to the door.)* I won't disturb him.

GESCHWITZ: I won't keep you.

SCHIGOLCH: I'll be off.

GESCHWITZ: How dark it's getting.

SCHIGOLCH: It'll get darker.

GESCHWITZ: I'm maimed.

SCHIGOLCH: Everyone has to be gone.

GESCHWITZ: I can't.

SCHIGOLCH: At least I can, thank God.

GESCHWITZ: I can't go and I can't stay.

SCHIGOLCH: Being so flat-chested I suppose you want to play the pater-familias.

GESCHWITZ: I've learned to wait.

SCHIGOLCH: Then wait quietly. Makes more sense than playing her rival. Who knows, maybe you'll fill out.

GESCHWITZ: She sent me up.

SCHIGOLCH: Then I'm bound to run into her. *(Goes off through the middle door.)*

GESCHWITZ: *(Alone.)* I'm maimed.—She said so.—I'm maimed. *(Sits down in the wicker chair beside the door.)* She may be right. I've waited three years. She used me as a murder weapon. She deceived me—deceived me and deceived me. Three whole years for one minute. Maybe if she saw me in my death throes at her feet.—All I have left is my life. She has all the rest—all—except for my life. The shares—the bank books—the bonds—the rents—my honor—my happiness—and still I wait. What will she give me when I'm dead? Will she cry? I don't think so. Can't believe in a loving God anymore—a God who maimed me. I believed in him once—believed for a long time. But not when I'm maimed—not when I'm maimed!—When he comes—I'll shoot him! Everyone else is whole—complete—every guttersnipe. They can make her dance for joy! Just not *me!* Not *me!* Only *I* can't! The only one who can't! Why—why—why—why—must I be the one who's damned—?

(Long pause. LULU opens the door and lets DR. HILTI enter.

GESCHWITZ remains unmoving in the chair beside the door, unnoticed by the others.)

LULU: What are you doing out so late?

HILTI: I've been to the theater. The Alhambra.

LULU: Ah! You've seen Constantinople, then?

HILTI: Yes, yes. Indeed!

LULU: How did you like it?

HILTI: Oh—it was very nice.

LULU: Yes.—Did you see the Turkish coffeehouse?

HILTI: Yes. Certainly. I've never seen such beautiful girls.

LULU: They're very prettily dressed—the Turkish dancing girls.

HILTI: Ah, yes. Two thousand women lifting their right leg at the same time!

LULU: You saw that?

HILTI: Yes. And then the left leg! I've never seen such beautiful girls before!

LULU: Haven't you?—You're not English, are you?

HILTI: No. I've only been here two weeks. Were you born in London?

LULU: No. I'm French.

HILTI: Ah, vous êtes Française?

LULU: Oui, monsieur, je suis Parisienne.

HILTI: Are you?

LULU: A true Parisienne, yes. My mother is a cashier at the Café Calypso. She once sold fish on the boulevards. My father is a member of the nobility. I haven't seen him in a while. He lives in the Faubourg St. Honorée.

HILTI: I just came from Paris. I was there for a week. Every day I went to the Louvre.

LULU: What did you do there?

HILTI: Admired the pictures. But I'm not French. I'm from Zurich, in Switzerland.

LULU: Ah, then you speak Swiss French.

HILTI: No. Zurich is in German Switzerland.

LULU: You speak German, then?

HILTI: Do you?

LULU: A bit. One of my old lovers was a German. From Berlin, I believe.

HILTI: What a relief you speak German!

LULU: *(Leading him to the chaise longue.)* Come here, sweetie. You'll spend the night? *(Kissing his eyes.)* You have such lovely eyes.

HILTI: I've only got five shillings on me.

LULU: Let me see, my darling.

HILTI: *(Emptying his purse.)* Here. It's all I ever carry away from home.

LULU: *(Taking the money and pocketing it.)* It'll do—just because it's you—because you have such sweet eyes. Put your arms around me.

HILTI: Oh, God, God, God, Jesus God! *(LULU kisses him.)* Oh, Jesus—I've never been with a woman before! This is my first—

LULU: Little liar!

HILTI: No, I mean it! Believe me! I imagined it all so differently!

LULU: Why did you marry so young?

HILTI: Marry?! Me? I'm not married!

LULU: Go on!

HILTI: No, Jesus, it's true!

LULU: Then what do you do?

HILTI: I'm a lecturer. I read philosophy at the university.

LULU: You mean it? You've never slept with a woman?

HILTI: I swear. I'm from a very old Basel family. I'm an aristocrat. As a student all I got was two francs pocket money.

LULU: I believe you said you're a philosopher?

HILTI: That's right. Yes.

LULU: Tell me, then—aren't there any women in Zurich?

HILTI: In Zurich?

LULU: Yes.

HILTI: Oh, you bet! Zurich's got fifty-five whorehouses. But only married men go there.

LULU: I see. Were you short of money?

HILTI: Oh, I wanted to pig around, all right! But I had better use for my money. Married men can't help needing it, but their wives are too ugly for them.

LULU: What kind of "pigging around" do you Swiss do?

HILTI: Just pigging. You know. The same as you.

LULU: Me?—But I make love.

HILTI: It's all the same! What else is it but pigging around? It's *all* pigging around!

LULU: Then why did you come here?

HILTI: Because now I need it. I'm engaged to be married. Just this evening I got engaged to a girl from a very old Basel family. She works here as a governess.

LULU: Is she pretty?

HILTI: Yes, she's worth two million. But now I need it. I have to be able to do it if I'm to get married. I'm really nervous, you know? To see what it's like?

LULU: *(Tossing her hair back.)* How lucky can I be! *(Gets up and takes the lamp.)* Whenever you're ready, professor! Nous verrons—*(Leads HILTI into her room and locks the door from inside.)*

GESCHWITZ: *(Motionless, pulls a small black revolver from her bag and holds it to her forehead.)* Come, my darling.—Come—

HILTI: *(Tears the door open from inside and rushes out.)* Jesus Christ! There's a body in there!

LULU: *(Lamp in hand, holds him by the sleeve.)* Stay with me—

HILTI: A dead man! A corpse!

LULU: *(Clinging to him.)* Stay with me! Stay with me!

HILTI: *(Freeing himself.)* There a dead body in—Jesus God! Filthy!

LULU: *(Embracing his legs.)* Stay with me!

HILTI: How do I get out of here? *(Looks around for the door and catches sight of GESCHWITZ; grabbing at his hair.)* The devil! It's the devil!

LULU: *(Crying out.)* Please—stay! Stay!

HILTI: Filthy business! Filthy, filthy business! Jesus God! *(Goes out through the middle door.)*

LULU: *(Jumping up.)* Stay—stay—stay—*(Rushes after him.)*

GESCHWITZ: *(Letting the revolver sink.)* Hanging is better. I would never hear anything again. What has life got in store for me? Pain, pain. I could jump from the bridge. The water's cold. Same as my bed. Which is colder? The water? My bed? In Paris the railings weren't so high. You're not cold long. I could dream—of her—to the end.—Hanging is better!—She's cold, too.—Or stab myself. I could just as well—stab myself.—But I'm not brave enough for that. No. That could never be. How often I've dreamt—that she kissed me. Just one more minute. No, no, no. Something always comes between.—Hanging is better.— I could never cut my wrists. That could never be. I can't poison myself.—Hanging is better. It's so dirty, so dirty, so dirty. Hanging! *(Hiding the revolver.)* I can't shoot myself. I can't jump in the Thames. The water's too clean!—Hang myself! *(Suddenly jumping up.)* God knows! *(She takes the rug strap from the wall, climbs onto the chair, attaches the strap to a hook in the wall above the door frame, places the strap around her neck, pushes the chair from under her with her foot, and falls to the floor.—She feels along the strap and finds the hook that was torn from the wall.)* Damned life! Damned life! Damned life! *(She stands for a while leaned against the wall; then in a tearful voice.)* Lulu—

Lulu—if only—I could still—if only I could still—if this were only a
test—if only I didn't have to go—Lulu—let me speak to your heart—
just once—just open your heart to me once—then everything—everything will be good!—I'll wait. I'll wait.—But at least promise
me—Lulu—then I won't have to go—not yet! Not till I've been
happy—just once. I know that. I know that now.—Or I'd suffer
through all eternity. God doesn't want that. He doesn't want it, so he
won't let me go! He wants me to be happy—once—just once.—
Lulu!—Listen to him!—Lulu!—He's speaking to you—for me! Listen
to him!—Lulu!—He'll punish you, he'll punish you! (*Drags herself
stage right, sinks to her knees in front of LULU's picture, and folds her
hands.*) My angel!—My love!—My star!—I worship you! I cherish you!
Who has suffered more? Who gave you more? Your laughter is so full
of joy! Who has been more patient?—Your skin is soft as snow.—Your
heart is just as cold.—Have pity on me!—Have pity!—Pity!

LULU: (*Leads in JACK; to GESCHWITZ, her eyes ablaze.*) You're still here?
(*JACK is a stocky, thickset figure with elastic movements, pale face, inflamed
eyes, scrofulous nose, high-arched, heavy eyebrows, down-turned mustache,
thin beard, matted side-whiskers, and fire-red hands with chewed finger-
nails. When speaking he goes from one pose to another at the same time
keeping his eyes lowered. He wears a dark overcoat and a bowler hat.*)

JACK: Who's this?

LULU: My sister.

JACK: Your sister?

LULU: She's mad. She's always in the way.

GESCHWITZ: (*Cringing back like a dog.*) I didn't hear you.

JACK: Will she disturb us?

LULU: No—stay, stay! Don't go, please—

JACK: You have a beautiful mouth when you speak.

LULU: (*Opening the door, to GESCHWITZ.*) Get out! Wait on the steps!

JACK: Don't send her away!

LULU: (*Closing the door.*) Will you stay with me?

JACK: How much do you want?

LULU: All night—?

JACK: You have a strong, pretty chin. Your lips are like bursting cherries.

LULU: You'll no sooner see me than you'll leave—tell me you have to get
home.

JACK: Liar!

LULU: Oh, God, oh, God—

JACK: You understand your business. You're not English.

LULU: No.

JACK: What, then?

LULU: German.

JACK: Where did you get your beautiful mouth?

LULU: From my mother.

JACK: I know that.—How much do you want?

LULU: Whatever you like.

JACK: I can't waste money. I'm not Baron Rothschild.

LULU: Will you stay all night?

JACK: No, I haven't got time.

LULU: Why won't you stay all night?

JACK: I'm a married man.

LULU: You'll say you missed the last bus and had to spend the night with a friend.

JACK: Time is money. How much?

LULU: A pound.

JACK: Good evening. *(Goes to the door.)*

LULU: *(Holding him back.)* Stay!—Stay! *(JACK goes past GESCHWITZ to the cubbyhole down right, opens it, and taps around inside.)* I live with my sister.

JACK: *(Coming back.)* You're insolent!

LULU: I am not insolent!—You can pay me tomorrow.

JACK: When I'm asleep, you'll roll me.

LULU: I don't do that.

JACK: Why else do you want me to stay all night? *(LULU is silent.)* That's suspicious.

LULU: Give me whatever you like.

JACK: Your mouth is the best part of you.

LULU: Half a sovereign—*(JACK laughs and goes to the door. She holds him back.)* Don't leave! I beg you!

JACK: How much?

LULU: Nothing—nothing at all.

JACK: Nothing? What does that mean? *(LULU throws GESCHWITZ, who has pulled herself up against JACK, to the floor.)* Let her go! This isn't your sister.—She loves you.

LULU: We're sisters-in-law—

JACK: *(Approaches GESCHWITZ and strokes her head.)* We don't hurt each other. We understand each other. Don't we? *(Fondling her cheek.)* Poor beast—

(GESCHWITZ cringes back and throws him poisonous glances.)

LULU: Are you a bugger?

JACK: *(Holding GESCHWITZ by the strap around her neck.)* What's that?—What is that?

LULU: She's insane. I told you. If you'd rather go with her—

JACK: *(Holding GESCHWITZ firmly by the strap, to LULU.)* Tell me how much you want.

LULU: Give me eight shillings.

JACK: Too much.

LULU: If that's too much—!

JACK: How long have you been walking the streets?

LULU: Two years.

JACK: I don't believe you.

LULU: Since my birthday.

JACK: Why'd you lie?

LULU: What am I supposed to say?

JACK: You're still wet behind the ears!

LULU: It's my first day.

JACK: How many have you serviced?

LULU: First there was a gentleman. He was mad as a hatter. Wouldn't let me say a word. Covered my mouth. I couldn't either laugh or groan. That was real exciting!—I could have bitten off his nose!

JACK: And then?

LULU: Won't you stay with me?

JACK: Then?

LULU: Then there was a nigger. We started fighting over the money. He didn't want to pay. Promised to pay afterwards—

JACK: And then?

LULU: Oh, how I'd love for you to stay all night!

JACK: I pay in advance.

LULU: I don't want money.

JACK: Who followed the black man?

LULU: Nobody.—A philosopher.—Said he'd never touched a woman. He wanted to practice on me for his wedding night. He swore like a trooper. He said he was Swiss. He was a virgin. He cleared out fast enough.

JACK: Why's that?

LULU: Because of that animal on the floor there.

JACK: *(Holding GESCHWITZ by the strap.)* Did she attack him?

LULU: He was disappointed. He thought it would be different.

JACK: Were you ever a mother?

LULU: I don't know what you mean.

JACK: Did you ever have a child?

LULU: No. Never.—Why?

JACK: Because your mouth is still so fresh.

LULU: What's the matter with my mouth?

JACK: Tell me how much you want.

LULU: I was a nice looking woman.

JACK: How much do you want if I stay all night?

LULU: Give me five shillings.

JACK: Sorry.—*(Going to the door.)* Sleep tight—

LULU: *(Stopping him.)* Four—

JACK: Do you live with a friend?

LULU: I'm all alone—with my sister.

JACK: *(Pointing left.)* What's in there?

LULU: My kitchen.

JACK: Kitchen?

LULU: There's no window.

JACK: *(Stomping his foot.)* Who lives down below?

LULU: Nobody.—The room's for rent.

JACK: Would three shillings do?

LULU: Yes.

JACK: I don't have that much—

LULU: Two—

JACK: I sized you up by your walk.

LULU: Have you seen me before?

JACK: Never.—I saw your back. I followed you.

LULU: My skirt is torn behind.

JACK: I was right, too. I saw your body was perfectly formed.

LULU: You see that from behind?

JACK: I saw by the way you put your foot down. I said to myself, she must have a very expressive mouth.

LULU: You seem to have taken a fancy to my mouth.

JACK: Yes. Indeed. You're intelligent. You're generous. You're ambitious. You're all right at heart.

LULU: What harm can that do—?

JACK: I saw that when you were walking on the sidewalk.

LULU: You're original.

JACK: I was coming behind you.

LULU: What are you staring at me for?

JACK: All I have is a shilling

LULU: Yes, and you're excited.

JACK: It's three years since I slept with a girl.

LULU: All right. Give me the shilling.

JACK: How did you make ends meet before today?

LULU: Parlor maid.

JACK: Parlor maids have rougher hands than you.

LULU: I had a rich friend. Give me your shilling.

JACK: You've already loved too much today.

LULU: Yes—

JACK: *(Pulling out his purse.)* I'll need sixpence change—

LULU: I haven't a penny.

JACK: You have to. I need to take a bus tomorrow morning.

LULU: Why are you trembling so?

JACK: Come on. Look in your pocket.

LULU: *(Looking in her pockets.)* Nothing—nothing—

JACK: I'll just have a look.

LULU: That's all I've got. *(Holds a ten-shilling piece in the palm of her hand.)*

JACK: I want the half sovereign.

LULU: I'll get it changed tomorrow morning.

JACK: Give it to me.

LULU: You're richer than me.

JACK: If I stay all night with you—*(LULU gives him the money and takes up the lamp from the flower stand. He notices Lulu's portrait.)* You're a society woman. You took care of yourself.

LULU: *(Opening the door to the cubbyhole down right.)* Come on, come on—

JACK: We don't need light.

LULU: In the dark?

JACK: Why not? It's going out. It stinks.

LULU: That's true. *(Places the lamp on the flower stand.)*

JACK: What's the use of that stink? *(About to turn down the lamp.)*

LULU: Let it burn.

JACK: The moon's shining.

LULU: Come on—

JACK: As you like.

LULU: Why don't you come?

JACK: I'm afraid—

LULU: *(Throws her arms around his neck and kisses him.)* I wouldn't do you any harm. I love you. You're like a baby. You're too bashful. You look puzzled. Why don't you look at me?

JACK: I don't know if I can do it.

LULU: You, too? Yes, yes. *(Her hand beneath his overcoat.)* What more do you want? Don't let me beg you any longer. No need to be afraid of me. I was never ill.

JACK: Doesn't it shame you—to sell your love?

LULU: What else could I do?

JACK: That's very mean.

LULU: You love me! You have pity on me!

JACK: I've never found a more beautiful girl in the street.

LULU: *(Holds him in her arms.)* Come on.—I'm not as bad as I look—

JACK: All right. *(Follows LULU into the cubbyhole.)*

GESCHWITZ: *(Alone, writes with her index finger on the floorboards.)* You planted—this love—in my heart—dearest—child—what can I do— my finger bleeds—I'm—I'm too hot—there's still something—I must think about—Lulu—*(The lamp goes out. On the floorboards beneath the windows are two glaring squares. Everything in the room is clearly to be made out. She speaks as if in a dream.)* When it gets dark—when it gets dark—she's my only thought—especially—when it gets dark. If only she hadn't—married—I'll have to think about that.—I'm so dirty, so dirty!—I still have to think about—if my father—hadn't married—I'd never have seen her—never seen—if my mother—together—they make them—the children—then why am I—maimed—I won't marry. —I—I once knew someone—Lulu—Lulu—*(Jumping up.)* Oh!—Oh! *(Shrieking is heard from the right. LULU, barefoot, and in a slip, tears the door open, screaming, and holds it shut from the outside.)*

LULU: Help! Help! Martha!

(GESCHWITZ rushes to the door, pulls out her revolver, aiming it at the door, at the same time pushing LULU behind her.)

GESCHWITZ: *(To LULU.)* Let go!

(JACK, bent double, tears open the door from the inside and runs a knife through GESCHWITZ, who fires a single shot toward the ceiling and collapses howling. JACK has posted himself in front of the door leading out.)

LULU: *(Downstage left.)*—Oh!—Oh!—Oh, God—

(Pause. GESCHWITZ, her head slumped into her neck, stretches the revolver toward LULU.)

GESCHWITZ:—Lulu—

(JACK pulls GESCHWITZ toward him, backward, by the strap and takes the gun from her hand.)

LULU: Police!—Police!

JACK: *(Points the revolver at LULU.)* Be quiet!

GESCHWITZ: *(Death rattle.)* He—won't—shoot—

(JACK lunges at LULU and tries to grab hold of her. LULU flees to the door leading out. JACK throws himself against the door.)

JACK: Got you!

LULU: *(Staggering backward.)* He'll slit open my belly!

JACK: Shut up!

(JACK throws himself to the floor and tries to get his hands around her feet. LULU escapes into her room down left and leans on the door from the inside. Her screams are heard.)

LULU: Help!—Help!—Help!—Police!—Police!

(JACK, knife in hand, attempts to force open the door. GESCHWITZ tries to stand and falls on her side.)

GESCHWITZ:—My angel!—My angel!

LULU: *(From inside.)* Murder!—Murder!—Help!

JACK: *(Working on the door, to himself.)* No prettier mouth in the whole wide world.

(The door gives way. JACK forces his way in. For a moment there is no sound other than the groaning of GESCHWITZ.)

LULU: *(From inside, suddenly screaming.)* No!—No!—Have pity!—Pity!

(JACK, carrying LULU in his arms, comes through the door, and crosses the room diagonally. LULU puts both hands against his forehead in an attempt to resist him; screams.) Murder!—Murder!—Murder!—You're ripping me up—

JACK: The bed's occupied.

LULU: *(Using all her voice.)* Police!

JACK: *(Puts her down, holds her head tightly, and bores his thumbs between her teeth.)* I'll make you quiet yet! *(LULU escapes him. JACK throws himself against the door to the hall.)* Goddamn—(Sweat drips from JACK's hair and his hands are bloody. He breathes from the depth of his chest cavity and stares at the floor with eyes bulging from his head.) This is some piece of work—(LULU looks wildly around, every limb trembling, suddenly grabs hold of the whiskey bottle, breaks it on the table, and

rushes toward JACK, the jagged edge pointed at him with her right hand.
JACK lifts his right foot and propels her onto her back. He stays quietly
where he is. LULU, hands across her belly and knees drawn up to her chest,
writhes on the floor.)

LULU: Oh—Oh—Oh—

GESCHWITZ: Lulu, I can't!

(JACK rapidly collects himself, lifts LULU from the floor, and carries her
stage right.)

LULU: *(Flinging her legs about.)* Martha!—He's slitting me!—He's slitting
me!

(JACK carries her into the cubbyhole.)

GESCHWITZ: Help!—Help!—Murder!—Help!

LULU: *(From inside.)*—Oh!—Oh!—Oh!—Oh!—Oh!—Oh, don't!—
Don't!—No!—No!

GESCHWITZ: *(Calling up her last strength to drag herself to the door.)*
Lulu!—Murder!—Police! Police!

(JACK returns from stage right after a pause, unbuttons his overcoat, and
hides a small package wrapped in newspaper in the breast pocket. He gropes
his way diagonally through the room and disappears through the door to
LULU's room.)

LULU: *(In the cubbyhole, whimpering.)* Oh—oh—oh—

GESCHWITZ: Lulu—my love!

(JACK returns from LULU's room with a full wash basin, sets it on the
flower stand, and washes his hands.)

JACK: I'd never have thought of a thing like that. What a phenomenon!
Never in two hundred years! What a lucky dog to find this curiosity!

GESCHWITZ: Lulu!—Are you alive?—My angel—

JACK: When I'm dead and my collection goes up for auction, the London
Medical Association will pay three hundred pounds for this prodigy
I've conquered tonight. The professors and students will say: This is
astonishing!—Not even a towel around. What a hole in the wall—
poor as hell—

GESCHWITZ: Say something—Lulu—

JACK: Well—*(Throws back GESCHWITZ's dress and dries his hands on her*
white petticoat.)

JACK: This monster has nothing to fear from me. *(To GESCHWITZ.)* It'll
be over for you in a second. *(Goes out through the middle door.)*

GESCHWITZ: *(Alone by the cubbyhole downstage right, pulls herself along*
on both arms toward the half-open door, leaving a thin trace of blood

behind her.) Once more—my angel—once more—to see—you—once more—I love—I love—love—I am—in misery—*(Her elbows collapse beneath her.)* Shhhh—it—*(Dies.)*

END OF PLAY

THE TENOR

A Farce in One Act
1897

CAST OF CHARACTERS
GERARDO *Imperial and Royal Court Singer*
MRS. HELEN MAROVA
PROFESSOR DÜHRING
MISS ISABEL COEURNE
MÜLLER *hotel proprietor*
A VALET
A PAGE BOY
A PIANO TEACHER

SETTING
The scene is the salon of a luxurious hotel suite. There is a main entrance and two side doors. Downstage left, a window with heavy, closed curtains. Stage right, a grand piano. Behind it, a Japanese screen in front of a fireplace. Large open trunks are scattered about. Gigantic laurel wreaths lean against armchairs and a plethora of bouquets are placed around the room, with a pile of them on the piano.

TIME AND PLACE
A large German city in the last years of the nineteenth century.

A pretentiously furnished room in a hotel. There is a center door, with other doors at the sides. Downstage right is a window with heavy closed curtains. At right, a piano. Behind the piano, a Japanese screen which covers the fireplace. Large, open trunks stand about, and gigantic laurel wreaths rest on upholstered armchairs. No end of bouquets are distributed about the room. A heap of other bouquets are piled on top of the piano. A VALET enters with an armful of clothes from the adjoining room and packs them in one of the large trunks. He straightens up when there is a knock at the door.

VALET: Yes?—Come in!

PAGE BOY: There's a woman downstairs asking if Mr. Gerardo is in.

VALET: Mr. Gerardo is not at home. *(The PAGE BOY exits. The VALET goes into the adjoining room and reenters with another armful of clothes. With a knock at the door, he puts down the clothes and goes to the door.)* Hm, who could that be, I wonder? *(Opens the door and receives three or four large bouquets, walks downstage with them, and lays them carefully on the piano; then busies himself once more with his packing. Another knock; he goes to the door, opens it, and receives a handful of letters of all colors, walks downstage, and examines the addresses.)* "Mr. Gerardo."— "Mr. Court Singer."—"Monsieur Gerardo."—"Gerardo, Esq."— "Most Honorable Sir."—That one's from the chambermaid:—"Mr. Gerardo, Royal and Imperial Singer to the Court."—*(Places the letters on a salver and continues his packing.)*

GERARDO: *(Entering.)* Why haven't you finished packing!—How much time do you need?

VALET: Another moment, sir.

GERARDO: I wish you'd hurry. I have several things to see to before I leave. Well now, what have we here? *(Reaching into one of the trunks.)* Good God, man! Weren't you ever shown how to fold a pair of pants? *(Removing the piece of clothing from the trunk.)* You call this packing? You might have something to learn from me after all. Though you ought to know more of such matters than I. This is the way one takes hold of a pair of pants. Then you hook them up here at the top, like so. And then you take hold of these two buttons. Do you see the buttons? Here? Everything depends on these two buttons. Then—you pull—the pants legs straight. There! Now!—And then you—fold them—in two—you see?—Like that! A pair of pants will keep its shape for a hundred years folded like that!

VALET: *(Very respectful, his eyes cast down.)* Perhaps Mr. Gerardo was a tailor once?

GERARDO: I beg your pardon?! No, I'm afraid not. Simpleton! *(Handing him the pants.)* There you are, pack them up again. But I wish you'd hurry, if you don't mind.

VALET: *(Bent over the trunk.)* Some letters came for you, sir.

GERARDO: *(Walking toward the right.)* Thank you, I've just noticed them.

VALET: And flowers, sir!

GERARDO: Yes. Thank you. *(Takes the letters from the salver and falls into an armchair in front of the piano.)* Just see you get through as soon as possible. *(The VALET goes off into the adjoining room. GERARDO opens the letters, rushes through them with a radiant smile, crumples them, and throws them under his chair. He reads aloud from one of them.)* "—if only I might belong to you, who are a god to me! How little it would cost you to make me so endlessly happy for the remainder of my life! If only you would consider—" *(Then to himself.)* Good God! I'm supposed to sing Tristan tomorrow in Brussels and I can't remember a single note! Not a single note! *(Looking at his watch.)* Half past three. That leaves me another three-quarters of an hour. *(A knock at the door.)* Come in!

PAGE BOY: *(Lugging in a cooler of champagne.)* I was told to put this in your room, sir.

GERARDO: What? Who's downstairs?

PAGE BOY: I was told to put this in Mr. Gerardo's room.

GERARDO: *(Rising.)* What is it? *(Relieving him of the cooler.)* Oh! Thank you. *(The PAGE BOY exits. GERARDO lugs the cooler downstage.)* Good God, now what am I to do with this! *(Reads the card accompanying it; then calls.)* George!

VALET: *(Enters from the adjoining room with an armful of clothes.)* This is the last of them, sir. *(Distributes them in the various trunks and locks them.)*

GERARDO: Very well.—And I am at home to no one.

VALET: Yes, I know, sir.

GERARDO: To no one.

VALET: You may rest assured, sir. *(Giving him the keys to the trunks.)* The keys, sir.

GERARDO: To no one!

VALET: The trunks will be taken down at once. *(About to leave.)*

GERARDO: One moment—

VALET: *(Returns.)* Yes, sir?

GERARDO: *(Gives him a tip.)* To *no* one!

VALET: Thank you very much, sir. *(Goes off.)*

GERARDO: *(Alone, looking at his watch.)* Still a half hour left. *(Searches out the piano score of* Tristan und Isolde *from beneath the flowers on the piano, and sings in half-voice while pacing back and forth.)*
Isolde! Geliebte! Bist du mein?
Hab ich dich wieder? Darf ich dich fassen?
(Clears his throat, plays two thirds on the piano, and begins anew.)
Isolde! Geliebte! Bist du mein?
Hab ich dich wieder?
(Clears his throat.) What abominable air in this room! *(Sings.)*
Isolde!—Geliebte!
I feel as if I had a weight of lead around my neck! I need some air!—Air! *(Goes to the window and tries to find a cord to pull back the curtain.)* Oh, for heaven's sake, where is it! Oh, yes, the other side. Here we are. *(Rapidly pulls back the curtains, and, seeing MISS COEURNE in front of him, throws back his head in a gesture of wild despair.)* Good God!

MISS COEURNE: *(Sixteen years old, in a blue dress, loose blond hair, a bouquet of red roses in her hands, speaks with an English accent, and looks GERARDO directly in the eye.)* I beg of you, please, don't send me away.

GERARDO: What do you suggest I do with you, then? Lord knows I never asked you to come here. You would be doing me an injustice, young woman, if you blamed me for my action, but, you see, I'm scheduled to sing tomorrow evening. I must confess, I chose to have this last half hour to myself. In fact, I gave specific orders that no one, absolutely no one, no matter who it might be, was to be admitted.

MISS COEURNE: *(Coming forward.)* Please don't send me away. You must understand. I heard you sing Tannhäuser yesterday evening, and I came here only to offer you these roses, and—

GERARDO: And? Well? Well, what?

MISS COEURNE: And myself! I really don't know whether I'm expressing all this correctly.

GERARDO: *(Grasps the back of a chair, and after a short struggle with himself, shakes his head.)* Who are you?

MISS COEURNE: Miss Coeurne.

GERARDO: I see.—Yes, of course.

MISS COEURNE: I suppose I'm still only a foolish child.

GERARDO: Yes, I know. All right now, young lady, come here. *(Sits in an armchair and pulls her in front of him.)* We must have a serious talk, you and I, such as you have never yet heard in all your short life, and which—if I am not mistaken—you are in some need of.—Simply because I am an artist, I have—now please understand me correctly. Let me see—you are how old?

MISS COEURNE: Twenty-two.

GERARDO: I'm afraid, my dear, you are sixteen, or seventeen at best. You have made yourself seem somewhat older in order to appear more desirable to me.—Well?—But you're foolish all the same. And my capacity as an artist in no way requires me to help you escape your foolishness. Now you mustn't misunderstand me.—Well? Why are you staring like that?

MISS COEURNE: I said I was foolish because I thought that's how you like girls in Germany.

GERARDO: I happen not to be German, my child, but nonetheless—

MISS COEURNE: And so? I happen not to be so very simple.

GERARDO: Nor am I a nursemaid.—I suspect that isn't quite the right word, since—since in any case you are no longer a child.

MISS COEURNE: No. Fortunately! Not any longer!

GERARDO: But, my dear young lady, don't you see—you have your tennis parties, you have your skating clubs, you go bicycle riding, you can take trips into the mountains with your girlfriends, you can swim, ride, dance. You have absolutely everything a young girl could possibly want. Why then, my dear young woman, have you come here to me?

MISS COEURNE: Because I despise all those things. Because I find them so terribly boring.

GERARDO: You're quite right. I wouldn't think of correcting you. I must confess, I also find something more in life. But you see, my child, I'm a man, and I'm thirty-six years old. Don't worry; the time will come when you, too, will have a fuller sort of life. When you're two years older, I'm certain there will be someone for you; and then you'll no longer need to come here to me, to someone who never asked for you and whom you know no better than—than all the rest of Europe knows him.—Nor will you have to hide behind window curtains to taste of the—the higher life. *(MISS COEURNE breathes heavily.)* Well?—You have my sincerest thanks for your roses. *(Pressing her hand in his.)* Will that satisfy you for today?

MISS COEURNE: Old as I am, I've never so much as thought of a man, until yesterday I saw you on stage as Tannhäuser. And I promise you—

GERARDO: No, you must promise me nothing, child! What good could possibly come from what you might promise me? The inconvenience would be entirely yours.—I speak to you now as a father speaks to his daughter. You can thank God your indiscretion hasn't landed you in some other artist's hands. *(Presses her hand in his.)* Let this be a lifelong lesson, and be satisfied.

MISS COEURNE: *(Her handkerchief at her face, more to herself, but without tears.)* Am I so ugly?

GERARDO: Ugly?—Why ugly?—You're young and you're indiscreet! *(Rises nervously, walks toward the right, returns, puts his arm around her waist and grasps her hand.)* Now listen to me, child! Why should you be ugly just because I sing, just because I happen to be an artist by profession?—The first thing you think is: "I'm ugly, I'm ugly!" It's the same wherever I go. But why must it happen just as I'm leaving? And especially when I have to sing *Tristan* tomorrow evening—! Don't misunderstand me. But being a singer doesn't require me to praise your youth and beauty. But that doesn't make you ugly. You must appeal to other men. Men who live under less of a strain than I. How could I possibly say such a thing to you!

MISS COEURNE: No, you'd never say it, but you'd think it.

GERARDO: Be reasonable, child! You have no right to ask me what I think about you. Whatever I may think is of no importance whatever. I assure you. You must take my word as an artist—I beg of you—I'm being honest with you. I am, unfortunately, a human being, and I cannot possibly see any creature suffer, however mean. *(Looks critically at her, but honorably.)* But I feel very sorry for you, child. I can say that, especially after you conquered your maidenly pride in waiting here for me. But, my dear young woman, you must consider my way of life. You must consider how important *time* is to me. Why, just yesterday, two, perhaps three hundred lovely, attractive young girls of your age saw me on the stage as Tannhäuser. Suppose every one of them made the same claims upon me as you? What would become of my singing? Of my voice? How could I maintain my art? *(MISS COEURNE sinks into a chair, covers her face, and weeps. He sits down on the arm of her chair, bends over her sympathetically.)* Don't you know, child, that it's a sin for you to cry just because you're young? You have a whole lifetime ahead of you. Be patient. You should be proud of your youth, happy. How glad the rest of us would be—even if we live the lives of artists— to begin life all over again.—And please, you mustn't be ungrateful for having heard me yesterday. You must spare me that tragic epilogue.

Am I to blame that you fall in love with me? Everyone falls in love with me. That's why I'm there. My manager insists I show myself to the public in this grand manner. There's more to it than singing, you understand. I have no choice but to play Tannhäuser that way. You must be kind now, dear child. Let me have these few remaining moments to prepare for tomorrow.

MISS COEURNE: *(Rises, dries her eyes.)* I can't imagine another girl acting as I have.

GERARDO: *(Directing her toward the door.)* Quite right, my child.

MISS COEURNE: *(Gently resisting, sobbing.)* At least, not if—

GERARDO: Not if my valet were guarding the door downstairs.

MISS COEURNE:—if—

GERARDO: If the girl is as lovely and attractive as you.

MISS COEURNE:—if—if—

GERARDO: If she has heard me only once as Tannhäuser.

MISS COEURNE: *(With renewed intensity.)* If she's as respectable as me!

GERARDO: *(Pointing to the piano.)* Before you leave I want you to take a look at those flowers. Let them be a warning to you, in case you again think of falling in love with a singer. Look how fresh they all are. I either let them wilt, or go to waste, or—or give them to the porter. And look at these letters. *(Lifts a handful of letters from the salver.)* You needn't be afraid. I don't know a single one of the women who've written them. I leave them all to their fate. What else can I do? But—and you may be certain of this—every one of your attractive young girl friends is among them.

MISS COEURNE: *(Pleading.)* Well, I'll never hide myself like this again. Never again.

GERARDO: Child, child, I don't have time! I'm sorry, but I'm just about to leave. I've told you already how sorry I am for you. But my train leaves in twenty-five minutes. What more do you want?

MISS COEURNE: A kiss.

GERARDO: *(Straightening up to full height.)* From me?

MISS COEURNE: Yes.

GERARDO: *(Taking her by the waist, with dignity, but sympathetically.)* This is a desecration of art, child. Can you imagine this is why they pay my weight in gold? Put on a few years and have a bit more respect for the chaste goddess to whom I have dedicated my life and work.— You have no idea who I mean, do you?

MISS COEURNE: No.

GERARDO: Yes, I'm aware of that. But so you won't think I've been too harsh with you, I'll give you my photograph. In exchange for your word that you'll leave me.

MISS COEURNE: Yes.

GERARDO: Very well. *(Goes behind the table and signs one of his photographs.)* Try to interest yourself more in the opera than in the people on stage. Who knows, you might even find great satisfaction in it.

MISS COEURNE: *(To herself.)* I'm still much too young.

GERARDO: Become a martyr to music! *(Comes forward and gives her the photograph.)* You're still much too young, but—it might help you all the same. You mustn't see me as the famous singer, but as an unworthy tool in the hands of an exalted master. Look around you at the married women you know. Every one of them, Wagnerians! Study his libretti, learn to feel his leitmotifs. That will protect you from further indiscretions.

MISS COEURNE: Thank you.

(GERARDO leads her out and in leaving presses the bell. He returns and takes up the piano score; goes toward the left, when he hears a knock.)

GERARDO: Come in!

VALET: *(Enters panting and out of breath.)* At your service—sir—

GERARDO: Are you guarding the door downstairs?

VALET: Not at the moment, sir.

GERARDO: I can see that—simpleton! And you're allowing no one up?

VALET: Three ladies downstairs were inquiring about you, sir.

GERARDO: You have the strictest orders to let no one up—no matter what they tell you.

VALET: And these letters came for you, sir.

GERARDO: Yes. Very well. *(The VALET places the letters on the salver.)* You have the strictest orders to let no one up!

VALET: *(In the doorway.)* Very good, sir.

GERARDO: Not even in exchange for a life-annuity, understand?

VALET: Of course, sir. *(Goes off.)*

GERARDO: *(Alone, tries to sing.)*

Isolde! Geliebte!—Bist du—

I should think these women would get tired of me after a while.—But then there are so many of them in the world.—And I'm all alone.— Each man bears his yoke, and must bear it. *(Goes to the piano and strikes two thirds.)*

(PROFESSOR DÜHRING, seventy years old, completely in black, with a

long, white beard, a wine-reddened aquiline nose, gold-rimmed spectacles, frock-coat and top hat, with an opera score under his arm, enters without knocking. GERARDO turns around.)

GERARDO: What do you want!

DÜHRING: Mr. Gerardo, I—I have—

GERARDO: How did you get in here!

DÜHRING: I waited for you for two hours down on the sidewalk, Mr. Gerardo.

GERARDO: *(Recollecting.)* Now let me see, you are—

DÜHRING: I stood downstairs on the sidewalk for two whole hours. What else could I do?

GERARDO: But, my dear sir, I have no time to—

DÜHRING: Well, I won't play the whole opera through right now.

GERARDO: But I have no time.

DÜHRING: You have no time! What do you expect me to say to that! You are thirty years old. You have been successful in your art. You can continue practicing it for the rest of your life. All I ask of you is to listen to your part in my opera. You promised me you would when you came to town.

GERARDO: What's the use, sir? I'm not my own master.

DÜHRING: I beg of you, sir, I beg of you, I beg of you! Look here at this old man on his knees before you; an old man who has known nothing in this world but his art. I know what you will say to me, you, a young man, who has been carried on high as though on angel wings. You would say to me: "If you would find Fortune, then you must not seek her." Do you believe that when a man has harbored only one thought for fifty years, he could possibly have overlooked any means within human possibility? First one grows flippant and then serious again. One tries to find his way by cunning; then he becomes a lighthearted child again; and then again a serious artist—not for ambition's sake, not for the sake of conviction, but because one can do nothing else, because one is cursed and damned to it by a cruel omnipotence, who sees the lifelong torment of its creature as a pleasing offering! I call it a pleasing offering because our kind rebels as little against its artists' fate as the slave of a woman against his seductress, as little as a dog against the whip of its master.

GERARDO: *(In despair.)* I have no power—

DÜHRING: Don't you see, my dear sir, that these tyrants of antiquity, who, for their own pleasure, had their slaves slowly tortured to death, were children, nothing but innocent little angels in comparison with that divine Providence which thought to create them in its own image!

GERARDO: Even if I do understand you, sir—

DÜHRING: *(While GERARDO tries several times to interrupt him, though in vain, follows him around the room, and repeatedly blocks his way to the door.)* You don't understand me. You can't understand me. How could you have had the time to understand me? Fifty years of fruitless labor, sir, is something you cannot understand, if you are the darling of Fortune as you are. But I shall try to give you an approximate understanding of it. As you can see, I'm too old to take my own life. The only proper time to do that is at twenty-five, and I'm afraid I've missed my opportunity. I must live my life to its conclusion; my hand has grown too unsteady. But what does a man of my age do? You ask me how I got here. You put your valet on guard at the door downstairs. I didn't try to slip past him; I've known for fifty years what he would always say: "The gentleman is not at home." And so I stood at the corner of the building for two hours in the rain, with my score under my arm, until I saw him go upstairs for a moment. Then I followed him, and while you were speaking to him in here, I concealed myself on the staircase—just where I don't think I need tell you. And then, after he had gone down again, I came in. Imagine a man my age doing that to reach someone who might be his grandson. I beg of you, sir, I beg of you, I beg of you, don't let this moment be fruitless for me as well, even if it costs you a whole day, an entire week. It's for your benefit as well as mine. When you came here one week ago to begin your guest appearances, you promised you would let me play my opera for you; and I have come here daily ever since. You were either rehearsing or entertaining female guests. And now you're ready to depart, and an old man will have spent a whole week in vain, waiting on the street. It would cost you no more than a single word: "I will sing your Hermann." It would mean the performance of my opera. Then you will thank God that I was so insistent, because even though you sing Siegfried, sing Florestan—there is no more thankful a part in your repertoire for a man of your ability than that of my Hermann. Then they will draw me out of my obscurity with loud acclaim and perhaps I will be able to give the world just a part of what I might otherwise have given them if they had not cast me from them like a leper. But the great material gain of my struggle will fall, of course, to you—

(GERARDO has finally leaned against the mantelpiece, and drums on the

marble slab with his right hand, when he notices something behind the screen. After having investigated the matter, he suddenly stretches out his hand and pulls out a female piano teacher dressed in gray. With outstretched fist at her collar, he leads her in front of the piano and out through the middle door.)

GERARDO: *(After locking the door behind her, to DÜHRING.)* Please, don't let this interrupt you!

DÜHRING: You see, every year ten new operas are performed which become impossible after the second performance; but only every ten years does a good opera come along which lives. And my opera is a good one, it is stageworthy, it will be a financial success. If you like, I can show you letters from Liszt and Wagner and Rubinstein, in which these gentlemen look up to me as though to a higher being. And why has it remained unperformed until this very moment? Because I have not lowered myself to the marketplace. It's like the young girl who for three years has been the toast of all the balls, but who has forgotten to become engaged. But another generation is on its way. And you know what our court theaters are. Oh, I can assure you that they are fortresses compared with which the armorplate of Metz and Rastatt is mere tin. They would rather dig up ten dead composers than admit even a single live one. All I ask of you is to lend me a hand in surmounting these fortress walls. You are inside them at thirty, and I, a man of seventy, stand outside. It would cost you a single word to let me in, while I vainly batter my gray head against its walls. That's why I've come to you. *(Very passionately.)* And if you are not absolutely inhuman, if your success has not killed off the last trace of sympathy for your fellow artists, then you cannot help but hear my plea.

GERARDO: I'll let you know for certain in a week. I will play through your opera. If you'll give it to me now, I'll take it with me.

DÜHRING: No, Mr. Gerardo, I'm too old for that now. In a week's time, according to your chronology, I will long have lain under the earth. I've been through that often enough. *(Strikes with his fist on the piano.)* Hic Rhodus, hic salta! For five years now I've called on the manager of our Royal Theater, Count Zendlitz. "What have you there for me, my dear Professor?"—"An opera, Excellency."—"Oh, so you've written a new opera. How marvelous!"—"No, Excellency, I haven't written a *new* opera. I've written an *old* opera. I wrote the opera thirteen years ago."—It wasn't this one I have here, it was my *Maria de' Medici.*— "You must let us have it, then? We're forever looking for new works. We can't cheat our way through with the old works very much longer.

My secretary travels from one theater to another without finding a single thing, and you, who live here in our very midst, withhold your production in proud disdain of the common world!"—"But, Excellency," I said to him, "I'm not withholding anything from anyone. Heaven as my witness. I delivered my opera to your predecessor, Count Tornof, thirteen years ago, and after three years I had to go back myself to find it again, and not a single person had looked at it." "Well, you just leave it here with us now, my dear Professor. In a week at the latest you shall have our decision."—And with that he slipped my score from under my arm and fired it down, as fast as humanly possible, into the bottom drawer, and that's where it lies today! And, white-haired child that I am, I went home and said to my Gretchen: "They're looking for a new opera at the theater. It's as good as on the stage right now." A year went by, she died and left me—she was the only one left who had been with me when I wrote it. *(Daubs and dries his tears.)*

GERARDO: I cannot help but feel the greatest sympathy for you, but—

DÜHRING: That's where it lies to this day!

GERARDO: Maybe you really are a child with white hair, yet I must confess, I doubt I can help you.

DÜHRING: *(In a violent rage.)* Yet you can stand there and watch an old man drag himself along on the same path on which you won your glorious victories! Tomorrow perhaps you may be on your knees before me, boasting of having known me; and yet today you recognize nothing more in the death-rattle of a creative artist than an unfortunate mistake; you are unable to wrest so much as half an hour from your greed of gold to help free me from the chains that weigh me down!

GERARDO: Very well, my good man, play for me, play for me! Come, sit down!

DÜHRING: *(Sits at the piano, opens his score, and strikes two chords.)*—No, no, that's not it, that's not it at all. I must get used to it again first. *(Strikes three chords, then turns more pages.)* That's the overture; I won't keep you here for that.—Now here is the first scene. *(Strikes two chords.)* This is where you stand at the deathbed of your father!—One moment, if you don't mind, I really must get my bearings.

GERARDO: Perhaps all you say is true. But I'm afraid you're misjudging my position.

DÜHRING: *(Plays a confused orchestration, and sings with a deep, grating voice.)*
Der Tod, der Tod, auch hier im Schlosse,
Wie er in unseren Hütten hauset:
So mäht er gross wie klein—

(Interrupting himself.) No, no, that's the chorus. I only wanted to play it for you because it's quite good. Now here is where you come in. *(Resumes the accompaniment and sings in a croaking voice.)*
Was ich gelebt bis zu dieser Stunde
War Morgengrauen. Von tückischen Geistern
Aufs Blut gefoltert, irrt ich umher.
Mein Aug' ist tränenleer!
Lass mich nur einmal noch die weissen Haare küssen—
(Interrupting himself.) Well?! *(Since GERARDO does not answer; violently irritated.)* These anemic, threadbare, plodding geniuses who give themselves such airs! Their technique is so sublime that it makes them sterile at twenty, impotent! Meistersingers, philistines, that's what they are, whether they're destitute or in public favor! They satisfy their hunger from cookbooks not from Nature! They think they've found her secret—naïveté! Ha, ha! Tastes like plated brass! They start off trying to make art instead of living first! They make music for musicians instead of for mankind that yearns for it! Blind, narrow, ephemeral creatures! Poor senile boys, dried up in the heat of Wagner's greater sun! *(Grasping GERARDO violently by the arm.)* Do you know where I first grab an artist when I find one?

GERARDO: *(Steps back somewhat frightened.)* Where?

DÜHRING: *(Placing his right hand around the wrist of his own left hand in order to feel his pulse.)* Before anything else, I grab him here! Here, right here, do you see? And if I feel nothing here!—Please, let me continue playing. *(Paging in the score.)* I won't go through the whole monologue for you. Anyway, there isn't time. Here we are, scene three, end of Act One. This is where the wage-earner's child, who grew up with you in the castle, suddenly enters. Now listen—this is after you have taken leave of your highly respected mother. *(Reading rapidly through the text in the score.)* Damon, wer bist du?—Darf man herein? *(To GERARDO.)* No, that's her line! *(Reading further.)* Bärbel!—Ja, ich bin's. Dein Vater ist gestorben?—Dort liegt er. *(Plays and sings in an extreme falsetto.)*
Hat mir gar oft meine Locken gestreichelt,
Wo er mich sah, war er freundlich zu mir.
O weh, das ist der Tod,
Die Augen sind geschlossen—
(Interrupting himself, looking at GERARDO with eyes wide.) Is that music or what?

GERARDO: Possibly.

DÜHRING: *(Striking two chords.)* Something more than the *Trompeter von Säckingen?*

GERARDO: Your confidence forces me to be honest with you. I can't imagine how my influence could be of any benefit to you.

DÜHRING: In other words, what you are trying to say is that the music is antiquated.

GERARDO: On the contrary! I should rather say that it's modern.

DÜHRING: Or modern. Excuse me, Mr. Gerardo, for that slip of the tongue. But that happens all the time to a man my age. One manager will write me: "We cannot produce your opera because its music is antiquated." And another writes: "We cannot produce it because it is much too modern."—In plain words, they both mean the same thing: "We want nothing to do with an opera by you, because as a composer you don't count!"

GERARDO: But I'm a Wagnerian singer, sir; I'm not a critic. If you want your opera produced, then you must apply to those gentlemen who are paid to know what is good art and what is bad. My judgment in matters of this sort count less the more I am regarded and prized as a singer.

DÜHRING: My dear Mr. Gerardo, you may be consoled that I, too, hold little trust in your judgment. What do I care about your judgment! I know what to expect from a tenor. I'm playing my opera for you so you'll say to me: "I want to sing your Hermann, I want to sing your Hermann!"

GERARDO: That will get you nowhere, sir. I must do what I'm asked; I'm bound by my contracts. It makes little difference whether you stand downstairs on the street for a week. To you a day more or less means nothing. But if I fail to leave here by the next train, I'm washed up. Who knows, perhaps singers who break their contracts will be given engagements in the next world. My chains are more tightly drawn than the harness on a carriage horse. My hand is open to anyone, even an absolute stranger, who asks me for material assistance; and yet, the sacrifice my calling demands of me—my happiness is worth far more than five hundred thousand francs a year. But ask the smallest expression of personal freedom of me, and you're asking too much of the slave I am. I cannot sing your Hermann so long as you do not count as a composer.

DÜHRING: But you must let me continue. You'll even learn to like it.

GERARDO: *(Buttoning his coat.)* If only you realized, sir, how much of what I desire I must deny myself; and how much I must take upon myself, for which I have not the slightest desire! Nothing remains but these two eventualities. You have been nothing but a free man your entire life. How can you complain of not putting yourself in the marketplace? Why don't you *put* yourself in that marketplace?

DÜHRING: Oh, the haggling—the shouting—the commonness—I've tried it a hundred times.

GERARDO: One must do what he is able, and not what one is unable to do.

DÜHRING: Everything must be learned first.

GERARDO: One must learn what one is able to learn. How do I know that's not the case with your composing?

DÜHRING: But I am a composer, Mr. Gerardo!

GERARDO: What you mean is, you've devoted your entire intellectual and spiritual powers to the writing of your operas.

DÜHRING: Quite right.

GERARDO: And, of course, you've had no energy left to arrange a performance.

DÜHRING: Quite right.

GERARDO: The composers I know go about it the other way around. They slap their operas together the best they're able and save their spiritual powers for *arranging* a performance.

DÜHRING: I could never be that kind of artist!

GERARDO: I suspect they would feel the same about you, sir. And yet, they are the ones who count. One must *be* something. Name me one famous man who didn't count. If one happens not to be a composer, then he sees to it that he's something else, and why be unhappy because of it? I was something else, too, before I became a Wagnerian singer; something at which no one could possibly doubt my proficiency; and I was completely satisfied. It's not for us to say what we were intended for in this world. If it were, anyone could come along. Do you know what I was before they discovered me?—A paperhanger's apprentice. Do you know what that is? With paste. I don't try to hide my lowly origins. Imagine what would have happened to me if, as a paperhanger, I'd decided to become a Wagnerian singer! Do you know what they'd have done with me?

DÜHRING: Sent you straight to the madhouse.

GERARDO: And quite right they would have been, too. Any man not satisfied with what he is will get absolutely nowhere in his life. A healthy man works at what he's successful in; and if he's unsuccessful then he chooses something else. You mentioned the judgment of your friends. It's an easy matter to be acknowledged by anyone, especially when it costs them nothing. Since I was fifteen I've been paid for every bit of work I've done, and not to have been paid would have been a disgrace. Fifty years of fruitless thrashing about! That should have convinced anyone of the impossibility of his dreams. What have you got out of life? You've wasted it in the most sinful way possible! I have never in my life striven for anything extraordinary; but of one thing I can certainly assure you, sir: since earliest childhood I have never been so idle as to stand around on the street for an entire week. And when I think that as an old man I may have to do just that—I speak only for myself now, sir—I don't know where I'd find the courage to look any man in the face.

DÜHRING: But with an opera like this!—It's not for myself I'm doing this, but for my art!

GERARDO: *(Laughing scornfully.)* You overestimate art, my good man. Believe me, art is not what people are made to believe it is.

DÜHRING: But there's nothing higher on earth.

GERARDO: This view is shared only by people like yourself, people who have an interest in making such a view prevail. Except for you, no one really believes it.—We artists are a luxury of the bourgeoisie; they're always outbidding one another to pay for us. If you were right, then how, for example, was an opera like *Walküre* possible, that deals with matters the exposure of which the public finds highly offensive? Yet when I sing Siegmund, the most solicitous of mothers think nothing of bringing their thirteen- and fourteen-year-old daughters. When I'm on the stage not a single member of the audience pays attention to what's happening. Because if they did, they'd storm out of the place. That's what happened when the opera was new. But now they've accustomed themselves to ignoring it. They're as little aware of what happens on stage as of the air that separates them from that stage. *That, you see, is the meaning of what you call art!* And to this you have sacrificed fifty years of your life! We artists have the task of exhibiting ourselves to the public night after night under one pretense or another. This public interest extends even to our private lives. Every breath we draw is public property. And because we subject ourselves to this for money, no one knows whether to idolize us the more or scorn us just that much more. Go out, discover how many people came to the theater yesterday to hear me sing, and how many came to gape at me as though I were the Emperor of China. Have you any idea what the public demands of art? They want to be able to shout *Bravo!* to throw flowers and wreaths onto the stage, to have something to talk about, to let themselves be seen, to cry *oh!* and *ah!* and at times to unhitch the horses from an artist's carriage—this is what the public demands, and I satisfy their demands. If they pay me half a million, I reciprocate by giving work to a legion of cabmen, writers, milliners, florists, and tavernkeepers. I make money circulate. I make blood circulate. Young girls become engaged, old maids get married, wives fall victim to their house guests, and grandmothers find no end of material for gossip. Accidents and crimes are brought about. A child is trampled to death at the box-office, a woman has her pocketbook stolen, a gentleman goes insane during a performance. All of which makes business for doctors, lawyers—*(Seized by a fit of coughing.)* And I'm to sing *Tristan* tomorrow in Brussels in my condition!—This is not vanity on my part, but to free you from your delusion. The standard for evaluating a man's importance is the world, not the inner conviction he assimilates through years of contemplation. I didn't put myself in the marketplace either; I was discovered. There is no such thing as a misunderstood genius! We aren't even the masters of our own fate; man is born to be a slave!

DÜHRING: *(Who has been paging through his score.)* Please, you must hear the first scene of the second act. It's a prospect in a park, you see, just like in that famous painting: *Embarquement pour Cythere—*

GERARDO: I've already told you I don't have time. And what could I get out of your hopping from one scene to the next?

DÜHRING: *(Slowly packing up his score.)* I'm afraid, Mr. Gerardo, you're misjudging me. I am not as known to the rest of the world as I may be to you. You will find me mentioned often enough in the writings of Richard Wagner. And I can assure you: if I were to die today, my works would be performed tomorrow. That is as certain as that my music will endure. I have a letter every day from my Berlin publisher, inquiring what chance there is of my imminent death.

GERARDO: All I can say is that since the death of Wagner there hasn't been even the slightest call for new operas. Perform new music and you'll have every conservatory, every artist, and every last member of the public at your throat. If you want to see your operas on the stage, then write the kind of music that could pass for what's played today; copy them, that's all it takes; steal your operas piecemeal from the Wagnerian repertoire. Only then can you count with any reasonable accuracy on having your work produced. My stupendous success of last night should prove that the old music will be with us for years to come. And my thoughts on this matter are no different from those of any other artist, of any other manager, or of any member of the paying public. Why go out of my way to have the new music whipped into me when the old music has already cost me so much inhuman torment!

DÜHRING: *(Offering him his trembling hand.)* I'm afraid I'm too old to learn to steal this late in life. One must begin such things young, or he will never learn.

GERARDO: Please don't be offended.—But—my dear sir—if you will permit me—you see, the thought that life has been such a struggle for you—*(Very rapidly.)* Well, the fact is that I've received five hundred marks too much for—

DÜHRING: *(Looks at him wide-eyed, then suddenly turns to the door.)* No, no, sir, please, no.—I would just as soon you didn't finish.—No, no, please! That's not at all why I came.—Please, sir, please!—You see, a great wise man once said: They are every one of them good-natured!—No, Mr. Gerardo. I didn't ask you to listen to my opera to extort money from you. My child is far too precious to me for that.—No, Mr. Gerardo, I'm sorry—*(Goes off through the middle door. GERARDO accompanies him.)*

GERARDO: Thank you, sir. It was my pleasure. *(Alone, he comes back, sinks into a chair opposite the cooler of champagne, and looks at the bottles.)* Who am I raking all this money together for? For my children? If only I had any children! For my old age? Perhaps—if I'm not all used up inside of two years!—Then I can say:

> Alas, alas,
> Where has the hobby gone!

HELEN: *(A radiant beauty, twenty years old, dressed in street clothes, with a muff, enters, extremely excited.)* I suppose you thought he could keep me out of here!—Why else would he be standing down there guarding the door!

GERARDO: *(Has jumped up.)* Helen!

HELEN: You knew perfectly well you'd see me again!

VALET: *(In the doorway that she has left open, his hands at his cheeks.)* I did what I could, Mr. Gerardo, but the lady—

HELEN: Boxed your ears!

GERARDO: Helen!

HELEN: Am I to stand around and be insulted?!

GERARDO: *(To the VALET.)* You may go.

> *(The VALET exits.)*

HELEN: *(Puts her muff on the chair.)* I can't live without you any longer. You will either take me with you or I shall go to my death.

GERARDO: Helen!

HELEN: I shall go to my death. You would be severing my very existence if you were to part from me! My mind and heart are no more. If I must experience another day like yesterday, without seeing you, then I shall never live through it. I haven't the strength. I beg of you, Oscar, take me with you! I beg of you, for my life's sake!

GERARDO: But I can't.

HELEN: You can if you want to. What do you mean, you can't? Leave me and you're the cause of my death. Those are no empty words. I'm not threatening you with them. They're the truth. I'm as certain of that as I now feel the beat of my own heart. I'm dead without you. And so you must take me with you. It's your duty as a human being. Even if only for a while.

GERARDO: On my word of honor, Helen, I can't. On my word of honor.

HELEN: But you must, Oscar, you must. Whether you want to or not, you must accept the consequence of your actions. Life is precious to me, and you and life are one. Take me with you, Oscar. Take me with you, unless you'd have my blood on your conscience.

GERARDO: Do you remember what I told you the first day I saw you in this very room?

HELEN: Yes! Yes! But what good is that to me now?

GERARDO: That sentiment must have no part of our relationship?

HELEN: What good is that to me now? I didn't know you then. I didn't know what a man could be like until I knew you. You knew that it would happen, you knew. Otherwise you'd never have made me promise not to make a scene at your departure. And what wouldn't I have promised you then if you'd asked me. That promise is my death. Leave me now and you've cheated me of my life.

GERARDO: I can't take you with me.

HELEN: My God, I knew before I came that you'd say that. I knew when I came. It stands to reason. You say that to every woman. And why should I be any better than they? I'm one of hundreds. I'm a woman among millions of women. I know all about it.—But I'm sick, Oscar. I'm sick unto death. I'm sick with love. I'm nearer to death than to life. It's all your doing, and you can save me without sacrificing anything, without assuming any burden. Why can't you then?

GERARDO: *(Emphasizing every word.)* Because my contract binds me not to marry or to travel in the company of women.

HELEN: *(Perplexed.)* But what could possibly prevent you?

GERARDO: My contract.

HELEN: You mean you're not allowed to—?

GERARDO: I'm not allowed to marry before my contract has expired.

HELEN: And you're not allowed to—?

GERARDO:—to travel in the company of women.

HELEN: I don't understand such a thing. Whom could it possibly concern?

GERARDO: My manager.

HELEN: Your manager? What business could it be of his?

GERARDO: It *is* his business.

HELEN: You mean because it might—affect your—voice?

GERARDO: Yes.

HELEN: But that's childish.—*Does* it affect your voice?

GERARDO: No.

HELEN: Does your manager believe in this nonsense?

GERARDO: No, he doesn't believe in it either.

HELEN: I don't understand. I can't comprehend how a—respectable human being could sign such a contract!

GERARDO: I am an artist first—and then I am a human being.

HELEN: Yes, I believe you. You're a great artist. An eminent artist. Then why can't you understand that I love you? Is this the only thing that your great mind can't understand?—I'm contemptible to you because you're the only man who has ever made me feel his superiority, the only man I've ever wanted to please. I did everything to hide from you what you meant to me—I was afraid of boring you. But yesterday I experienced what no woman should ever have to endure. If I weren't so in love with you, Oscar, you'd think more of me. That's the most terrible thing about you. You despise the woman whose whole world you are. I'm nothing now, nothing but an empty shell. Now that your passion has consumed me, you want to leave me here like this. But my life will go with you, Oscar. So take along this flesh and blood, too— it belongs to you—unless you want it to perish.

GERARDO: Helen—

HELEN: Your contract! What are contracts to you! Who ever heard of a contract that couldn't be gotten around in some way! Why are contracts made? You mustn't use your contract as a weapon to murder me. I don't believe in your contracts. Let me go with you, Oscar. You'll see, he won't even mention breach of contract. He won't, I know he won't, I know human nature. And if he does, then there will always be time for me to die.

GERARDO: But we have no right to each other, Helen. You're no more free to follow me, than I'm free to take such a responsibility upon myself.—I don't even belong to myself. I belong to my art—

HELEN: Your art, your art! What could I possibly care about your art! I've clung to your art only so you'd pay attention to me. Could Heaven make a man like you, to let him make a fool of himself night after night? How can you boast about it? You can see I'm willing to ignore that you're an artist. What couldn't one ignore in a demigod like you. If you were a criminal, Oscar, I'd feel the same about you. I can't control myself. I lie in the dust before you as I should always lie. I should always entreat your mercy as I entreat it now. I should always be lost in you as I am lost at this moment. And death should always be before my eyes as it stands there now.

GERARDO: *(Laughing.)* Helen, Helen! What's all this about death! Women as capable of enjoying life as you are can't commit suicide. You know the value of life better than I. You're too sensible to throw your life away. You should leave that for others to do—half-human beasts and dwarfs—the ones nature has treated like stepchildren.

HELEN: Oscar—I never said I was going to shoot myself. When did I ever say such a thing? Where would I get the courage? I said I'd die unless you took me with you; die in the way a person dies of any sickness, because I'm only alive when I'm with you. I can live without everything else—without home, without children—but not without you. I simply can't live without you.

GERARDO: *(Uneasy.)* Helen—calm yourself. Or you'll force me to do something terrible. I have exactly ten more minutes. This scene you're making is not sufficient for me to break my contract. Your state of mind will not justify me in front of any judge. I can give you ten minutes more. If in that time you can't control yourself, Helen—well, I simply can't leave you in this condition.

HELEN: I don't care if the whole world sees me lying here.

GERARDO: Consider the risk you're taking.

HELEN: As if I still had anything to risk.

GERARDO: Your social position.

HELEN: All I can lose is you.

GERARDO: And your family?

HELEN: My family doesn't exist except for you.

GERARDO: But I don't belong to you.

HELEN: I have nothing to lose but my life.

GERARDO: And your children?

HELEN: *(Flaring up.)* Who took me away from them, Oscar? Who robbed my children of their mother?

GERARDO: Did I make advances to you?

HELEN: *(With the greatest passion.)* No, no! You must never believe that! I threw myself at you then and I would throw myself at you now! Neither my husband nor my children could have held me back! If I die, then I'll have known what life is, Oscar! Through you! I have you to thank that I've come to know myself! And I do thank you for it, Oscar! I do!

GERARDO: Helen—listen to me quietly.

HELEN: Yes. Yes. We still have ten minutes.

GERARDO: Listen to me quietly.

(They both sit on the divan.)

HELEN: *(Staring at him.)* I have you to thank for it.

GERARDO: Helen—

HELEN: I'm not asking for you to love me. All I ask is to breathe the same air as you.

GERARDO: *(Struggling to maintain his composure.)* Helen—a man like me can't be bound by the conventional ways of life. I've known society women in every country of Europe. And they've always made scenes when it came time for me to leave. Yet we always knew what we owed to our positions. But I've never been faced with an outburst such as yours.—Helen—not a day goes by but I'm tempted to run off to some idyllic Arcadia with one woman or another. But one must always be conscious of his duty. You're bound by duty the same as I. And there's no higher law than duty.

HELEN: I think I know better by now, Oscar, what the highest of laws is.

GERARDO: All right, what? Your love for me, I suppose? That's what they all say! Whatever a woman sets her mind to is good, and whoever opposes her is bad. You can thank our comic playwrights for that. To get full houses they turn the world upside-down. They call it great-souled when a woman sends her family and children to perdition just to indulge her senses. I'd like to live like a turtledove, too. And yet I've always obeyed my duty. But if after duty pleasure again presented itself, I have always enjoyed myself to the fullest. The person who fails his duty, has no right to make even the slightest demands on any human being.

HELEN: *(Turned away, dreamily.)* That will never bring the dead to life again.

GERARDO: *(Nervously.)* But, Helen, I'm trying to give you back your life. I want to give you back what you've sacrificed to me. Please take it, Helen, please. And for God's sake, don't make more of it than it is.—How can a woman humiliate herself so disgracefully? Where is your pride? How contemptuously you'd have dismissed me if I'd fallen in love with you, if I had shown any jealousy.—What am I in the eyes of your society friends? A man who makes a fool of himself every night.—Would you sacrifice yourself to a man whom a hundred women have loved before you, and whom a hundred more women will love after you, and who will not let themselves be discountenanced for so much as a second because of it? Would you have your passion made ridiculous in the sight of God and the world?

HELEN: *(Looking away from him.)* I know very well I'm asking for unheard of things from you, but—what else can I do?

GERARDO: *(Calmingly.)* Helen, I've given you all I could have given you. I couldn't have been more to you if you had been a princess. To have done any more for you would have meant your death.—You must set me free now.—I can understand how difficult it is, but—in such cases one often feels on the verge of death. I'm often apprehensive for my own life—art as a profession is likely to unstring anyone's nerves. It's hard to believe how easily one gets over it.—You must resign yourself to the fact that our life is but a chance occurrence. We didn't seek one another out because we loved each other; we simply loved each other because we found one another. *(Shrugging his shoulders.)* You tell me I must bear the consequences of my own actions, Helen?—Could you seriously blame me, Helen, for not turning you away when you came here under the pretense of having me judge your voice?—No, I think you value your advantages far too much for that; you know yourself too well; you're too proud of your beauty to be guilty of such an action.—Weren't you really quite certain of your victory when you came here?

HELEN: *(Turned away.)* To think of what I was a week ago! And—and to see what I am now!

GERARDO: *(Very matter-of-factly.)* Helen, I want you to ask yourself this question: What choice does a man have in a situation like this? You're generally known to be the most beautiful woman in this city. Shall I, as an artist, assume the reputation of a no-good idler, who shuts himself in his room from all his women visitors?—Then there's a second eventuality: that I do receive you, but pretend not to understand what you want of me. That, of course, without my even trying, would give me the reputation of being a simpleton.—The third eventuality—and it is a dangerous one—is: that I declare to you, quietly and politely, precisely what I have just told you. But, as I said, it's very dangerous. For apart from the fact that you'd accuse me of being vain and a conceited ass, it would certainly place me in a most curious light.—And if I refused the honor you offered me I'd become a contemptible and helpless puppet, a target for your woman's wit, a scarecrow for you to tease and scoff at with impunity for as long as you like. And then when you've charmed me to distraction, you'd put me on the rack.—What choice have I left? *(HELEN stares at him, looks about helplessly, shudders and struggles to answer him.)*

GERARDO: And so, there's only one thing to do. To make an enemy who—despises me, or—to make an enemy who—at least has some respect for me. And—*(Stroking her hair.)*—Helen—no man would want to be despised by a woman of such universally praised beauty as you.—Can you still ask to come with me? Does your pride still permit it?

HELEN: *(Shedding torrents of tears.)* My God, my God, my God, my God, my God!

GERARDO: Your social position made it possible for you to challenge me. And you used that advantage. I'd be the last to censure you for that. And so you mustn't censure me if I lay claim to my own rights.—No man was ever more honorable to a woman than I to you. I told you that sentiment could have no part in our relationship. I told you that my profession hindered me from binding myself in any way. I told you that my—engagement here would be over today—

HELEN: *(Rising.)* My head feels like it's going to burst! Words, words, words, words!—I'm choking! *(Grasping her heart and her throat.)* Here, and here! Oscar—it's not as easy as you think. A woman more or less like myself—has done her duty, she's given life to two children. What would you say—what would you say, Oscar, if tomorrow I went out and—and made another man as happy as I have you? What would you say to that, Oscar?—Say something.—Tell me—

GERARDO: I have nothing to say. *(Looking at his watch.)* Helen—

HELEN: Oscar! *(On her knees.)* My life! My life! I'll never ask you again! Ask anything of me you like! Except that! Except that I should die! You don't know what you're doing! You're beside yourself! You have no control! The *last time!* You detest me because I love you. Don't let time pass in vain. Save me! Save me!

GERARDO: *(Pulls her up forcibly.)* Helen, listen to me, listen. Listen to me!

HELEN: *(To herself.)* If I must!

GERARDO: Helen—how old are your children?

HELEN: One is six and the other is four.

GERARDO: Both girls?

HELEN: No.

GERARDO: Is the four-year-old a boy?

HELEN: Yes.

GERARDO: And the six-year-old is a girl?

HELEN: No.

GERARDO: Then they're both boys?

HELEN: Yes.

GERARDO: Have you no pity for them?

HELEN: No.

GERARDO: How happy I'd be if they were mine! Helen—would you give them to me?

HELEN: Yes.

GERARDO: *(Half joking.)* Suppose I were as exacting as you—suppose I took it in my head and said I love this woman and no other and I would never love any other!—I can't marry her! I can't take her with me. And yet I have to leave.—What could I possibly do with you?

HELEN: *(From here on grows steadily more calm.)* Yes, yes.—Of course.—I understand.

GERARDO: You may be certain, Helen, that there are millions of men in the world like me. I'm not such a very splendid specimen of a man. Our meeting should have taught you something. You say that you can't live without me. How many men do you know? The more of them you know, the less regard you'll have for them. And you'll never again think of taking your life for any man's sake. You'll think no higher of men than I of women.

HELEN: To you we're one of a kind. But that's not true.

GERARDO: I'm serious, Helen. No one loves just this or that particular person, unless he's a fool and knows only one person. Everyone loves his own kind and can find them anywhere, as long as he knows how to go about it.

HELEN: And when a person finds one of his own kind, is it certain he'll be loved in return?

GERARDO: Helen, you have no right to complain about your husband. You should have known yourself better. Every young girl is free to make her own choice. There's no power on earth to compel a girl to belong to a man she doesn't like. A woman is free of any such assault. That's the kind of nonsense those women would like to convince the world of; women who've sold themselves for some material gain; women who'd like to escape their obligations.

HELEN: *(Smiling.)* Breach of contract?

GERARDO: *(Striking himself on the chest.)* If I sell myself, then at least they're dealing with an honest man!

HELEN: *(Smiling.)* Then is a person who loves—not honorable?

GERARDO: No!—Love is nothing but a stupid bourgeois virtue. Why, the farmer who yokes his wife to the plow, along with his oxen, wants to be loved the same as any other. Love is an escape for any good-for-nothing or coward!—In the great world in which I live, every human being has his acknowledged worth. When two people join themselves, they know perfectly well what to expect. They have no need of love.

HELEN: *(Once more in a gently pleading way.)* Then show me this great world of yours.

GERARDO: Helen—would you sacrifice your whole happiness and your family's for a momentary pleasure?

HELEN: No.

GERARDO: Do you promise you'll go back to your family—quietly?

HELEN: Yes.

GERARDO: And you won't go and die—not even as one dies of a sickness?

HELEN: Yes.

GERARDO: Do you promise me that?

HELEN: Yes.

GERARDO: And you'll be content with your duties as a mother—and as a wife?

HELEN: Yes.

GERARDO: Helen!

HELEN: Yes.—What more do you want of me!—I'll promise anything.

GERARDO: That I can leave here without any trouble?

HELEN: *(Rising.)* Yes.

GERARDO: May I have just one more kiss?

HELEN: Yes—yes—yes—yes—yes—

GERARDO: *(After having kissed her copiously.)* In a year from now, Helen, I shall sing here again.

HELEN: In a year from now!—Oh, I shall look forward to that!

GERARDO: *(With feeling.)* Helen! *(HELEN presses his hand, takes the muff from the chair, pulls out a revolver, shoots herself in the head, and collapses.)* Helen! *(Wavering backward then forward and then sinking down in a chair.)* Helen!
(Pause. The PAGE BOY enters and looks at GERARDO and HELEN.)

PAGE BOY: Sir.—Mr. Gerardo!
(GERARDO doesn't move. The PAGE BOY goes to HELEN. GERARDO jumps up, runs to the door, and bumps into the hotel proprietor, MÜLLER, drawing him forward.)

GERARDO: Send for the police! I must be arrested! If I leave I'm a beast, and if I stay here I'm ruined, I'll have broken my contract! I still have—*(Looking at his watch.)*—I still have one minute and ten seconds. Please! Hurry! I must be arrested!

MÜLLER: Fritz, get the nearest policeman!

PAGE BOY: Yes, sir, right away!

MÜLLER: Run as fast as you can! *(The PAGE BOY exits. To GERARDO.)* Don't let it worry you, Mr. Gerardo, sir. Things like this happen here all the time.

GERARDO: *(Kneels down beside HELEN and grasps her hand.)* Helen!— She's still alive! She's still alive! *(To MÜLLER.)* Once I'm arrested, it will be a perfectly legal excuse!—What about my trunks?!—Is the carriage at the door?

MÜLLER: It's been there for twenty minutes, sir. *(Goes to the door and admits the VALET who carries down one of the trunks.)*

GERARDO: *(Bent over HELEN.)* Helen!—*(To himself.)* Well, I guess it can't do me too much harm! *(To MÜLLER.)* Haven't you called a doctor yet?

MÜLLER: We phoned the doctor at once, sir. He'll be here any time now.

GERARDO: *(Grasping HELEN under the arms and half raising her.)* Helen!—Don't you recognize me, Helen!—The doctor will be here any time now!—It's your Oscar, Helen!—Helen!

PAGE BOY: *(In the middle door, which has remained open.)* Not a policeman in sight, sir.

GERARDO: *(Forgetting everything, jumps up, letting HELEN fall back onto the carpet.)* I have to sing *Tristan* tomorrow in Brussels! *(He collides with several pieces of furniture, and rushes out through the middle door.)*

END OF PLAY

The Marquis of Keith

1900

Cast of Characters

CONSUL CASIMIR *a merchant*
HERMANN CASIMIR *his son, fifteen years old*
THE MARQUIS OF KEITH
ERNST SCHOLZ
MOLLY GREISINGER
ANNA, COUNTESS WERDENFELS *a widow*
SARANIEFF *a painter*
ZAMRIAKI *a composer*
SOMMERSBERG *a writer*
RASPE *a police inspector*
OSTERMEIER *proprietor of a brewery*
KRENTZL *a master builder*
GRANDAUER *a restaurateur*
MRS. OSTERMEIER
MRS. KRENTZL
BARONESS VON ROSENKRON *a divorcée*
BARONESS VON TOTLEBEN *a divorcée*
SASHA
SIMBA
A BUTCHER'S HELPER
A BAKERY WOMAN
A PORTER
PATRONS OF THE HOFBRÄUHAUS

Time and Place

1899, late summer; Munich

ACT ONE

A study, the walls of which are covered with pictures. In the rear wall to the right there is a door leading into the hallway, and to the left a door leading into a waiting room. A door in the right wall leads into the living room. Downstage left is a writing table on which unrolled plans are lying; on the wall beside the writing table is a telephone. There is a divan downstage right, with a smaller table in front of it; somewhat upstage is a larger table. Bookcases with books; musical instruments, bundles of notes and documents. The MARQUIS OF KEITH is seated at the writing table engrossed in one of the plans. He is a man of about twenty-seven, medium height, slender, and bony; he would have an exemplary figure if not for the limp in his left leg. His features are vigorous, though at the same time nervous and hard. He has piercing gray eyes, a small blond mustache. His unmanageable short, straw-blond hair is carefully parted in the middle. He is dressed in a suit well chosen for its social elegance, but by no means foppish. He has the rough, red hands of a clown. MOLLY GREISINGER enters from the living room and places a covered tray on the table in front of the divan. She is a plain sort of creature, brunette, somewhat shy and harassed, wearing a plain house dress, but at the same time she possesses large, black, soulful eyes.

MOLLY: There you are, my sweet. Tea, caviar, and cold cuts. Did you know you were up at nine this morning?

KEITH: *(Without moving.)* Thank you, my dear.

MOLLY: You must be starved. Any word yet on the Fairyland Palace? Will it be built?

KEITH: Can't you see I'm busy?

MOLLY: Mm. Always when I come in, too. It seems I know you only from the gossip of your lady friends.

KEITH: *(Without turning in his chair.)* I knew a woman once who covered both ears whenever I talked business. "Come and tell me when you've *done* something!" she would say.

MOLLY: Unlucky me—your knowing all kinds of women. *(A bell rings.)* Now who could that be? *(Goes into the hall to open the door.)*

KEITH: *(To himself.)* Poor creature!

MOLLY: *(Returns with a card.)* A young gentleman to see you. I told him you were busy.

KEITH: *(Having read the card.)* Just who I wanted to see!

(MOLLY brings in HERMANN CASIMIR and goes off into the living room.)

HERMANN: *(A fifteen-year-old student in an extremely elegant cycling costume.)* Good morning, Baron.

KEITH: To what do I owe the honor?

HERMANN: I suppose I should come right out with it. I was at the Café Luitpold last night with Saranieff and Zamriaki. I told them I absolutely had to have a hundred marks. Saranieff suggested I come to you.

KEITH: All Munich thinks I'm an American railroad tycoon.

HERMANN: Zamriaki said you always have cash on hand.

KEITH: I patronize Zamriaki because he's the greatest musical genius since Richard Wagner. But these highway robbers are not proper company for you.

HERMANN: I find them interesting nonetheless. I discovered them at a meeting of the Anarchists.

KEITH: Ah, revolutionary gatherings. Fine way to start your life. Your father must be delighted.

HERMANN: Why doesn't my father let me leave Munich!

KEITH: Because you're not old enough.

HERMANN: At my age I can learn more from *real experience* than from scooting around on a *school bench!*

KEITH: Real experience deprives you of your natural abilities. And in your situation especially. The son of our greatest German financial genius. What does your father think of me?

HERMANN: My father never speaks to me.

KEITH: But he does speak to others.

HERMANN: That may be. I'm at home as little as possible.

KEITH: That's unfortunate. I've followed your father's financial operations since before my days in America. Your father rejects the possibility that there's anyone as clever as himself. It's why he refuses to join my enterprise.

HERMANN: I could never lead a life like my father's. I'd be miserable.

KEITH: Suppose your father just doesn't know how to interest you in his profession?

HERMANN: The important thing isn't merely to live; but to learn everything about life and the world.

KEITH: A desire that will lead you to ruination. Take my word for it.

What you must learn is to live within the circumstances of your birth. It will guard you against degrading yourself quite so cheerfully.

HERMANN: By pumping you for money? Is wealth the highest value, then?

KEITH: Theoretically, perhaps. These values are called "higher" because they're founded on money. And they're *possible* only *because* of money. You, of course, are free to devote yourself either to an artistic or a scientific profession because your father has already made a fortune. If in doing so, however, you disregard the world's guiding principle, then you are deliberately dropping your inheritance into the hands of swindlers.

HERMANN: If Jesus Christ had chosen to act according to this guiding principle—

KEITH: Just bear in mind that Christianity liberated two-thirds of mankind from slavery. Not a single idea—social, scientific, or artistic—revolves around anything other than property. That's why the Anarchists are the sworn enemies of ideas. And don't expect the world to change in this regard. Man adjusts or man is eliminated. *(Has sat down at the writing table.)* I'll give you the hundred marks. But do come around sometime when you aren't in need of money. How long since your mother died?

HERMANN: Three years this spring.

KEITH: *(Handing him a sealed note.)* Take this note to Countess Werdenfels, Brienner Strasse 23. Give her my best regards. I haven't any cash on me today.

HERMANN: Thank you, Baron.

KEITH: *(Showing him out; as he closes the door behind him.)* Thank you, it was my pleasure. *(With this he returns to the writing table, rummaging in the plans.)* His old man treats me like a dog-catcher. Hm, I must arrange a concert as soon as possible. Public opinion will then force him into joining my enterprise. If worst comes to worst, I will simply have to do without him. *(A knock at the door.)* Come in! *(ANNA, THE WIDOWED COUNTESS WERDENFELS enters. She is a voluptuous beauty of thirty: white skin, turned-up nose, sparkling eyes, luxuriant chestnut-brown hair. He goes to meet her.)* So, here you are, my queen! I've just sent young Casimir to you with a small request.

ANNA: So that was the young Casimir, was it?

KEITH: *(After kissing her hastily on the mouth, which she has offered to him.)* He'll be back if he doesn't find you.

ANNA: He doesn't in the least resemble his father.

KEITH: Let's forget about his father, shall we? I've approached some people whose social ambitions assure me of their enthusiasm for my enterprise.

ANNA: But everyone knows that old Casimir loves to patronize young artists—especially if they are female.

KEITH: *(Devouring ANNA with his eyes.)* One look at you, Anna, and I'm another person. You're the living pledge of my good fortune. But won't you have some breakfast? There's tea, caviar, and cold cuts.

ANNA: *(Sits on the divan and eats.)* I have a lesson at eleven. I dropped in for only a moment. Madame Bianchi tells me that in a year's time I could be Germany's leading Wagnerian soprano.

KEITH: *(Lighting a cigarette.)* Perhaps in a year you'll be doing so well that the greatest Wagnerian sopranos will be seeking *your* patronage.

ANNA: Fine, yes! But it's difficult for me, with my limited woman's intelligence, to imagine reaching the heights so soon.

KEITH: I quite agree with you. Personally, I allow myself to be pulled along without resistance till I can comfortably say: "This is where I will build!"

ANNA: And in that, my dear, I shall be your most faithful accomplice. For some time now my delirious love of life has brought me to thoughts of suicide.

KEITH: One man steals what he wants, the other receives it as a gift. When I went out into the world, my boldest aspiration was to end up a village school master in Upper Silesia.

ANNA: And little did you dream that one day Munich would lie at your feet.

KEITH: All I knew of Munich was from a geography class. If my reputation isn't exactly spotless, remember the depths I rose out of.

ANNA: I pray fervently every night for some infusion of your energy.

KEITH: Energy? Me? Nonsense.

ANNA: You couldn't live without constantly battering your head through one stone wall after another.

KEITH: Unfortunately, I can't breathe in a bourgeois atmosphere. It's the major limitation to my talent. If that explains my achievement, then I take no credit for it. Then, of course, there are those who find themselves rooted on a certain social plane where they vegetate without ever coming into conflict with the world.

ANNA: You, of course, emerged full-blown from the heavens.

KEITH: But a bastard nonetheless. Intellectually my father was a promi-
nent man, especially in mathematics and the other exact sciences, and
my mother was a gypsy.

ANNA: If I had your skill in reading people's faces, I could grind their
noses into the dust with the tip of my toe.

KEITH: Gifts of that sort cause more distrust than they're worth, and
bourgeois society has always secretly despised me for it. It's society's
very timidity—quite against its own will—that has made my reputation. The higher I climb, the more they trust me. One day the crossing of the philosopher with the horse-thief will be fully appreciated.

ANNA: The only topic of conversation these days is your Fairyland Palace.

KEITH: The Fairyland Palace is a rallying point for my powers, nothing
more. I have no intention of auditing account books for the rest of my
life.

ANNA: And what about me? Do you think I want to take singing lessons
the rest of my life? You said the Fairyland Palace was to be built for me.

KEITH: For you to dance around on your hind legs the rest of your life
and be crucified by those nitwits of the press? What you need are a few
more highlights in your past.

ANNA: Well, I certainly can't pull a family-tree from my hat like the
Mesdames von Rosenkron and von Totleben.

KEITH: Nor would I envy them for it, my dear.

ANNA: I certainly hope not! What feminine charms *should* I envy them
for?

KEITH: I inherited these ladies when I took over the concert agency. Once
I'm established they can peddle radishes or write novels for all I care.

ANNA: I care more about the shine on my shoes than about any feelings
you may have for me. And do you know why? Because you are the
most inconsiderate creature I've ever known. All you care about is your
own sensual gratification. If you were to leave me, I'd feel only pity for
you. Just take care *you* aren't the one who gets left.

KEITH: (*Caressing ANNA.*) My life has a long history of sudden reversals,
and now I'm seriously considering building a house—a house with
high ceilings, a park, and a broad flight of stairs leading to the
entrance. Ah! and with a contingent of beggars in the driveway to
complete the picture. The past is over for me and I won't be turning
back. It's too often been a life-and-death struggle. I wouldn't advise a
friend to take my career as a model.

ANNA: You're indestructible.

KEITH: Yes, and I attribute that to everything I've achieved up to now. You know, Anna, if we'd been born in two separate worlds, we'd have had to find one another.

ANNA: I'm not exactly destructible myself.

KEITH: Even if Providence hadn't destined us for each other because of our similarity of tastes, there's one other thing we have in common—

ANNA: A robust constitution.

KEITH: *(Sits beside her and caresses her.)* As far as women are concerned, intelligence, health, sensitivity, and beauty are inseparable; any one of which leads inevitably to the other three. If these traits are intensified in our children—*(SASHA, a thirteen-year-old errand boy in livery jacket and knee breeches, enters from the hallway and places an armful of newspapers on the center table.)* What has Councilor Ostermeier to say?

SASHA: The Councilor gave me a letter. It's there with the newspapers. *(Goes off into the waiting room.)*

KEITH: *(Having opened the letter.)* I can thank your being with me here for this! *(Reads.)* "—I have frequently been told about your plans and am extremely interested. I shall be at the Café Maximilian at noon today—" The world has just now been placed in the palm of my hand! And if old Casimir decides to come along, I can simply turn him my backside. With these "worthy" gentlemen on my side, my power is absolute.

ANNA: *(Has risen.)* Could you give me a thousand marks?

KEITH: Broke again?

ANNA: The rent is due.

KEITH: That can wait till tomorrow. Don't worry about it.

ANNA: Whatever you say. Count Werdenfels prophesied on his deathbed that one day I would learn about life's less agreeable side.

KEITH: If he had appreciated you more he might still be alive.

ANNA: His prophecy has yet to be fulfilled.

KEITH: You'll have the money tomorrow at noon.

ANNA: *(While KEITH accompanies her out.)* No, please. I'll come for it myself.

(The stage remains empty for a moment. Then MOLLY GREISINGER enters from the living room and clears away the tea things. KEITH returns from the hallway.)

KEITH: *(Calling.)* Sasha! *(Removes one of the pictures from the wall.)* This will have to see me through the next two weeks.

MOLLY: Do you really think we can continue living this way?

SASHA: *(Enters from the waiting room.)* Baron?

KEITH: *(Gives him the picture.)* Go over to Tannhäuser's. Tell him to put this Saranieff in his window. He can have it for three thousand marks.

SASHA: Very good, Baron.

KEITH: I'll be along in five minutes. Wait! *(He takes a card from his writing table on which "3000 M" is written and slips it into the picture frame.)* Three thousand marks! *(Goes to the writing table.)* But first I must dash off a newspaper article about it.

(SASHA goes off with the picture.)

MOLLY: I'd just once like to see the smallest result from all this big talk!

KEITH: *(Writing.)* "The Aesthetic Ideal in Modern Landscape Painting."

MOLLY: If Saranieff could paint, you wouldn't have to write newspaper articles about him.

KEIT:H *(Turning around.)* I beg your pardon?

MOLLY: I know, you're busy.

KEITH: You were saying?

MOLLY: I received a letter from Bückeburg.

KEITH: From your mama?

MOLLY: *(Finds the letter in her pocket and reads.)* "You are both welcome at any time. You could move into the two front rooms on the third floor. That way you could wait quietly until your transactions in Munich are completed."

KEITH: Can't you understand, my dear, that these little letters of yours are undermining my credit?

MOLLY: There's no bread for tomorrow.

KEITH: Then we'll dine out. The Hotel Continental?

MOLLY: I wouldn't be able to swallow a bite for fear the bailiff was here attaching our beds.

KEITH: He's still working on that. Why can that little head of yours think only about food and drink? Life would be so much happier if only you saw its brighter side. You have the most incorrigible fascination with misfortune.

MOLLY: No, *you!* Other people breeze through life without a worry. They live for one another in comfortable houses with no threat to their happiness. And here *you* are, with all your talents, running around like a madman, ruining your health, and still we're penniless.

KEITH: When have you ever gone hungry! Is it *my* fault you never spend anything on clothes? When I've finished writing this article, I'll have three thousand marks. Take a cab, buy everything you can think of on the spur of the moment.

MOLLY: He'll as likely pay three thousand marks for that picture as I am to wear silk stockings for you!

KEITH: *(Rises unwillingly.)* You're a jewel!

MOLLY: *(Throws her arms around his neck.)* Have I hurt you, darling? Forgive me! Please! But I honestly believe what I just said.

KEITH: If the money doesn't last beyond tomorrow, I won't regret the sacrifice.

MOLLY: *(Wailing.)* I know it was hateful of me. Beat me!

KEITH: The Fairyland Palace is as good as built.

MOLLY: Then at least let me kiss your hand. Please let me kiss your hand.

KEITH: I hope I can maintain my composure over the next few days.

MOLLY: Why won't you let me? How can you be so inhuman?

KEITH: *(Pulls his hand out of his pocket.)* It's time you took stock of yourself, my dear; otherwise you might be in for a big surprise.

MOLLY: *(Covering his hand with kisses.)* Why won't you beat me? I know I deserve it!

KEITH: You're cheating yourself of happiness with all the devices a woman has at her disposal.

MOLLY: *(Jumps up indignantly.)* I'm not frightened by these flirtations of yours! We're too close, you and I. Once that bond breaks, you're free; but as long as you're down on your luck, you're mine.

KEITH: Fearing my good fortune more than death will be your undoing, Molly. If tomorrow my hands are free, you won't stay another moment.

MOLLY: Good! As long as you know.

KEITH: But I'm not *down* on my luck!

MOLLY: Just let me work here only till your hands are free.

KEITH: *(Sits again at the writing table.)* Very well, do as you will. But you know how I dislike women who work.

MOLLY: I refuse to be a monkey or parrot for your sake. And I can't very well ruin you by standing over a washtub, instead of running around with you, half-naked, to fancy dress balls.

KEITH: This doggedness of yours is really quite superhuman.

MOLLY: It's certainly beyond *your* comprehension.

KEITH: Even if I *did* understand, it still wouldn't help you.

MOLLY: *(Triumphantly.)* There's no need to rub your nose in it, my dear. But I *will* spell it out to you, if you like. I wouldn't be one bit happier if I thought myself better than God made me—*just because you love me!*

KEITH: That goes without saying.

MOLLY: (*Triumphantly.*) Because you can't live without my love. Keep your hands as free as you like. Whether I stay is up to me entirely. All that's required is that I leave you a few remnants of love for your other women. Let them deck themselves out as vulgarly as they please; it saves me the boredom of going to comedies. You and your ideals! I know all about that!—If it ever came to your carrying any of them out—and fat chance there is of that! I'd gladly be buried alive.

KEITH: You should learn to take what fortune offers you.

MOLLY: (*Tenderly.*) Just what *does* it offer me, my love? We had these same endless fears in America, too. And in the end everything always fell apart. In Santiago you weren't elected president, and you were nearly sentenced to death when on the decisive evening we failed to have brandy on the table. Do you remember how you shouted: "A dollar, a dollar, a republic for a dollar!"?

KEITH: (*Jumps up enraged and goes to the divan.*) I was born into this world a cripple, but I refuse to condemn myself to be a slave because of it. And just because I was born a beggar, I *will not* deny myself life's most extravagant luxuries as my rightful inheritance.

MOLLY: You'll never do more than look at them from the outside, no matter how long you live.

KEITH: Only death can change what I've just said. And death would think twice before coming, afraid of making a fool of himself. If I die without having lived, I'll come back as a ghost.

MOLLY: Your trouble is a swelled head.

KEITH: But *I am justified!* When you were fifteen and an irresponsible child, you left school and ran off with me to America. If we part now, and you are left to your own devices, you'd come to the worst end possible.

MOLLY: (*Throws her arms around his neck.*) Then come to Bückeburg with me! My parents haven't seen their Molly for three years. They'll give you half their money, they'll be so happy! And how well we could live there together.

KEITH: In Bückeburg?

MOLLY: All troubles end sometime.

KEITH: (*Freeing himself.*) I'd rather pick up cigar butts in cafés.

SASHA: (*Returns with the picture.*) Tannhäuser says he can't put the picture in his window. Tannhäuser says he already has a dozen pictures by Saranieff.

MOLLY: So what else is new.

KEITH: That's why I keep you here. *(Goes to the writing table and tears up the piece of paper.)* At least I needn't write a newspaper article about it. *(SASHA goes into the waiting room after placing the picture on the table.)*

MOLLY: These Saranieffs and Zamriakis are people of another cut entirely. They know how to turn people's pockets inside out. The two of us are just too simple for the great world.

KEITH: Your kingdom is not yet come. Leave me alone. Bückeburg will just have to wait.

MOLLY: *(As the bell rings in the corridor, claps her hands maliciously.)* The bailiff! *(She hurries to open the door.)*

KEITH: *(Looks at his watch.)* What else can we sacrifice to fortune?

MOLLY: *(Accompanies ERNST SCHOLZ into the room.)* The gentleman refuses to give me his name.

(ERNST SCHOLZ is a slender, extremely aristocratic figure of about twenty-seven; black wavy hair, a Vandyke beard, and under his strong elongated eyebrows large water-blue eyes with an expression of helplessness.)

KEITH: Gaston! Where have you come from?

SCHOLZ: Your welcome is a good sign. I've changed so that I presumed you'd never recognize me.

(MOLLY, after looking at SCHOLZ, decides against removing the breakfast dishes for fear of disturbing the two men. She goes into the living room without the dishes.)

KEITH: You seem worn out. But then life never really was a game.

SCHOLZ: At least not for me. That's precisely why I've come. It's on your account that I'm here in Munich.

KEITH: Thank you. Whatever I have left over from my business is yours.

SCHOLZ: I know how bitter a struggle life is for you. But now I want to get to know you personally. I would like to place myself under your spiritual guidance for a time; but only on one condition: that you permit me to put my financial resources at your disposal.

KEITH: But why? I'm just about to become director of a gigantic corporation. And I assume you're not doing badly yourself. If I'm not mistaken, we last saw each other four years ago.

SCHOLZ: At the legal convention in Brussels.

KEITH: You had just passed your state examination.

SCHOLZ: And you were writing for every newspaper around. You may recall how I reproached you for your cynicism at the ball in the Palace of Justice.

KEITH: You had fallen in love with the daughter of the Danish ambassador, and you broke out in a rage when I maintained that women are by nature a far more materialistic breed than men, even after experiencing the finest of luxuries.

SCHOLZ: I see you're no different now from when we were children—an unscrupulous monster. And you were absolutely right.

KEITH: I've never been more flattered.

SCHOLZ: I'm a broken man. However much I may detest your view of life from the depths of my soul, as of this moment I entrust you with the riddle of my existence—which, by the way, I consider to be insoluble.

KEITH: Good God! I see you're finally shaking off melancholy and coming out from under your cloud!

SCHOLZ: This is no cowardly capitulation on my part. I've done all in my power to solve this riddle and failed every time.

KEITH: At least it's behind you now. During the Cuban Revolution I was to be shot with twelve conspirators. Naturally I fell down at the first shot and played "dead" until they came to bury me. From that day on I felt myself master of my fate. *(Jumping up.)* We assume no obligations at birth, and we have nothing to throw away except our life. Living on after death is outside the rules. That time in Brussels, I believe, you intended going into the civil service?

SCHOLZ: I decided on the Ministry of Railroads.

KEITH: I never understood why, with your enormous wealth, you never chose to live the life of a great lord, in accord with your tastes.

SCHOLZ: I intended, first, to become a useful member of human society. Had I been born the son of a day-laborer it would have happened as a matter of course.

KEITH: One can help one's fellow men best by working to one's own advantage. The further my interests extend, the greater the number of people I can provide with the means of livelihood. Whoever imagines that by doing his job and feeding his children he's accomplishing something useful is merely pulling the wool over his own eyes. The children would be grateful if they'd never been born, and a hundred poor devils are struggling for the same job.

SCHOLZ: I could see no reason why I should stroll through the world, a worthless idler, just because I was rich. I have no artistic talent, and I didn't think myself insignificant enough to be satisfied with a happy marriage and the raising of children.

KEITH: Then you've given up the civil service?

SCHOLZ: *(Hangs his head.)* Because I was the cause of a terrible disaster while I still held office.

KEITH: On my return from America, someone who had met you the year before in Constantinople said you'd been traveling for two years, but were back and soon to be married.

SCHOLZ: I broke the engagement three days ago. I've never been more than half a man. Since the day I came of age, I've been convinced that I couldn't enjoy my existence until I'd justified it through honest work. This point of view has led me to seek pleasure out of a sheer sense of duty, nothing else, as though I were doing penance. But every time I intended to open my arms to life, I became paralyzed by the memory of the unfortunate souls who lost their lives horribly because of my exaggerated conscientiousness.

KEITH: What *is* all this?

SCHOLZ: I changed one of the railroad's regulations. There was the constant danger that it couldn't be carried out to the letter. Naturally my fears were exaggerated, but with every day I saw the disaster draw nearer. I lack the intellectual equilibrium of people who come from homes worthy of human beings. The day after my regulation was introduced two express trains collided. Nine men, three women and two children lost their lives. I had to inspect the scene myself. It isn't my fault I'm still alive after seeing it.

KEITH: And then you traveled.

SCHOLZ: I went to England, to Italy, but still felt cut off from human activity. In pleasant, happy surroundings, amid deafening music, I suddenly hear a piercing cry, because I am unexpectedly reminded of the disaster. Even in the Orient I lived like a frightened owl. To be quite honest, ever since the day of the disaster I've been convinced that I can buy back my joy in living only through self-sacrifice. But to do so I must have access to life. I had hoped to find that access a year ago when I became engaged to a lovely girl of lower-class origins.

KEITH: You intended her to become Countess Trautenau?

SCHOLZ: I am no longer Count Trautenau. I don't expect you to understand that. The press did everything possible to contrast my name and rank with the disaster I had caused. I felt bound by duty to my family to assume another name. For two years now I have been Ernst Scholz. That way my engagement could arouse no surprise; but disaster would have come from that as well. In her heart, no spark of love; in mine, only the need for self-sacrifice; our association, an endless chain of trivial misunderstandings. I've given the girl an ample dowry to make her a desirable match for someone of her station. She was so happy with her new-won freedom that she could scarcely express herself. And now, finally, I must learn the difficult art of forgetting myself. We can look death in the eye with clear consciousness; but no one can really live till he has forgotten himself.

KEITH: *(Throws himself into a chair.)* My father would turn over in his grave if he knew that you—were asking for my advice.

SCHOLZ: It's called: life contradicting bookish wisdom. Believe me, your father contributed his share toward my one-sided development, too.

KEITH: My father was as selfless and conscientious as the mentor and tutor of a Count Trautenau had to be. You were his model student, I his whipping-boy.

SCHOLZ: Don't you remember how our chamber maids at the castle used to kiss you, and even more passionately when I was around? *(Rising.)* The next two to three years will be spent—with no exception—*(tears in his voice.)* teaching myself to be a sensualist.

KEITH: Let's go to the dance this evening out at Nymphenburg! That's as gauche as anything our kind can possibly do. But with all the rain and sleet pouring down on my head I feel enticed to bathe myself in the mire again.

SCHOLZ: I'm not eager for the yells and cries of the marketplace.

KEITH: There won't be a loud word spoken. Just a hollow roar like the ocean uprooted from its depths. Munich is Arcadia and Babylon simultaneously. The silent Saturnalian frenzy that grips the soul at every turn has a fascination for even the most jaded.

SCHOLZ: Jaded? How? I've never in my life had a moment's pleasure.

KEITH: We'll have to keep the crowd at a distance. My appearance in such places attracts them like flies to carrion. But I promise you, you'll forget yourself, all right. Not just tonight, but three months from now when you think back on this evening.

SCHOLZ: I've even asked myself whether it's not my tremendous wealth that's at the root of my misfortune.

KEITH: *(Indignant.)* That's blasphemy!

SCHOLZ: I've seriously considered renouncing my wealth as I have my title. That would benefit my family only during my lifetime, of course. In any case, I can dispose of my property on my deathbed; which is to say, after it has ruined my life. If from my youth onward, given my moral earnestness and industry, I'd had to struggle for my livelihood, I would now be in the middle of a brilliant career instead of an outcast.

KEITH: On the other hand, you might be wallowing with your lower-class girl in the most common sort of trashy lovemaking and then be cleaning the dirty boots of your "fellow men."

SCHOLZ: I'd make that exchange anytime, and gladly.

KEITH: Just don't fantasize that this railroad disaster is what's keeping you from enjoying life. You feed off these memories only because you're too dull to arrange for more delicate nourishment.

SCHOLZ: You may be right. It's why I've come to you for spiritual guidance.

KEITH: We'll find something to sink our teeth into tonight. I'm afraid I can't invite you to breakfast with me. I have a business meeting at twelve with a local bigwig. But I'll give you a few lines to take to my friend Raspe. Spend the afternoon with him; we'll meet at six tonight at the Hofgarten Café. *(Has gone to the writing table and writes a note.)*

SCHOLZ: What sort of business are you in?

KEITH: I'm an art dealer, I write for the newspapers, and I have a concert agency— none of it worth talking about. You've come just at the right time to see the founding of a gigantic concert hall being built exclusively for my artists.

SCHOLZ: *(Takes the picture from the table and examines it.)* You have a nice picture gallery.

KEITH: *(Jumping up.)* I wouldn't take ten thousand marks for that. A Saranieff. *(Turning it around.)* You hold it this way.

SCHOLZ: I know nothing about art. While traveling, I didn't set foot inside a museum.

KEITH: *(Gives him the note.)* The gentleman is an international authority on crime; so don't be too open with him at first. Really a charming man. People never know whether they ought to keep an eye on me, or whether I'm here to keep an eye on them.

SCHOLZ: Thank you for your kind reception. At six tonight, then, the Hofgarten Café.

KEITH: Then off to Nymphenburg. And thank you for finally having confidence in me. *(KEITH accompanies SCHOLZ out. The stage is empty for a moment. Then MOLLY GREISINGER enters from the living room and clears the tea service from the table. KEITH returns immediately; calling.)* Sasha! *(Goes to the telephone and rings.)* Seventeen thirty-five. Inspector Raspe!

SASHA: *(Enters from the living room.)* Baron?

KEITH: My hat! My overcoat!

(SASHA hurries into the hall.)

MOLLY: Please, I beg of you, you mustn't have anything to do with this patron. He wouldn't be here unless he wanted to exploit us.

KEITH: *(Speaking into the telephone.)* Thank God you're there! Just wait ten minutes. You'll see for yourself. *(To MOLLY, while SASHA helps him into his overcoat.)* I must hurry to the newspaper offices.

MOLLY: What should I answer mama?

KEITH: *(To SASHA.)* A carriage!

SASHA: At once, Baron. *(Goes off.)*

KEITH: Give her my deepest regards. *(Goes to the writing table.)* The plans—the letter from Ostermeier—tomorrow morning all Munich must know that the Fairyland Palace will be built!

MOLLY: Then you're not coming to Bückeburg?

KEITH: *(The plans rolled up under his arm, he takes his hat from the table, center, and puts it on at a rakish angle.)* Can you imagine him a sensualist! *(Goes off hurriedly.)*

END OF ACT ONE

ACT TWO

In the Marquis of Keith's study the center table is laid with breakfast: champagne and a large dish of oysters. The MARQUIS OF KEITH leans against the writing table with his left foot on a stool, while SASHA, kneeling in front of him, buttons his shoes with a buttonhook. SCHOLZ stands behind the divan as he strums on a guitar he has taken from the wall.

KEITH: What time did you get back to your hotel this morning?

SCHOLZ: *(With a radiant smile.)* Ten.

KEITH: Wasn't I right to leave you alone with that charming creature?

SCHOLZ: *(Smiling blissfully.)* After last night's discussions about art and modern literature, I wonder if I shouldn't start taking lessons from the girl. I was even more amazed when she asked to wait on your guests at your garden party—the one you say will astonish all of Munich.

KEITH: She considers it an honor. But let's not talk about the garden party now. I'm leaving for Paris tomorrow for a couple of days.

SCHOLZ: This comes at a most inopportune time for me.

KEITH: Come along then. One of my artists will sing for Madame Marquesi before making her debut here.

SCHOLZ: And relive the mental torments I suffered in Paris?

KEITH: I thought last night's experience might help you over that hurdle? All right, then, spend your time during my absence with Saranieff. We're bound to run into him somewhere today.

SCHOLZ: The girl last night said Saranieff's studio was a chamber of horrors, full of every abomination known to man. And then she ran on in the most delightful way about her childhood; how when she was a girl in the Tyrol she spent all summer sitting in cherry trees, and how on winter evenings, till dark came on, she'd go sleighing with the village children. How can such a girl consider it an honor to serve at your party!

KEITH: It helps her fight the unspeakable contempt that bourgeois society has for her.

SCHOLZ: But how do they justify such contempt? How many hundreds of women in the best social circles have their lives ruined because the wellspring of life has dried up in them! Whereas in her it overflows it banks. This young girl's joy in life is no sin. Not like the soul-stifling discord my parents endured during twenty years of marriage!

KEITH: What is sin!

SCHOLZ: Yesterday I was so certain I knew. But today I can confess openly what thousands upon thousands of respectable people like me have experienced: that the man whose life is an empty failure is bitterly envious of the creature who has wandered from the path of the virtuous.

KEITH: The happiness of these creatures wouldn't be so despised were it not the most unprofitable business imaginable. Sin is nothing more than a mythic name for bad business. Good business is simply the way of the existing social order. No one knows that better than I. I, the Marquis of Keith, despite my reputation in Munich, despite my European reputation, am just as much outside the boundaries of society as that girl. Why else would I be giving the garden party? You have no idea how it pains me not to be able to receive the poor thing as one of my guests. It will be in far better taste if she comes as hired help.

SASHA: *(Has risen.)* Shall I call a carriage for the Baron?

KEITH: Yes. *(SASHA goes off. KEITH stamps his feet securely into his boots.)* You've read, I suppose, that the Fairyland Palace Company was established yesterday?

SCHOLZ: How could I have seen a newspaper since yesterday?

(They both take their places at the breakfast table.)

KEITH: It all depends on a brewer, a master builder, and a restaurateur. They are the caryatids that must support the pediment of the temple.

SCHOLZ: Incidentally, your friend Raspe, the police official, is a charming person.

KEITH: He's a scoundrel; I like him for quite another reason.

SCHOLZ: He's told me he was originally a theology student, but too much studying cost him his faith, and he tried getting it back the same way as the prodigal son.

KEITH: He sank lower and lower till finally the arm of the law caught him up and returned him to his faith by detaining him for two years under lock and key.

SCHOLZ: The girl absolutely failed to understand why I'd never learned to ride a bicycle. She thought it very reasonable of me not to have ridden a bicycle in Asia and Africa because of wild animals. But she thought I ought certainly to have begun in Italy.

KEITH: I'll warn you again, my friend: don't be too open with people. Truth is our most priceless possession and we can never be too sparing with it.

SCHOLZ: Is that why you assumed the title "Marquis of Keith"?

KEITH: I have as much right to be called "Marquis of Keith" as you have to be called "Ernst Scholz." I'm the adopted son of Lord Keith, who in the year 1863—

SASHA: *(Enters from the hall, announcing.)* Professor Saranieff.

(SARANIEFF enters. He wears a black Prince Albert coat with sleeves somewhat too long, light trousers which are somewhat too short, thick shoes, and glaring red gloves. His rather long, unruly black hair is cut straight all the way around; on a black ribbon in front of his eyes that are filled with anticipation he wears a pince-nez à la Murillo. His profile is expressive, and he sports a small Spanish mustache. After greeting them he hands his top hat to SASHA.)

SARANIEFF: From the bottom of my heart, dear friend, I wish you the best of good fortune. The cables at last are cut and the balloon free to rise.

KEITH: The command of my enterprise awaits me: I'm afraid I can't invite you to breakfast.

SARANIEFF: *(Sitting down at the table.)* Then I shall release you from the obligation.

KEITH: Sasha, set another plate!

(SASHA has hung up the hat in the hall and goes off into the living room.)

SARANIEFF: I'm surprised the great Casimir's name isn't included on the board of directors of the Fairyland Palace.

KEITH: The reason is that I don't wish to waive credit for being the creator of my own work. *(Introducing them.)* Saranieff, the painter— Count Trautenau.

SARANIEFF: *(Taking a glass and plate and helping himself; to SCHOLZ.)* Count, I already know you inside and out. *(To KEITH.)* Simba was just with me; she's sitting this very moment for a Boecklin.

KEITH: *(To SCHOLZ.)* Boecklin was a great artist himself. *(To SARANIEFF.)* You really needn't boast about these tricks of yours!

SARANIEFF: Make me famous, and I'll have no need for such tricks. I'll pay you thirty percent for life. Consider Zamriaki for a moment. His mind is already tottering like a rotting fence post. And why? Because he insists on immortality by honorable means.

KEITH: My only concern is his music. For the genuine composer the mind is always a hindrance.

SCHOLZ: To want immortality requires an extraordinary love of life.

SARANIEFF: *(To SCHOLZ.)* Incidentally, our Simba described you to me as a most interesting person.

SCHOLZ: Yes, I can well imagine she doesn't meet old grumpusses like me every day.

SARANIEFF: She categorized you as a Symbolist. *(To KEITH.)* Then she raved on about some up-coming party with a gigantic fireworks display for the Fairyland Palace.

KEITH: You don't dazzle dogs with fireworks, but rational men feel insulted if you refuse them. In any case, I'm going to Paris for a few days first.

SARANIEFF: They've asked your opinion on a joint German-French mutual aid treaty, have they?

KEITH: Just keep it to yourself!

SCHOLZ: I had no idea you were also active in politics!

SARANIEFF: Is there anything the Marquis of Keith isn't active in?

KEITH: I won't have it said I took no interest in my own times.

SCHOLZ: Aren't your own affairs enough to keep you occupied if you take life seriously?

SARANIEFF: I'd say you take life too *damned* seriously! Did some washer woman in the village of Gizeh, at the foot of the pyramids, manage to give you the wrong collar by mistake?

SCHOLZ: You appear to have been fully informed about me. May I visit you someday in your studio?

SARANIEFF: If you like, we can have our coffee there right now. You'll even find your Simba there.

SCHOLZ: Simba?—Simba? What's all this talk about Simba? She told me her name was Kathi!

SARANIEFF: Her real name is Kathi; but the Marquis of Keith dubbed her Simba.

SCHOLZ: *(To KEITH.)* Undoubtedly because of her stunning red hair.

KEITH: I'm sorry, but I have no information on the subject.

SARANIEFF: She's made herself comfortable on my Persian divan and is just now sleeping off her hangover from yesterday. *(MOLLY GREISINGER enters from the living room and lays a place for SARANIEFF.)* My heartiest thanks, dear madam; but as you can see, I've already finished. You'll pardon me, I hope, if I haven't taken the opportunity of kissing your hand.

MOLLY: Save your compliments for more worthy occasions! *(The bell rings in the corridor; MOLLY goes to answer it.)*

KEITH: *(Looks at his watch and rises.)* You will have to excuse me, gentlemen. *(Calls.)* Sasha!

SARANIEFF: *(Wiping his mouth.)* Ah, but we'll go with you, of course. *(He and SCHOLZ rise.)*

(SASHA enters from the waiting room with the coats and helps KEITH and SCHOLZ put theirs on.)

SCHOLZ: *(To KEITH.)* Why didn't you tell me you were married?

KEITH: Here, let me straighten your tie. *(He does so.)* You must give more attention to your outward appearance.

MOLLY: *(Returns from the hall with HERMANN CASIMIR.)* The young Casimir wishes to see you.

KEITH: *(To HERMANN.)* Did you deliver my kind regards yesterday?

HERMANN: The Countess herself was waiting for money from you!

KEITH: Wait here just a moment. I'll be right back. *(To SCHOLZ and SARANIEFF.)* Gentlemen?

SARANIEFF: *(Takes his hat from SASHA.)* With you through thick and thin!

SASHA: The carriage is waiting, Baron.

KEITH: Sit with the driver! *(SCHOLZ, SARANIEFF, KEITH, and SASHA go off.)*

MOLLY: *(Gathering the breakfast dishes together.)* What can you possibly want in this madhouse! You'd be much more sensible to stay home with your mama!

HERMANN: *(Wanting to leave the room at once.)* My mother happens not to be alive, dear lady; but I wouldn't want to bother you.

MOLLY: Oh, for heaven's sake, don't go! You're not bothering anyone. I just don't understand how parents can be so inhuman as not to protect their children from associating with these highway robbers. I once had a happy home like yours, and at the same age, and no wiser, without even thinking, I took a leap straight into the bottomless pit.

HERMANN: *(Considerably agitated.)* My God, I *must* find a way! I'll be ruined if I stay in Munich any longer! But the Marquis is bound to refuse me his help if he even suspects what I have in mind. Please, madam, please, don't betray me!

MOLLY: If only you guessed my state of mind right now, you wouldn't be in the least worried about my concern with your problems! I just hope you don't end up in a worse fix than me. If my mother had let me work, as I am now, instead of sending me ice-skating every free afternoon, I'd still have a life of happiness ahead of me!

HERMANN: But—if you're so miserable and you know—well, that you could still be happy, why—why don't you get a divorce?

MOLLY: Oh, God! Don't talk about things you don't understand! To get a divorce, you have to be married first.

HERMANN: I'm sorry, I—I thought you were.

MOLLY: God knows, I don't want to complain about anyone! But to get married in this world you first need papers. And having papers is beneath his dignity! *(A bell rings in the corridor.)* Morning till night, this place is like a post office! *(Goes off into the hall.)*

HERMANN: *(Pulling himself together.)* Why do I go shooting my mouth off like that!

MOLLY: *(Leads in the COUNTESS WERDENFELS.)* You may wait here for my husband if you like. He should be back very soon. May I introduce you?

ANNA: Thank you. We've met.

MOLLY: Of course! Then I won't be needed. *(Goes into the living room.)*

ANNA: *(Sits down on the bench of the writing table beside HERMANN and places her hand on his.)* Tell me now, my dear, what you do at school that you need so much money?

HERMANN: I won't.

ANNA: But I'd like very much to know.

HERMANN: I can believe that!

ANNA: You're very stubborn.

HERMANN: *(Pulls his hands from hers.)* I will not be bargained with!

ANNA: Who's bargaining? Don't flatter yourself. You see, I divide human beings into two large classes. The young and interesting and the old maids.

HERMANN: In your opinion, of course, I'm an old maid.

ANNA: Well, unless you can tell me why you need all that money—

HERMANN: But how can I? I'm an old maid!

ANNA: On the contrary. I could tell from the first that you were young and interesting.

HERMANN: And I am, too; or I'd be content to stay here in Munich.

ANNA: But you're dying to get out into the world!

HERMANN: And now, I suppose, you want to know where. Paris—London.

ANNA: Paris is quite unfashionable these days.

HERMANN: I don't really care about going to Paris.

ANNA: Then why not stay here in Munich? You have a father with more money than—

HERMANN: Because there's nothing here to experience! I'll die if I stay in Munich, especially if I have to spend more time at school. An old school friend writes me from Africa that when you're unhappy in Africa you're ten times happier than when you're in Munich.

ANNA: Let me tell you something. Your friend is an old maid. Don't go to Africa. Stay here in Munich with us and *really* experience something.

HERMANN: But that's impossible here!

(MOLLY shows in POLICE INSPECTOR RASPE. RASPE, in his early twenties, is dressed in a light-colored summer suit and straw hat and has the innocent childlike features of an angel by Guido Reni; short blond hair, the beginnings of a mustache. When he feels himself being watched he clamps his blue pince-nez onto his nose.)

MOLLY: My husband will be back shortly, if you would care to wait. May I introduce you—

RASPE: I really don't know, dear madam, if it would be of any real service to the Baron if you introduce me.

MOLLY: All right then!—Goodness! *(She goes into the living room.)*

ANNA: May I say that your precautions are quite superfluous? We have met.

RASPE: *(Seating himself on the divan.)* Hm. I'm afraid I shall have to recollect—

ANNA: When you have sufficiently recollected yourself, then I should like to ask you not to introduce me either.

RASPE: How is it I've never heard you spoken of here?

ANNA: What's in a name? I was told that you spent two years in total solitude.

RASPE: And you, of course, revealed to no one that you knew me in my glory days.

ANNA: Whom haven't we known in his glory days!

RASPE: You're quite right. Pity is blasphemy. What could I do? I was the sacrifice of the insane confidence everyone had in me.

ANNA: And now you're young and interesting again?

RASPE: I now make use of that same insane confidence everyone had in me for the well being of my fellow men. By the way, can you tell me something more specific about this sensualist?

ANNA: I'm terribly sorry; he hasn't been put through his paces for me yet.

RASPE: It's really quite astonishing. A certain gentleman by the name of Ernst Scholz—wants to train here in Munich to become a sensualist.

ANNA: And for that reason the Marquis of Keith introduces him to a police official?

RASPE: He's quite harmless. Scarcely knowing what to do with him, for his education's sake I took him to the Hofbräuhaus. It's quite near.

(MOLLY opens the entrance door and shows in CONSUL CASIMIR. He is a man in his middle forties, rather heavy set, dressed in opulent elegance; a full face with a luxuriant black beard, powerful mustache, bushy eyebrows, and hair parted carefully down the center.)

MOLLY: My husband is not at home. *(Goes off.)*

CASIMIR: *(Without greeting anyone, goes straight toward HERMANN.)* There is the door! To think I have to hunt you down in this den of thieves!

HERMANN: You'd never have come looking for me here if it didn't look bad for your business!

CASIMIR: *(Threatening him.)* Will you be quiet! Move! Or do I have to show you how!

HERMANN: *(Pulls out a pocket revolver.)* Don't touch me, papa! Don't touch me! I'll shoot myself if you touch me!

CASIMIR: You'll pay for this when I get you home!

RASPE: Why should he let himself be treated like an animal?

CASIMIR: Must I be insulted here as well?

ANNA: *(Approaches him.)* Please, sir, this is bound to cause an accident. Calm down first. *(To HERMANN.)* Be reasonable now; go home with your father.

HERMANN: There's nothing to go home *for!* If I drank myself into a stupor because I don't know why I'm alive, he'd never even notice!

ANNA: Then calm down and tell him what you have in mind. Just don't threaten your father with that revolver. Give me that thing.

HERMANN: Is that what you thought I wanted?

ANNA: You won't regret it. I'll give it back to you when you've quieted down. Do you take me for a liar? *(HERMANN hesitantly gives her the revolver.)* Now ask your father to forgive you. If you have a spark of honor in you, you can't expect your father to take the first step.

HERMANN: But I will not be destroyed!

ANNA: First ask his forgiveness. You'll know then that he can be reasoned with.

HERMANN: I—I beg you to—*(He sinks to his knees and sobs.)*

ANNA: *(Trying to raise him.)* Aren't you ashamed of yourself! Look your father in the eye!

CASIMIR: He has his mother's nerves!

ANNA: Prove to your father that he can have confidence in you. Go home now, and when you've quieted down you will tell your father all about your plans and your wishes. *(Leads him out.)*

CASIMIR: *(To RASPE.)* Who is this woman?

RASPE: This is the first time in two years I've seen her. At the time she was a saleswoman in a shop on Perus Strasse. Her name was Huber, if I'm not mistaken. If you'd care to know anything further—

CASIMIR: Thank you. At your service! *(Goes off.)*

(MOLLY enters from the living room to remove the breakfast dishes.)

RASPE: Excuse me, madam. Did the Baron really intend to return before dinner?

MOLLY: For God's sake, don't ask me such ridiculous things!

ANNA: *(Returns from the hall; to MOLLY.)* May I help you with that?

MOLLY: You ask if you can help—*(She puts the serving tray back down on the table.)* Let whoever wants to clear the table! *I* didn't eat off it! *(Goes off into the living room.)*

RASPE: That bit with the boy was extremely well done.

ANNA: *(Sits down at the writing table.)* I envy him the carriage his father is taking him home in.

RASPE: Tell me, whatever became of that Count Werdenfels who used to give one champagne party after another two years ago?

ANNA: That happens to be my name now.

RASPE: I should have guessed! Would you convey to the Count my sincerest congratulations on his choice.

ANNA: I'm afraid that's no longer possible.

RASPE: Obviously then you've separated.

ANNA: Yes, obviously. *(Voices are heard in the hallway.)* I'll explain it to you some other time.

(KEITH enters with OSTERMEIER, KRENTZL, and GRANDAUER, all of them more or less large-bellied, bleary-eyed Munich Philistines. SASHA follows.)

KEITH: What a remarkable stroke of luck! I can introduce you at once to one of our leading artists. Sasha, remove this mess! *(SASHA goes into the living room with the breakfast dishes. KEITH introduces them.)* Mr. Ostermeier, the brewery proprietor; Mr. Krentzl, the master builder; Mr. Grandauer, the restaurateur: the caryatids of the Fairyland Palace— Countess Werdenfels. But your time is limited, gentlemen, and you did come to see the plans. *(Takes the plans from the writing table and unrolls them on the center table.)*

OSTERMEIER: Take your time, my friend. Five minutes one way or the other won't matter.

KEITH: *(To GRANDAUER.)* Would you hold this, please.—What you see here is the large concert hall with its retractable ceiling and skylight, so that in the summer it can serve as an exhibition palace. Next to it here is a smaller theater, one I intend to make a popular venue by decorating it in the most modern taste, something, shall we say, that is a cross between a dance hall and a mortuary. Modernity is always the cheapest and the most effective way to advertise.

OSTERMEIER: Hm—you haven't forgotten the lavatories, eh?

KEITH: Here you see detailed sketches of the cloak room and the toilet facilities.—And here, my dear Krentzl, is the façade: driveway, pediment, and caryatids!

KRENTZL: I sure wouldn't want to be one of them caryatids!

KEITH: Just a joke, sir, just a joke.

KRENTZL: What'd my old lady have to say if I let myself be chiseled into one of them caryatids way up there, and even worse, on a Fairyland Palace!

GRANDAUER: As you know, my main concern for the restaurant is space.

KEITH: We have proposed, my dear Grandauer, to devote the entire ground floor to the restaurant.

GRANDAUER: You can't go crowding folks into a place for eats and drinks like you can for listening to that music.

KEITH: And for afternoon coffee, my dear Grandauer, you will find we have a terrace on the mezzanine with a magnificent view of the grounds along the Isar.

OSTERMEIER: Begging your pardon, old friend, do you think we could have a look at your preliminary expense sheet.

KEITH: *(Producing a sheet of writing.)* Four thousand shares at five thousand comes to approximately twenty million marks.—I'm operating on the assumption, gentlemen, that each of us subscribes for forty preferred shares, and that we pay for them at once. The estimated dividend, as you can see, is extraordinarily low.

KRENTZL: Looks like all we need is the go-ahead from the local authorities.

KEITH: That's why, in addition to the shares, we are going to issue a number of interest-drawing bonds and place a portion of them at the city's disposal for worthy purposes.—The proposal is that the members of the governing board receive ten percent of the net profit before deductions for depreciation and reserves.

OSTERMEIER: Quite right. Can't ask for more than that.

KEITH: As far as the stock market is concerned, we'll need to work some on that. I'm going to Paris tomorrow for that very purpose. Two weeks from today we will celebrate with our founders' party at my villa on Brienner Strasse.

(ANNA winces.)

OSTERMEIER: Sure would be nice to get Consul Casimir to join up by the time the party comes along!

KRENTZL: That's the best idea yet, you know? With Casimir with us the authorities *couldn't* say no—not to *anything!*

KEITH: It is my hope, gentlemen, to call a general meeting of the board before the party. At that time you will see how I have taken into consideration your suggestions regarding Consul Casimir.

OSTERMEIER: *(Shakes his hand.)* So, have a pleasant trip to Paris, my friend. Let's hear from you. *(Bowing to ANNA.)* I take my leave, madam. My compliments.

GRANDAUER: With all respects. I wish you a good afternoon.

KRENTZL: Best regards. Good day!

(KEITH leads the gentlemen out.)

ANNA: *(After he has returned.)* What can you possibly be thinking of, announcing your founders' party at my house?!

KEITH: I'll have a dress made for you in Paris that will render it quite unnecessary for you to be able to sing. *(To RASPE.)* And you, sir—I will expect that at the founders' party you will utilize all your charm to bewitch the wives of our three caryatids.

RASPE: I doubt the ladies will be disappointed.

KEITH: *(Giving him some money.)* Here are three hundred marks. I'm bringing fireworks back from Paris, the likes of which the city of Munich has never seen.

RASPE: *(To ANNA.)* He got it from the sensualist.

KEITH: I use every mortal according to his talents, and I must recommend a certain degree of caution in regard to my very dear friend Raspe.

RASPE: When a man looks, as you do, as though he'd been cut from the gallows, making his way honestly through life is no art. I'd be curious to know where you'd be today if you had my angelic face!

KEITH: With a face like yours, I'd have married a princess.

ANNA: *(To RASPE.)* If I'm not mistaken, you had a French name when we were first introduced.

RASPE: Having become a useful member of human society, I no longer indulge in French names.—Permit me to pay you my respects. *(Goes off.)*

ANNA: My serving staff is simply not large enough to handle big suppers!

KEITH: *(Calls.)* Sasha!

SASHA: *(Enters from the waiting room.)* Baron?

KEITH: Would you care to help serve at my friend's garden party?

SASHA: That would be a real pleasure, Baron. *(Goes off.)*

KEITH: May I introduce you today to my oldest boyhood friend, Count Trautenau?

ANNA: I've never had much luck with counts.

KEITH: That doesn't matter. All I ask is that you don't discuss my domestic relations with him. The fact is he's a moralist, by nature and by conviction. He's already catechized me today regarding my domestic arrangements.

ANNA: Good Lord, the one who's training to become a sensualist?

KEITH: Oh, it's a total contradiction! Ever since I've known him, he's lived a life of sacrifice, without realizing that there are, in fact, two souls inside him.

ANNA: Mercy! I have trouble with just one! But I thought his name was Scholz.

KEITH: One of his souls is Ernst Scholz, the other Count Trautenau.

ANNA: Thank you, but no thank you. I want nothing to do with people who can't make up their minds.

KEITH: But he's a paragon of decision. The world has no more pleasures to offer him unless he starts in again from the bottom.

ANNA: Then let him start his climb, step by step.

KEITH: Why are you so upset?

ANNA: Because you're trying to pair me off with this frightful monster!

KEITH: He's gentle as a lamb.

ANNA: Thank you very much, but I don't invite incarnations of disaster into my boudoir!

KEITH: You're not understanding me. Just now I can't do without his confidence, and therefore I don't want to expose myself at this time to his disapproval. If he fails to get to know you, all the better for me: I won't have his reproaches to look forward to.

ANNA: One never knows where your calculations are going to lead.

KEITH: What did you have in mind?

ANNA: I thought you wanted me to play his little whore.

KEITH: How could you think such a thing!

ANNA: You said a moment ago you use every mortal according to his talents. By that standard, haven't I the talent of a whore?

KEITH: *(Taking her in his arms.)* Anna—I'm going to Paris tomorrow, not to look into the stock market or to buy fireworks, but because I need a breath of fresh air, because I need to stretch my arms, if I'm not to lose the image of myself that I have so carefully constructed here in Munich. Anna, would I be taking you with me to Paris if you didn't mean everything to me?—Do you know something, Anna? Not a night goes by but I dream of you with a diadem in your hair. If ever you asked me to pull down a star for you from the firmament, I wouldn't be afraid, I'd find the way and means to do it.

ANNA: Go on! Use me as a whore!—You'll see soon enough the kind of profit I yield!

KEITH: All I can think of at this moment is the concert dress I'll have made for you at St. Hilaire's—

SASHA: *(Enters from the hall.)* A Mr. Sommersberg would like to see you.

KEITH: Show him in. *(To ANNA, describing the dress.)* A silvery torrent of mauve silk and paillettes from shoulder to ankle, so tightly laced and cut so deep, front and back, that the dress will appear a glittering jewel on your slender body!

(SOMMERSBERG has entered. In his late thirties, deeply-lined face, hair and beard streaked with gray and unkempt. A heavy winter overcoat covers his shabby clothes; torn kid gloves.)

SOMMERSBERG: I am the author of *Songs of a Happy Man.* I don't look it.

KEITH: I looked like that once myself.

SOMMERSBERG: I would never have found the courage to come to you, except that I have had almost nothing to eat for two days.

KEITH: I've been there myself hundreds of times. How can I help you?

SOMMERSBERG: A little something—for lunch—

KEITH: Is that all the use you think I can be to you?

SOMMERSBERG: I'm an invalid.

KEITH: But you still have half a life ahead of you!

SOMMERSBERG: I've wasted my life living up to the expectations people had set for me.

KEITH: Perhaps you'll find a current to take you out to open sea again. Or are you afraid?

SOMMERSBERG: I can't swim; and here in Munich resignation isn't so hard to bear.

KEITH: Come to our founders' party in Brienner Strasse two weeks from today. You'll make some very necessary contacts there. *(Gives him some money.)* Here are a hundred marks. Keep enough of it to rent a dress suit for the evening.

SOMMERSBERG: *(Hesitantly taking the money.)* I feel as if I'm deceiving you—

KEITH: Just don't deceive yourself! And in doing so you will be doing a good turn for the next poor devil who comes to me.

SOMMERSBERG: Thank you, Baron *(Goes off.)*

KEITH: Don't mention it. *(Closes the door and puts his arms around ANNA.)* And now, my queen, we're off to Paris!

END OF ACT TWO

ACT THREE

A room overlooking a garden is lighted with electric lamps; a wide glass door in the right side wall leads into the garden. The middle door in the back wall leads into the dining room where dinner is being served. When the door is opened one sees the upper end of the table. In the left wall is a curtained door into the game room. Near the door is an upright piano. Downstage right, a lady's writing table; downstage left, a settee, chairs, and table, etc. In the upstage right corner there is a door which leads into the hallway. A toast is being drunk in the dining room. As the glasses clink, SOMMERSBERG, in shabbily elegant evening dress, and KEITH, in a full-dress suit, enter the salon through the center door.

KEITH: *(Closing the door behind him.)* You've drawn up the telegram?

SOMMERSBERG: *(Paper in hand, reading.)* "The founding of the Munich Fairyland Palace Company brought together yesterday evening a gathering of notable citizens of the convivial city on the Isar for a highly spirited garden party at the villa of the Marquis of Keith on Brienner Strasse. A magnificent fireworks display, lasting till after midnight, delighted the residents of the neighborhood. We wish to extend to this enterprise begun under such favorable auspices—"

KEITH: Excellent!—Whom can I send to the telegraph office—? *(SOMMERSBERG goes off into the hallway; at the same time ERNST SCHOLZ enters; he is in full-dress suit and overcoat.)* You've certainly kept us waiting long enough!

SCHOLZ: And I've merely come to tell you I can't stay.

KEITH: They're making a laughing stock of me! Old Casimir has already left me in the lurch; but at least he sent a congratulatory telegram.

SCHOLZ: I don't belong with people! You complain about being outside of society; I'm outside of humanity!

KEITH: Haven't you every pleasure now that a man can dream of?

SCHOLZ: Pleasure? What pleasure? This frenzied whirl of sensations I'm wallowing in makes me no different from a barbarian. True, I *have* learned to go into raptures over Rubens and Wagner. The disaster that once aroused pity in me has become almost insupportable in its ugliness. And I've become an aficionado regarding the artistic achievements of dancers and acrobats.—But after all this, I haven't made even one step of progress! It's because of my money that I'm treated like a human being. But no sooner do I want to *be* one than I find myself ramming into invisible walls!

KEITH: There are humans that are like weeds, they take root anywhere, and are uprooted just as easily. If they're the ones you envy, don't look to me for pity! The world's a damned sly beast and a bitch to conquer. But succeed once and you're proof against any misfortune.

SCHOLZ: If such phrases satisfy you, then there's nothing from you I can hope for. *(About to leave.)*

KEITH: *(Detaining him.)* Phrases? No! I'm beyond misfortune. We're too well acquainted, misfortune and I. Misfortune for me is an opportunity like any other. Any stupid ass can suffer misfortune; the trick is to exploit it to one's advantage.

SCHOLZ: You cling to the world like a whore to her pimp. You don't understand that a man who exists only for himself can become as loathsome to himself as carrion.

KEITH: Goddamn it, then be satisfied with this "piety" of yours! With this purgatory of earthly vice and joy behind you, you'll look down on this miserable sinner that I am like a Father of the Church!

SCHOLZ: If only I had my human birthright! Better to crawl into the wilderness like a beast than to apologize every step of the way for my very existence!—I can't stay here!—I met Countess Werdenfels yesterday!—How I offended her, I can only guess. Unintentionally I assumed the tone I use with our Simba.

KEITH: I've had more slaps from women than I have hairs on my head! But not one has ever laughed at me behind my back because of it!

SCHOLZ: I'm a man without breeding—and with a woman for whom I have the highest regard!

KEITH: The man whose every step from youth on has led to a spiritual conflict, can rule the world long after the rest of us have become food for worms! And that's *you!*

SCHOLZ: And then there's our Simba—playing the waitress here tonight! The world's most experienced diplomat never handled such a situation!

KEITH: Simba doesn't know you!

SCHOLZ: I'm not afraid she'll be too friendly with me; what frightens me is she'll be insulted if I ignore her for no good reason.

KEITH: How would *that* insult her? She knows a hell of a lot more about class distinction than you.

SCHOLZ: Oh, don't worry, I know about class distinction! They're the chains that teach us how utterly weak we are!

KEITH: And you suppose that *I* don't battle weakness? My conduct can be as correct as the course of the planets, my dress as elegant as a lord—it doesn't matter. There is nothing, nothing, that can change this plebeian hand into what it is not. You could as easily turn an imbecile into a paragon of intellect. With my intellectual gifts, I could long ago have enjoyed a better social position except for these hands.—Come, you'd do best to put your overcoat in the next room.

SCHOLZ: Leave me alone! I couldn't talk calmly with the Countess today if I wanted to.

KEITH: Then talk with the two divorcées; they're both experiencing conflicts similar to yours.

SCHOLZ: Both at once?!

KEITH: Neither one over twenty-five, absolute beauties, ancient Nordic aristocracy, and so ultramodern in their way of life that they make me feel like an old flintlock beside them.

SCHOLZ: I feel I'm not far from being a modern myself. *(Goes off into the game room; KEITH is about to follow him when SARANIEFF enters from the hallway.)*

SARANIEFF: Is there anything left to eat?

KEITH: Would you kindly leave your coat outside!—I haven't eaten all day long.

SARANIEFF: They're not so particular here. But first I must ask you something rather important. *(SARANIEFF hangs his hat and coat in the hallway; meanwhile SASHA in frock coat and satin breeches enters from the game room with a filled champagne cooler on his way into the dining room.)*

KEITH: When you set off the fireworks, Sasha, be careful with the big mortar. There's all hellfire in it.

SASHA: Oh, I'm not scared, Baron! *(Goes off into the dining room, closing the door behind him.)*

SARANIEFF: *(Returns from the hallway.)* Do you have any money?

KEITH: But you've just sold a picture! Why do you think I sent my friend to see you?

SARANIEFF: What can I get out of a squeezed lemon? You've already robbed him of all he has. It'll be three days before he can pay me a penny.

KEITH: *(gives him a note.)* Here are a thousand marks.

(SIMBA, a typical Munich girl, ruddy complexion, with nimble movements,

luxuriant red hair, in a tasteful black dress with white pinafore, enters from the dining room with a serving tray of half-empty wine glasses.)

SIMBA: The Councilor wants to toast the Baron another round.

(KEITH takes one of the glasses from the tray and goes to the table through the open door. SIMBA goes off into the game room.)

KEITH: Ladies and gentlemen! This evening signifies the beginning of an era for Munich that will eclipse all that has preceded it. We are creating a center in which all the arts of the world will be welcome. If our enterprise has caused general astonishment, then you must be mindful that only the truly astounding wins the greatest success. I empty my glass in honor of the principle which has ordained Munich a city of the arts, in honor of Munich's citizens and its lovely women.

(While the glasses are still clinking, SASHA enters from the dining room and goes into the game room. SIMBA enters from the game room with a platter of cheese under a glass cover on her way into the dining room.)

SARANIEFF: Simba! Are you blind?! Your sensualist is about escape your snare only to be reeled in again by the Countess from Perusa Strasse! Why?

SIMBA: What are you doing out here? Go inside! Sit at the table!

SARANIEFF: I? With the caryatids!—Simba! Think of all the marvelous money your sensualist has in his pockets! Do you want to have it devoured by the insane Marquis of Keith?!

SIMBA: Leave me alone, you hear? I'm workin'!

SARANIEFF: The caryatids have had enough cheese! Let them wipe their mouths and be done with it! *(Places the cheese platter on the table and takes SIMBA on his knee.)* Simba! Don't you care for me anymore? Must I continue begging twenty marks from the Marquis of Keith amid wailing and the gnashing of teeth, while you have access to thousand mark notes fresh from their source?

SIMBA: Oh, thanks a lot! I never been plagued by *any*one like this sensualist with his stupid compassion! He tells me I'm a martyr to civilization! You ever heard anything so crazy? A martyr to civilization! I tell *him,* I say: "Tell your *society* ladies that! They'll *love* it," I says, "you calling 'em martyrs to civilization, 'cause what're they otherwise? Nothin'!" Martyr to civilization he calls me, when I drink champagne and have all the fun I want!

SARANIEFF: If I were a woman, Simba, a woman of your qualities, this sensualist would have to pay for every muggy glance with an ancestral castle!

SIMBA: That's how he talks, all right! Askin' me why he's a man. Like there ain't enough ghosts in the world! Ever hear *me* ask why I'm a *girl?*

SARANIEFF: Nor do you ask us to throw away fifty million marks on some confounded idea of yours!

SIMBA: Oh, all those sad millions! You know, I only seen him laugh once since I met him. I told him, I told this sensualist, he had to learn to ride a bicycle. So he learned. We ride out to Schleissheim and while we're in the woods lookin' around a thunderstorm breaks out like the world was gonna end. Then, for the first time since I met him, he started in laughing. Oh, God, how he laughed! "There," I said, "there, *now* you're a sensualist! A *real* one!" Every stroke of lightning, he laughed!—The more it lightninged and thundered the crazier he laughed! "Don't go standin' there under the trees," I says, "that's where the lightning hits!"—"No lightning'll hit me," he says, and laughs and laughs!

SARANIEFF: Simba! Simba! You could have become an imperial countess on the spot!

SIMBA: Thanks a lot! A Social Democrat is what I could've become. Improve the world, humanitarianism, those are his specialties. No thanks, I ain't made for the Social Democrats. Too moralistic for me. They get into power once and good-bye champagne suppers.—You seen my lovey?

SARANIEFF: Seen your lovey? I thought *I* was your lovey!

SIMBA: That could be almost anybody!—I gotta watch out for him, he don't get tipsy, or the Marquis of Keith won't hire him for his new Fairyland Palace. *(SOMMERSBERG enters from the hallway.)* Here he is! Where you *been* all this time?

SOMMERSBERG: Sending a telegram to the newspapers.

SARANIEFF: Good God! Have graves begun to open? Sommersberg! Shame on you rising from the dead to be secretary of the Fairyland Palace!

SOMMERSBERG: *(Indicating SIMBA.)* This angel has restored me to the world.

SIMBA: Oh, go on, lovey!—He comes and asks me where he can get money.—"The Marquis of Keith," I says to him. "If he's all out, there ain't another penny in all Munich."

RASPE: *(Dressed in the most elegant evening clothes, a small chain with an Order on his chest, enters from the game room.)* Simba, this is simply scandalous, making the Fairyland Palace Company wait for its cheese!

SIMBA: *(Catches up the cheese platter.)* Holy Mother of God!—I'm comin'! Right now!

SARANIEFF: Why not just stay with the old crones you were hired to see to?

SIMBA: *(Taking RASPE's arm.)* You leave this bubby of mine alone, you hear?—You'd be pleased as punch if you was as handsome as him! Both of you!

SARANIEFF: Simba—you're a born whore!

SIMBA: I'm what?

SARANIEFF: You're a born whore!

SIMBA: One more time?

SARANIEFF: You're a born whore!

SIMBA: No, I ain't no born whore. I'm a born cheese toaster. *(Goes off into the dining room with RASPE.)*

SOMMERSBERG: I personally dictate her love letters for her.

SARANIEFF: Then it's you I have to thank for destroying my castles in the air! *(SASHA enters from the game room with a lighted lantern.)* Jesus, what are you all got up for! You expecting to find a rich countess to marry?

SASHA: I'm going to the garden to set off the fireworks. Wait'll you see the big mortar. That'll be an eye-opener! The Marquis says it's the fires of hell! *(Goes off into the garden.)*

SARANIEFF: His master's afraid of blowing himself up if he sets them off himself.—No wonder Dame Fortune never hoists him into the saddle! He'd ride the poor beast into the ground till it was a bag of bones. *(The center door opens and the guests leave the dining room.)* Come along, Sommersberg! Let's have our Simba dish us up a real Lucullan feast! *(The guests stream into the salon; at their head, RASPE between MRS. OSTERMEIER and MRS. KRENTZL; then KEITH with OSTER-MEIER, KRENTZL, and GRANDAUER; then ZAMRIAKI with BARONESS VON TOTLEBEN; and finally SCHOLZ and ANNA.— SARANIEFF and SOMMERSBERG sit down at the table in the dining room.)*

RASPE: Will their royal highnesses join me in a cup of exquisite coffee?

MRS. OSTERMEIER: My! There's no more gracious cavalier in all southern Germany!

MRS. KRENTZL: The gentlemen of our nobility could certainly take lessons from you!

RASPE: On my word of honor, ladies, this is the most glorious moment of my life. *(Goes off with both ladies into the game room.)*

OSTERMEIER: *(To KEITH.)* It was quite nice, you know, of old Casimir to send us a congratulatory telegram. But then, you see, my dear friend, old Casimir is a most cautious man.

KEITH: No matter! No matter! Old Casimir will have joined us by the time of our first general meeting. Won't you gentlemen have some coffee? *(OSTERMEIER, KRENTZL, and GRANDAUER go off into the game room.)*

BARONESS VON ROSENKRON: *(To KEITH, who is about to follow the gentlemen.)* Promise me now, Marquis, that you will allow me to study to be a dancer for the Fairyland Palace.

BARONESS VON TOTLEBEN: And me to be a trick rider!

KEITH: You have my word, divine ladies, the Fairyland Palace will not open without you!—What is it, Zamriaki? You're as pale as a corpse—

ZAMRIAKI: *(A slender, short, conservatory musician, with long, black wavy hair parted down the middle, speaks with a Polish accent.)* On my symphony I am working day and night. *(Takes KEITH to one side.)* You permit, Marquis, I like ask advance twenty mark on conductor salary for Fairyland Palace Orchestra.

KEITH: With the greatest pleasure. *(Gives him the money.)* Do you think, perhaps, you might give us a sampling of your new symphony soon in an up-coming concert?

ZAMRIAKI. I play Scherzo. Scherzo will be great success.

BARONESS VON ROSENKRON: *(At the glass door into the garden.)* My, just look at this sea of light! Look, Martha, look! Come, Zamriaki, take us into the garden!

ZAMRIAKI. I come, ladies! I come! *(He goes into the garden with BARONESS VON ROSENKRON and BARONESS VON TOTLEBEN.)*

KEITH: *(Following them.)* Good God, people, stay away from the big mortar! It's loaded with my most splendid rockets! *(Goes off into the garden.)* *(SIMBA closes the door from inside the dining room. ANNA and SCHOLZ stay behind alone in the salon.)*

ANNA: I can't imagine what in the world I could have taken amiss. This tactlessness you speak of, could it have been in your relations with some other woman?

SCHOLZ: Quite impossible. Please understand, I'm as happy as a person imprisoned since earliest childhood breathing free air for the first time. It's why I'm so uncertain of every step; afraid of losing my happiness.

ANNA: It must be fascinating to live in darkness without ever opening your eyes!

SCHOLZ: Countess, if I could exchange my life for one that strives for the common good, I'd never be able to thank my Creator enough.

ANNA: I thought you came to Munich to learn to be a sensualist?

SCHOLZ: Learning to be a sensualist is only a means to an end. You have my most sacred assurance of that. But don't think me a hypocrite because of it.—There's still so much good to fight for in this world! And I *will* find a place for myself in it. The more blows Fortune rains down on my head, the more precious this bag of bones will become, though it's been such a burden up to now. And there's one thing I am absolutely certain of: If ever I succeed in serving my fellow men, I will never, never once, take any credit for it! My path may lead me up or lead me down, no matter; I will always obey the terrible and ruthless instinct of self-preservation!

ANNA: Maybe the famous became famous because they couldn't endure living with us run-of-the-mill mortals.

SCHOLZ: You still don't understand me, Countess.—As soon as I've found my proper sphere of activity, I'll be the most modest and gracious company. I've already begun. I've been riding a bicycle here in Munich. It was as if I hadn't looked at the world since the days of my earliest childhood. Every tree, every body of water, the mountains, the heavens, they were all one great revelation that I seemed to have had a presentiment of in a former life.—May I invite you to a cycling party sometime?

ANNA: Say tomorrow morning at seven? Or aren't you one for getting up early?

SCHOLZ: Tomorrow morning at seven! My life has suddenly become an endless spring landscape!

ANNA: Just don't keep me waiting!

(ZAMRIAKI, BARONESS VON ROSENKRON, and BARONESS VON TOTLEBEN return from the garden. SIMBA enters from the game room.)

BARONESS VON ROSENKRON: Oh, but it's cold!—Martha, we'll have to take our shawls when we go out next. Play us a cancan, Zamriaki! *(To SCHOLZ.)* Do you dance the cancan?

SCHOLZ: I regret that I do not, madam.

BARONESS VON ROSENKRON: *(To BARONESS VON TOTLEBEN.)* Then we'll dance together. *(ZAMRIAKI has seated himself at the piano and begun playing a waltz.)* Do you call that a cancan, maestro?

ANNA: *(To SIMBA.)* But you *do* dance the waltz?

SIMBA: If madam wishes—

ANNA: Come!

(BARONESS VON ROSENKRON, BARONESS VON TOTLEBEN, ANNA, and SIMBA dance the waltz.)

BARONESS VON ROSENKRON: More tempo, please!

(KEITH returns from the garden and turns off all the electric lights but one, so that the salon is only dimly lighted.)

ZAMRIAKI: *(Breaks off playing with annoyance.)* I come with each beat closer to my symphony!

BARONESS VON TOTLEBEN: But why is it suddenly so dark?

KEITH: To show off my rockets better! *(He opens the door to the dining room.)* If you please, ladies and gentlemen—*(RASPE, MR. and MRS. OSTERMEIER, and MR. and MRS. KRENTZL enter the salon. SIMBA goes off.)* It pleases me to announce that in the next few weeks the first of our grand Fairyland Palace concerts will take place, concerts that will publicize our Munich enterprise. Countess Werdenfels will introduce us to some songs of very recent composition, while our conductor Zamriaki will personally direct excerpts from his symphonic poem *The Wisdom of the Brahmans.*

(General applause. In the garden a rocket rises into the air, casting a reddish shimmer into the salon. KEITH turns off all the electric lights and opens the glass door.)

KEITH: Into the garden, ladies and gentlemen! Into the garden if you want to see! *(A second rocket rises into the air as the guests leave the salon. KEITH, who is about to follow them, is held back by ANNA. The stage remains dark.)*

ANNA: What do you mean announcing I'm to take part in your Fairyland Palace concert?

KEITH: If you wait till your teacher proclaims you ready, you'll be old and gray without ever having sung a note. *(Throws himself into a chair.)* At last, at last this perilous tightrope act of mine is coming to an end! For ten years I've used every ounce of energy just to keep my balance.— From here on out the way is upwards!

ANNA: And just where do I get the cheek to appear in front of a Munich audience with my so-called singing?!

KEITH: But you were going to be the best Wagnerian soprano in Germany in two years.

ANNA: I was joking.

KEITH: How was I to know that!

ANNA: Concerts are prepared for months in advance!

KEITH: I haven't denied myself thousands of times, only to do what people *usually* do. If they happen not to like your so-called singing, they'll be left breathless by your brilliant Parisian gown.

ANNA: If only others saw me as you do!

KEITH: I'll make certain they use the right glasses!

ANNA: Every time I appear you see and hear the most fantastic things. You overrate my appearance as much as you overrate my art.

KEITH: *(Jumping up.)* I've never been suspected of overrating women, but I knew you inside out at first glance. Is it any wonder I spent ten years looking for you on two continents? We had met on numerous occasions, but you were always either in the clutches of a bandit like myself, or I was so down and out that there was no practical advantage in my entering your luminous social circle.

ANNA: If your love for me is making you lose your mind, what reason is that for me to heap the scorn of Munich on my back?

KEITH: Other women have heaped quite different things on themselves for my sake!

ANNA: I am not infatuated with you!

KEITH: It's what they all say! Surrender to your inevitable good fortune, why don't you? I'll inspire you with all the confidence you'll need for your debut—even if I have to drive you out there with a loaded revolver!

ANNA: Keep treating me like an animal and soon it'll all be over between us!

KEITH: You can be confident of one thing, that I'm a man who takes life damned seriously! Although I like to bathe in champagne, I can also, like few others, deny myself all of life's pleasures. Three whole days without having made at least one step of progress toward my goal are unbearable!

ANNA: It's about time, don't you think, that you reached that goal?

KEITH: Can you really suppose, Anna, that I'd arrange this concert if I weren't absolutely certain you'd turn it into a brilliant triumph? Let me tell you something: I'm a man of *faith*—*(In the garden a rocket rises hissingly into the air.)* I believe in nothing so firmly as that our efforts and sacrifices are rewarded in this world!

ANNA: You'd *have* to, to overwork yourself as you do!

KEITH: And if we aren't the ones rewarded, then our children will be.

ANNA: But you haven't any!

KEITH: You'll give them to me, Anna! Children with my intelligence, with robust, healthy bodies and aristocratic hands. And for that I'll build you a home fit for a queen, one that a woman of your stamp deserves! And I'll place a husband at your side with the power to fulfill every desire mirrored in your great, black eyes. *(Kisses her passionately. In the garden some fireworks are set off which for the moment bathe the couple in a dark red glow.)* Go into the garden. The caryatids are dying to kneel to their goddess!

ANNA: Aren't you coming, too?

KEITH: *(Turns on two of the electric lights so that the salon is dimly lighted.)* I need to dash off a newspaper article about our concert. It must appear in tomorrow morning's paper. In it I'll congratulate you in advance for your triumph.

(ANNA goes into the garden. KEITH sits at the table and notes down a few words. MOLLY GREISINGER, a colored shawl over her head, enters from the hallway excited and disturbed.)

MOLLY: I have to speak to you for a moment.

KEITH: As long as you like, my dear; you aren't disturbing me. Although I did tell you that you wouldn't be able to stand it at home alone.

MOLLY: Dear God, let some dreadful disaster overtake us! Nothing else can save us now!

KEITH: Then why don't you come with me when I ask you?

MOLLY: *(Shuddering.)* To your friends?

KEITH: The people in these rooms are the *business* that keeps us *alive!* But you can't bear to know I'm here with my thoughts and not with you!

MOLLY: And that surprises you?! You know, when you're around these people, you're not at all the same person; you're someone I've never known, never loved, someone I'd never have followed even a step, to say nothing of sacrificing home, family, happiness, everything.— You're so good, so wonderful, so dear!—But around these people—to me you're worse than—than dead!

KEITH: Go home and dress up a little. Sasha will go with you. You *mustn't* be alone tonight.

MOLLY: Yes, I'm just in the mood for getting all dolled up. You frighten me the way you carry on. It's as if the world would end tomorrow. I feel like I have to *do* something, *any*thing, to keep these horrors away from us.

KEITH: As of yesterday I began drawing an annual salary of one hundred thousand marks. You needn't fear dying of hunger any longer.

MOLLY: Don't joke! It's *me* you're sinning against. I almost can't bring myself to say what frightens me!

KEITH: Then how can I calm you? Tell me. I'll do it at once.

MOLLY: Come with me! Come with me out of this murderer's den where all they want is to destroy you. It's true; I've complained to others about you; but I did it because I couldn't go on watching your childish delusions. You're so stupid, stupid as stupid can be! You *are!* You let yourself be taken in by the lowest, commonest swindlers, and you patiently let them cut your throat.

KEITH: It's better to *suffer* injustice, my dear, than to *do* injustice.

MOLLY: Yes, but you need to know when it's *happening!*—But they make very certain your eyes stay tight closed. They flatter you, these people, saying what a marvel of cleverness and diplomacy you are! Only because your vanity strives for nothing higher! And all the while they're quietly and cold-bloodedly placing the rope around your neck!

KEITH: What is this terrible thing you're so afraid of?

MOLLY: *(Whimpering.)* I can't tell you. I can't make myself say it!

KEITH: Please say it; you *must*; then you'll be able to laugh about it.

MOLLY: I'm afraid—I'm afraid that—*(A muffled report sounds from the garden; MOLLY screams and falls to her knees.)*

KEITH: *(Helping her up.)* That was the big mortar.—Calm yourself now!—Come, have a couple glasses of champagne, then we'll go out and watch the fireworks together—

MOLLY: I've had *enough* fireworks in my head these last two weeks!—You were in Paris!—Who was with you in Paris!—I swear by everything that's holy, I'll forget that I ever trembled because of you, forget that I ever suffered for you, if only you will come with me now!

KEITH: *(Kisses her.)* Poor creature!

MOLLY:—A penny to the poor.—Yes, yes, I'm going—

KEITH: You're staying here; what are you thinking of! Dry your tears! Someone's coming up from the garden—

MOLLY: *(Throws her arms passionately around his neck and covers him with kisses.)* You're so dear!—so wonderful!—so good!—*(Lets loose of him, smiling.)* All I wanted was to see you, just once, just today, with your friends. There are times, you know, when I'm a little—*(Rotates her fist in front of her forehead.)*

KEITH: *(Wanting to hold her back.)* You're staying here, my—!
    (MOLLY rushes out through the hall door. SCHOLZ, limping and holding his knee, enters from the garden through the glass door.)

SCHOLZ: *(Very pleased.)* Please don't be alarmed!—Put out the light so they can't see me from out there. No one noticed anything. *(He drags himself to the chair into which he lets himself down.)*

KEITH: What is it?

SCHOLZ: Turn the lights out first.—It's nothing. The big mortar exploded! A piece of it struck me in the kneecap.

KEITH: *(Has put the light out; the stage is dark.)* That could only happen to you.

SCHOLZ: *(In a blissful voice.)* The pain's already beginning to subside.— Believe me, there's no happier creature under the sun! I won't be going cycling tomorrow with Countess Werdenfels, in any case. But so what! *(Jubilantly.)* I've triumphed over the evil spirits; happiness lies before me; I belong to life! From today on I am another man—*(A rocket rises from the garden and bathes SCHOLZ's features in a lurid glow.)*

KEITH: Good God—I almost didn't recognize you there for a moment!

SCHOLZ: *(Jumps up from the chair and hops about the room triumphantly on one foot, while holding onto his injured knee with his hands.)* For ten long years I regarded myself as an outcast! Outlawed by society! But it was all just imagination! Imagination! All of it—imagination!

END OF ACT THREE

ACT FOUR

In the garden room of Countess Werdenfels a number of enormous laurel wreaths are lying about on armchairs; a splendid bouquet of flowers is placed on the table. ANNA, COUNTESS WERDENFELS, dressed in an attractive morning costume, is found in conversation with POLICE INSPECTOR RASPE and HERMANN CASIMIR. It is forenoon.

ANNA: *(A piece of colored paper in her hand, to HERMANN.)* Thank you, my young friend, for the lovely verses you composed for me yesterday after our first Fairyland Palace concert.—*(To RASPE.)* But I find it most odd, sir, that on this morning in particular you should come to me with such serious rumors concerning your friend and benefactor.

RASPE: The Marquis of Keith is neither my friend nor my benefactor. Two years ago I asked him, as a psychiatric expert, to bear witness at my trial. He might have saved me a year and a half in prison. Instead, he dashed off to America with a fifteen-year-old girl!

SIMBA: *(In a tasteful maid's uniform, enters from the hallway and hands ANNA a card.)* The gentleman would like to see you.

ANNA: *(To HERMANN.)* Good Lord, your father!

HERMANN: *(Frightened, looking at RASPE.)* How could my father suspect I've come here!

RASPE: He didn't hear it from me.

ANNA: *(Lifts the curtain to the game room.)* Go in there. I'll send him on his way.

(HERMANN goes into the game room.)

RASPE: It's best, then, if I pay my respects and be on my way, too.

ANNA: Yes, that would be best.

RASPE: *(Bowing.)* Madam! *(Goes off.)*

ANNA: *(To SIMBA.)* You may show the gentleman in.

(SIMBA shows CONSUL CASIMIR in; he is followed by a lackey from whom he has taken a bouquet of flowers; SIMBA goes off.)

CONSUL CASIMIR: *(Handing her the flowers.)* You will permit me, madam, to extend to you my sincere congratulations on your triumph of yesterday evening. Your debut has taken all Munich by storm; you could not, however, have made a more lasting impression on any of your audience than you did on me.

ANNA: Even if that were true, I'm overwhelmed that you've come personally to tell me so.

CASIMIR: Do you have a moment?—It has to do with a purely practical matter.

ANNA: *(Invites him to be seated.)* I'm certain you'll find yourself on the wrong track.

CASIMIR: *(After both have been seated.)* We shall see presently.—I wanted to ask you if you would be my wife.

ANNA: But I don't understand—

CASIMIR: That's why I've come, to reach an understanding about it. Allow me to make it clear from the start; you will, of course, be required to give up the enticing career you embarked on yesterday evening.

ANNA: Surely you can't have considered this step thoroughly.

CASIMIR: A man of my age, madam, takes no ill-considered step. Later, yes—or earlier. Would you care to tell me what other scruples come to mind?

ANNA: Surely you must know that I can't answer such a proposal.

CASIMIR: I'm quite aware of that. I am, however, thinking of a time in the not too distant future, when you will be utterly free to make your own decisions concerning yourself and your prospects.

ANNA: At the moment I really can't imagine such a possibility.

CASIMIR: Today, you see, I'm the most respected man in Munich; tomorrow, however, I could find myself behind bars. I would find no fault with my best friend if he questioned whether to stand by me in such a reversal of fortune.

ANNA: Would you also not find fault with your wife if she considered the same question?

CASIMIR: My wife, certainly; my mistress, never. I'm not looking for an answer now. I refer to a time when you may find yourself with nowhere to turn or when the situation alters and frees you from all obligations; in short, then, for the time when you need someone to turn to.

ANNA: And that's when you'd make me your wife?

CASIMIR: All this must seem quite insane to you; and yet it does honor to your modesty. But as it happens, I am accountable only to myself. As you may know, I have two small children at home, girls of three and six. Then, as you might well imagine, there are other considerations— As for you, I take full responsibility that you will not disappoint my expectations—even in spite of yourself.

ANNA: I admire your self-confidence.

CASIMIR: You may have absolute confidence in me.

ANNA: But after a success like yesterday evening!—It was as if a new spirit had come over the people of Munich.

CASIMIR: Believe me, I sincerely envy the founder of the Fairyland Palace for his subtle shrewdness. I must also compliment you in particular on your choice of a dress for yesterday evening. You exhibited such confidence in how it showed off your figure to best advantage that I must confess I found it quite impossible to devote proper attention to your recital.

ANNA: Please don't think the applause inflated my opinion of my artistic capabilities.

CASIMIR: And if it did, I wouldn't blame you; but your teacher tells me that a success such as yours yesterday evening has brought misfortune to many. But there is one thing that you mustn't forget: Where would the most celebrated singer today be if rich men did not consider it their moral duty to listen to her without hope of return? No matter how splendid the salary may be in individual cases, the fact remains that these people almost always live on charity.

ANNA: I was amazed at the favorable reception given every number.

CASIMIR: *(Rising.)* Except for that unfortunate symphony of this Zamriaki. I have no doubt whatever that with time we will come to venerate the noise occasioned by this Zamriaki as a divine artistic revelation. Let us therefore allow the world its ways, hope for the best, and expect the worst. You will permit me, madam, to bid you good day. *(Goes off.)*

ANNA: *(Clasps her temples in both hands, goes to the game room, lifts the curtain and steps back.)* You didn't even close the door!

HERMANN CASIMIR: *(Enters from the game room.)* Who would ever have dreamed of such an experience!

ANNA: Go on now, so that your father will find you at home.

HERMANN: *(Noticing the second bouquet.)* The flowers are from him?—I seem to have inherited the proclivity from him.—Except that to *him* the expense means *nothing*.

ANNA: Where do you get money for such insane expenses?

HERMANN: The Marquis of Keith.

ANNA: Please, go now! You look worn. I hope your carouse didn't go on too long last night!

HERMANN: I helped save Zamriaki's life.

ANNA: Do you count that among your worthy accomplishments?

HERMANN: What better have I to do?

ANNA: It's all very well for you to feel for the unfortunate; but you needn't sit at the same table with them. Misfortune is contagious.

HERMANN: *(Significantly.)* The Marquis of Keith says the same thing.

ANNA: Go now! Please!

SIMBA: *(Enters from the hallway and hands ANNA a card.)* The gentleman would like to see you.

ANNA: *(Reading the card.)* "Representative of the South German Concert Agency." —Tell him to come back in two weeks.
(SIMBA goes off.)

HERMANN: What answer will you give my father?

ANNA: I think it's time you leave! You're becoming impertinent!

HERMANN: I'm going to London—even if I have to steal the money. Then my father will have no reason to complain about me.

ANNA: That's more to your benefit than to his.

HERMANN: *(Uneasily.)* I owe that much to my little sisters. *(Goes off.)*

ANNA: *(Reflects a moment, then calls.)* Kathi!

SIMBA: *(Enters from the dining room.)* Madam?

ANNA: I want to get dressed.
(A bell rings in the corridor.)

SIMBA: At once, madam. *(Goes to open the door.)*
(ANNA goes off into the dining room. Immediately following, SIMBA shows in ERNST SCHOLZ, who walks supported by an elegant crutch, limping on his stiff knee, and carrying a large bouquet of flowers.)

SCHOLZ: I've had no opportunity, dear child, to thank you for your tactful, sensitive conduct recently at the garden party.

SIMBA: *(Formally.)* Does the Baron wish to be announced to madam?

KEITH: *(Enters from the hallway in a light-colored overcoat, with a bundle of newspapers in his hand; removing his overcoat.)* Finding you here is a real act of Providence, I must say! *(To SIMBA.)* Why are you still here?

SIMBA: Madam has took me on as a housemaid.

KEITH: You see, I brought you luck.—Announce us!

SIMBA: Very well, Baron. *(Goes off into the game room.)*

KEITH: The reviews in the morning papers are quite enthusiastic! *(Sits at the table downstage, left, and pages through the newspapers.)*

SCHOLZ: Any word yet where your wife is staying?

KEITH: With her parents in Bückeburg. You disappeared suddenly during the banquet yesterday.

SCHOLZ: I had the most pressing need to be alone. How *is* your wife?

KEITH: Thanks; her father's on the verge of bankruptcy.

SCHOLZ: Surely you have enough left over to spare her family that!

KEITH: Have you any idea what yesterday's concert cost me?

SCHOLZ: You really do take things too lightly!

KEITH: What would you have me do, help you hatch the eggs of eternity?

SCHOLZ: If only I could transfer some of my excess sense of duty to you.

KEITH: God save me from that! I need all the flexibility possible to make the most of this success.

SCHOLZ: Thanks to you, today I can face life calmly and with confidence. And so I feel it my duty to speak as frankly to you as you spoke to me two weeks ago.

KEITH: The only difference is I haven't asked for your advice.

SCHOLZ: One *more* reason, then, for complete and open frankness. My exaggerated zeal for duty caused the death of twenty people; but *you* act as though one had *no* duty what*ever* to his fellow men. What's more, you en*joy* playing with people's lives!

KEITH: In my case all they come away with is a black eye.

SCHOLZ: *(With growing self-confidence.)* Then you're lucky! What you fail to realize is that others have the same claims to life's pleasures as you. And as for morality, that sphere of man's highest achievement, you haven't the meagerest understanding of it.

KEITH: You do remain true to yourself, don't you?—You come to Munich with the express purpose of training to be a sensualist, but by some oversight you train to be a moralist.

SCHOLZ: Because of the variegated life here in Munich, I've reached a modest yet all the more reliable evaluation of myself. During these last two weeks I've gone through such enormous inner transformations that if you care to listen I actually *can* speak as a moralist.

KEITH: *(Irritated.)* The fact is my good fortune galls you.

SCHOLZ: I don't believe in your good fortune! I'm so unspeakably happy that I could embrace the entire world, and quite honestly and sincerely I wish you the same. But as long as you jeer in your puerile way at life's highest values, you'll never have it. Before coming to Munich I appreciated only the *spiritual* significance of the relationship between men and women, because sensual gratification seemed vulgar to me. I've learned that it's the other way around. But you have never in your entire life valued a woman for anything higher than the sensual gratification she brings. As long as you refuse to make concessions to the moral order, as I have had to, you'll find that your good fortune is founded on quicksand!

KEITH: *(To the point.)* I'm afraid you have it all wrong. I can thank these last two weeks for my *material* freedom, and as a result I am finally able to *enjoy* my life. And you can thank these last two weeks for your *spiritual* freedom, and as a result *you* are finally able to enjoy *your* life.

SCHOLZ: With one difference: all *my* pleasures are concerned with becoming a useful member of human society.

KEITH: *(Jumping up.)* Why should anyone even *want* to become a useful member of human society?!

SCHOLZ: Because otherwise one's existence has no justification!

KEITH: My existence *needs* no justification! I *asked* no one for my existence and *from* that I deduce I am justified in existing *any way I choose!*

SCHOLZ: And so with utter peace of mind you resign your wife to a life of misery, the woman who shared with you every danger and hardship these last three years!

KEITH: What am I to do! My expenses are so monumental I haven't a penny left over for my own use. I paid up my share of the founding capital with the first installment of my salary. I considered for a moment appropriating the money given me to defray the costs of the preliminary work. But I can't do that. Or would you advise me otherwise?

SCHOLZ: Possibly I can let you have ten or twenty thousand marks if you can't help yourself in any other way. Just by chance I received a draft today from my steward in excess of ten thousand marks. *(Takes the draft from the portfolio and hands it to KEITH.)*

KEITH: *(Tears the paper from his hand.)* Just don't come to me tomorrow saying you want the money back!

SCHOLZ: I don't need it just now. The remaining ten thousand marks I'll need to send through my banker in Breslau.

ANNA: *(Dressed in elegant street clothes, enters from the game room.)* Forgive me, gentlemen, for keeping you waiting.

SCHOLZ: *(Hands her the flowers.)* I could not deny myself the pleasure, madam, of wishing you luck with all my heart on the first morning of your very promising artistic career.

ANNA: *(Places the flowers in a vase.)* Thank you. In last night's excitement, I completely forgot to ask how your injuries are doing.

SCHOLZ: God knows, they're not worth talking about. My doctor says if I wanted to I could be climbing mountains inside of a week. What pained me yesterday were the peals of scornful laughter that Zamriaki's symphony received.

KEITH: *(Has seated himself at the writing table.)* I cannot do more than give people the opportunity to show what they are capable of. Whoever doesn't make the grade, falls by the wayside. Conductors are not hard to come by in Munich.

SCHOLZ: Wasn't it you who said he was the greatest musical genius since Richard Wagner?

KEITH: Just because I *own* a nag doesn't mean I *call* it one. I have to be answerable at any moment for the accuracy of my accounts. *(Rising.)* I and the caryatids have just been to the city council. They were asked to consider whether the Fairyland Palace is something Munich really needs. The answer was unanimously in the affirmative. A city like Munich can't even begin to dream of all it needs!

SCHOLZ: *(To ANNA.)* I presume madam has world-embracing plans to discuss with her fortunate impresario.

ANNA: Thank you, no, not really. Leaving us already, are you?

SCHOLZ: May I have the honor of calling on you again in the next few days?

ANNA: My pleasure; you're always welcome.

(SCHOLZ has shaken KEITH's hand; goes off.)

KEITH: The morning reviews of your performance are quite enthusiastic.

ANNA: Any news about Molly?

KEITH: She's with her parents in Bückeburg; wallowing in an ocean of petit-bourgeois sentimentality.

ANNA: Next time we won't be so frightened for her! She also needed to prove how completely unnecessary she is to you!

KEITH: Thank God that violent passion for you is a book with seven seals. If a woman isn't capable of making a man happy, the least she wants is to set fire to the roof over his head.

ANNA: Nonetheless, you need to inspire a bit more confidence in your business enterprises! Sitting on a volcano day and night isn't a particularly pleasant experience.

KEITH: Why is everything I hear today a moral lecture?

ANNA: Because you act as though you were in constant need of being drugged. You don't know what rest is. I've discovered that when one is in doubt between one thing and another, the best thing is to do *nothing at all*. It's *doing* things that makes one susceptible to all kinds of unpleasantries. I do as little as possible and I've always been happy. How can you blame someone for distrusting you, when all you do is chase after luck day and night like a ravenous wolf?

self-conquest that I became reconciled to the moral attitudes current here in Munich. If my happiness were to be dashed to pieces *because* of that reconciliation so as to share in the happiness of my fellow man, it would be the most revolting farce!

ANNA: I thought your intention was only to become a useful member of human society!

SCHOLZ: I dreamed of bettering the world as a prisoner behind iron bars dreams of snow-covered mountains! There's only one thing now that I can still hope for, to make the woman I love so unspeakably so happy that she will never regret her choice.

ANNA: I'm sorry to have to tell you, but I'm rather indifferent toward you.

SCHOLZ: Indifferent? But I've never in my life had more proof of attraction from any woman than I've had from you!

ANNA: That's not my fault. Your friend described you to me as a philosopher who couldn't be bothered with reality.

SCHOLZ: It was reality that tore me *from* my philosophy! I'm not one of those who rail against earthly vanity all their lives, and then when they're deaf and lame, have to be kicked into submission by death!

ANNA: The Marquis of Keith is kept from misfortune by his confirmation verse! He considers it an infallible magical formula for keeping the police and bailiff at bay!

SCHOLZ: I don't stoop to believe in omens! If this fortune hunter is right, then at my confirmation I received just as infallible a formula against misfortune as he did. Our pastor gave me the saying: "Many are called, but few are chosen."—But that doesn't bother me! Even if I had *concrete proof* that I don't belong to the chosen, it would only strengthen me in my fearless battle against my destiny!

ANNA: Please spare me your fearless battles!

SCHOLZ: I'd rather *give up* reason than be convinced by it that there are people who, innocently and from the start, are shut off from all happiness!

ANNA: Complain about that to the Marquis of Keith.

SCHOLZ: I'm *not* complaining! The longer the hard school of misfortune endures the more hardened my intellectual resistance becomes. People like me are capable of transformation. *My soul is indestructible!*

ANNA: Congratulations!

SCHOLZ: It's the source of my irresistible power! The less you feel for me the greater and more powerful my love for you becomes, and the sooner do I see the moment when you will say to me: "I fought against you with all the power at my command, but I love you!"

ANNA: Heaven protect me from that!!

SCHOLZ: Heaven will *not* protect you from it! When a man with my strength of will, a will that is unbreakable, concentrates all his thought and endeavor on *one thing and one thing only*, then there are only two possibilities: either he achieves his goal or he loses his mind.

ANNA: Yes, I'm inclined to agree.

SCHOLZ: I'll take the chance! It all depends on which is more resistant, your lack of feeling or my mind. I expect the worst and will not look back till I've reached my goal; because if I'm unable to fashion a happy life out of the bliss that fills me now, then there's no hope for me. The opportunity will never offer itself again!

ANNA: I thank you from the bottom of my heart for reminding me of that! *(Sits down at the writing table.)*

SCHOLZ: This is the last time the world will lie before me in all its glory!

ANNA: *(Writing a note.)* That applies to me, too! *(Calls.)* Kathi! *(To herself.)* The opportunity will never offer itself to me again either.

SCHOLZ: *(Suddenly coming to himself.)* Why are you so mistrustful, madam?!—Why are you so mistrustful? You're mistaken, Countess! You're harboring a terrible suspicion—

ANNA: Are you still unaware of the fact that you are detaining me? *(Calls.)* Kathi!

SCHOLZ: I couldn't possibly leave you like this! Give me your assurance that you do not doubt my sanity!
(SIMBA enters with ANNA's hat.)

ANNA: Where were you so long?

SIMBA: I was afraid to come in.

SCHOLZ: Simba, you know better than anyone that I'm in possession of my five senses.

SIMBA: *(Pushing him back.)* Go on, don't talk so dumb!

ANNA: You will leave my maid alone. *(To SIMBA.)* Do you know the address of Consul Casimir?

SCHOLZ: *(Suddenly petrified.)*—The mark of Cain on my brow—

END OF ACT FOUR

ACT FIVE

All the doors in the Marquis of Keith's study are wide open. As HERMANN CASIMIR leans against the center table, KEITH calls into the living room.

KEITH: Sasha! *(Receiving no answer he goes into the waiting room; to HER-MANN.)* Excuse me. *(Calls into the waiting room.)* Sasha! *(Comes downstage; to HERMANN.)* So you're going to London with your father's consent. I can give you the best of recommendations to take with you to London. *(Throws himself onto the divan.)* In the first place I recommend you leave your German sentimentality at home. Social Democracy and anarchism are passé in London these days. But let me tell you one thing more: the only way to properly exploit one's fellow man is to appeal to the good in him. Therein resides the art of being liked, the art of getting what one wants. The more fully you take advantage of your fellow man, the more careful you have to be that you have right on your side. Never seek your own gain to the detriment of a virtuous man, but only to the detriment of scoundrels and block-heads. And now let me transmit to you the philosopher's stone: the most splendid business in the world is *morality*. I'm not yet at the point of having made it my business, but I wouldn't be the Marquis of Keith if I let the opportunity slip through my fingers entirely. *(The bell rings in the corridor. He calls.)* Sasha! *(Rising.)* I'll slap that rascal's ears! *(Goes into the hallway and returns with COUNCILOR OSTERMEIER.)* You couldn't have come at a more opportune moment, my dear Ostermeier—

OSTERMEIER: My colleagues on the Board of Directors, my dear friend, have commissioned me to—

KEITH: I have a plan to discuss with you that will increase our intake many times over.

OSTERMEIER: Do you want me to report at the general meeting that I failed again today to inspect your account books?

KEITH: You're raving, my dear Ostermeier! Why don't you explain to me calmly and impartially what this is all about?

OSTERMEIER: What it is about is your account books, dear friend.

KEITH: *(Irritably.)* To think I slave away for these bleary-eyed num-skulls—

OSTERMEIER: So he's right, then! *(Turning to leave.)* Your servant, sir!

KEITH: *(Tears open the drawer of the writing table.)* Here, you may revel all you like in the account books! *(Turning to face OSTERMEIER.)* Who's right?

OSTERMEIER: A certain Police Inspector Raspe, who bet five bottles of Pommery last night at the American Bar that you *don't keep* account books.

KEITH: *(Bridling.)* Quite right, I *don't* keep account books.

OSTERMEIER: Then show me your notebook.

KEITH: I have established a company, sir, I have *not* had time to set up an office!

OSTERMEIER: Then show me your notebook.

KEITH: *(Bridling again.)* I *have no notebook.*

OSTERMEIER: Then show me the deposit receipts from the bank.

KEITH: Can you actually think I took your money to let it out on interest?!

OSTERMEIER: Don't excite yourself, dear friend. Even if you don't keep books, at least you note down your expenditures elsewhere. An errand boy does that much.

KEITH: *(Tosses his memorandum book onto the table.)* There you have my memorandum book.

OSTERMEIER: *(Opens it and reads.)* "A silvery torrent of mauve silk and pailettes from shoulder to ankle."—That's all!

KEITH: Sir, I have served up one success to you after another. If, however, you choose to place obstacles in my path, then you may rest assured of one thing: you will never again see as much as one penny of your money, in this world or the next!

OSTERMEIER: Our shares in the Fairyland Palace aren't so bad off, my friend. We'll see our money again. Your servant! *(About to leave.)*

KEITH: *(Holding him back.)* Your snooping about is undermining the enterprise, sir! I beg your pardon; I'm excited; my feeling for the Fairyland Palace is that of a father toward his child.

OSTERMEIER: Then your worries about your child are over. The Fairyland Palace is secured and will be built.

KEITH: Without *me?*

OSTERMEIER: If need be, then without you, dear friend.

KEITH: But you can't do that!

OSTERMEIER: In any case you would be the last one to hinder us!

KEITH: That would be a low and rotten trick!

OSTERMEIER: Oh, that's good! It really is! Just because we refuse to be cheated by *you* any longer, you call *us* the cheats!

KEITH: If you're so sure you're being cheated, then sue me!

OSTERMEIER: What a marvelous idea, my friend! If only we weren't on the Board of Directors!

KEITH: What are you talking about! You're on the Board of Directors to support me in my work.

OSTERMEIER: And that's why I've come; but you don't seem to have anything to work at.

KEITH: My dear Ostermeier, I am a man of honor. You have no right to subject me to such abominable treatment. You take over the business side of the operation, and I'll manage the artistic. I admit to certain managerial shortcomings, but I was able to overlook them, knowing they would never occur again; and that once my position was secure, I would never be found guilty of even the slightest infraction.

OSTERMEIER: We could have talked of this yesterday when I was here with the other gentlemen; but you were more determined to talk our ears off. I might say to you even today: Let's make another stab at it— if only you had shown yourself to be sincere. But when all we hear are lies, well—

KEITH: *(Bridling.)* Then you may tell the gentlemen: I will build the Fairyland Palace just as surely as the idea burst full-grown from my brain. If, however, *you* build it—and you may tell the gentlemen this, too!—then I will blow the Fairyland Palace, together with its Board of Directors *and* its stockholders—sky high!

OSTERMEIER: I will give an exact accounting, neighbor! You know, I really don't like insulting people to their faces, not to mention throwing them out on their—Your servant, sir! *(Goes off.)*

KEITH: *(Staring after him.)*—on their asses! I thought as much. *(To HERMANN.)* Don't leave me now; I may go to pieces and wither away to nothing.—How is this possible? *(Tears in his eyes.)* After all those fireworks!—Am I to be driven like an outcast again from country to country?! No! No! I mustn't allow myself to be pushed against a wall!—This is the last time the world will lie before me in all its glory! *(Pulling himself up straight.)* No!—Not only am I not tottering *yet*, I'll take a leap that will astonish all of Munich. And while the city is still trembling with astonishment, I'll fall on its prostrate body, to the accompaniment of trumpets and drums, and tear it limb from limb. We'll see *then* who'll be the first to get to his feet! *(COUNTESS WERDENFELS enters. He rushes toward her.)* My queen—

ANNA: *(To HERMANN.)* Would you excuse us for a moment?

KEITH: *(Shows HERMANN into the living room, closing the door behind him.)* You look terribly self-confident today.

ANNA: That's quite possible. Every day since our Fairyland Palace concert, I've had a good half-dozen proposals of marriage.

KEITH: That means damned little to me!

ANNA: But not to me!

KEITH: *(Scornfully.)* Have you fallen in love with him?

ANNA: Whom do you mean?

KEITH: The sensualist!

ANNA: Are you making fun of me?

KEITH: Then whom *do* you mean?

ANNA: *(Indicating the living room.)* His father.

KEITH: And you want to talk with me about this?

ANNA: No, I just wanted to ask if there's been any sign of Molly.

KEITH: No, but what's this with Casimir?

ANNA: What's this with Molly?—Are you keeping her disappearance a secret?

KEITH: *(Uneasily.)* Frankly, I'm less afraid that she's had an accident than that her disappearance will pull the ground out from under my feet. Should that seem inhuman, I've at least paid for it by sitting out the last three nights in the telegraph office.—My crime against her is that in all the time we've known each other she's never once heard an angry word from me. She allows herself to be consumed with longing for her petit-bourgeois world where, packed in like sardines, they drudge and humiliate and love one another! No free view, no free breath! As much as possible and of the commonest sort!

ANNA: Suppose they don't find Molly, what then?

KEITH: I can be consoled with the prospect that once my house has collapsed about me, she will come back, penitent and smiling, and say: "I'll never do it again!"—Her goal has been reached; I can start packing.

ANNA: And what's to become of *me?*

KEITH: Up to this point you've gained the most from our enterprise and I hope you will continue to gain by it. You can't lose anything because you haven't invested anything.

ANNA: Are you so sure?!

KEITH:—I see—!

ANNA: I'm glad!

KEITH:—What did you answer him?

ANNA: I wrote saying I couldn't answer him just yet.

KEITH: To crawl away a coward at the end?—As victor to renounce your worth as a human being?

SCHOLZ: *(Flaring into a rage.)* I am *not* renouncing my worth as a human being! You have no cause to insult me, to jeer at me!—If a man forces himself, *against his will,* to accept the restraints I put upon myself now, *then* he may very *well* lose his worth as a human being. And yet, because of that, he remains relatively happy; he protects his illusions.—A man who comes to terms with reality dispassionately, as I am, resigns neither the respect nor the sympathy of his fellow men.

KEITH: *(Shrugs his shoulders.)* I'd take a little more time to think it over.

SCHOLZ: I've given it mature consideration. It's the last duty my destiny requires me to fulfill.

KEITH: Once you're in, getting out won't be so easy.

SCHOLZ: If I had even the slightest hope of getting out again, I'd never go in. The renunciation that I've burdened myself with, the self-conquest and joyful hope that I've wrested from my soul, I undertook in order to change my fate. I bewail God that there is no longer any doubt that I am different from other men.

KEITH: *(Very proudly.)* And I *praise* God that I have never *doubted* that I was different from other men!

SCHOLZ: *(Very calmly.)* Bewail God or praise God—until this very moment I have thought of you as the most cunning of scoundrels!—But I've given up even this illusion. A scoundrel counts on luck just as surely as an honorable man counts on good conscience not deserting him even in irrevocable misfortune. Your luck is as threadbare as mine, except that you don't know it. That's the horrible danger hanging over you!

KEITH: The only danger hanging over me is that tomorrow I'm out of money!

SCHOLZ: None of your tomorrows will have money, no matter how long you live!—I wish I knew you were safe from the hopeless consequences of your delusion. It's why I've come to see you this last time. I'm profoundly convinced that the best thing for you is to come with me.

KEITH: *(Cunningly.)* Where?

SCHOLZ: To the sanitorium.

KEITH: Give me the thirty thousand marks and I'll be right there with you.

SCHOLZ: Come with me and there will be no more need of money—ever. You'll find a more comfortable life than you may ever have known. We'll keep a carriage and horses, we'll play billiards—

KEITH: *(Embracing him.)* Give me the thirty thousand marks!! Shall I humiliate myself here at your feet? I could be arrested on the spot!

SCHOLZ: So it's gone that far, has it? *(Pushing him back.)* I don't give sums like that to madmen!

KEITH: *(Shouts.)* You're the madman!

SCHOLZ: *(Calmly.)* I'm the one come to his senses.

KEITH: *(Scornfully.)* If a lunatic asylum lures you because you've come to your senses—go right ahead!

SCHOLZ: You're one they have to bring there by force!

KEITH:—I suppose you'll reassume your title once you're there?

SCHOLZ: You've gone bankrupt on two continents in every conceivable way that bourgeois life permits!

KEITH: *(Venomously.)* If it is your moral duty to free the world of your superfluous existence, I'm sure there are more radical means than going for drives and playing billiards!

SCHOLZ: I tried that long ago.

KEITH: *(Shouts at him.)* Then what are you still doing here?!

SCHOLZ: *(Gloomily.)* I failed at that as I have at everything else.

KEITH: May I suppose you shot someone else—by mistake?

SCHOLZ: They cut the bullets from between my shoulders; near the spinal column.—This is the last time anyone will ever offer you a help-ing hand. You already know the sort of experiences that are in store for you.

KEITH: *(Throws himself on his knees and clasps SCHOLZ's hands.)*—Give me the forty thousand marks and I'm saved!

SCHOLZ: That won't save you from the penitentiary!

KEITH: *(Starts up in terror.)* Shut up!

SCHOLZ: *(Pleading.)* Come with me and you'll be safe. We grew up together; why shouldn't we wait for the end together, too? To bour-geois society you're a criminal and subject to all kinds of inhuman medieval tortures—

KEITH: *(Moaning.)* If you won't help me, then go, please, I beg of you!

SCHOLZ: *(Tears in his eyes.)* You mustn't turn your back on your only refuge! You didn't choose your pitiable fate anymore than I chose mine.

KEITH: Go! Go!

SCHOLZ: Come. Come.—As a companion I'll be gentle as a lamb. It would be a dim ray in the dark night of my life to rescue my boyhood friend from his terrible fate.

KEITH: Go! Please!

SCHOLZ:—I want you to entrust yourself to my guidance as of this moment—as I once wanted to entrust myself to you—

KEITH: *(Cries out in despair.)* Sasha! Sasha!

SCHOLZ: At least, then, don't forget that—that you have a friend who will welcome you at any time. *(Goes off.)*

KEITH: *(Crawling around on all fours, searching.)* Molly!—Molly!—This is the first time I've ever whimpered on my knees in front of a woman! *(Suddenly hears a sound from the direction of the living room.)* Oh, it's you? *(HERMANN CASIMIR enters from the living room.)* I can't ask you to stay here any longer. I'm not—I'm not quite well. I—I have to—to sleep on it first—to master the situation again. Have a good— a good—*(Heavy footsteps and many voices are heard from the front stairs.)* Listen—The noise! The uproar!—That's bad—

HERMANN: Close the door, then.

KEITH: I can't!—I can't!—It's her—!

(A number of patrons from the neighboring Hofbräuhaus drag in a lifeless MOLLY. Water drips from her body, her clothes hang from her in shreds. Her undone hair covers her face.)

BUTCHER'S HELPER: Here's the crook we're after! *(To the others behind him.)* Is it him? You bet! *(To KEITH.)* Look here what we fished up! Look here what we're bringin' you! Look here—if you got the guts!

PORTER: Pulled her out of the sewer! From under the iron grate! Must've been in the water a whole week!

BAKERY WOMAN: An' all the time the dirty tramp runs around with his shameless pack! Ain't paid for his bread in six weeks! Lets his poor wife beg at all the shops for something to eat! Would've made a stone cry the way she looked at the end!

KEITH: *(Retreats backwards to the writing table, while the crowd presses around him with the body.)* I beg of you, please, calm down!

BUTCHER'S HELPER: Shut your mouth, you bastard! I'll clout you one!—Over there! Look!—Is it her or not? Look at her, I said!

KEITH: *(Has grabbed from the writing table HERMANN's revolver left there earlier by Countess Werdenfels.)* Touch me just once and I'll use this!

BUTCHER'S HELPER: What's the bastard say?—What's he say?—You goin' to give me the revolver?—Ain't you done enough to her, you shit? Give it here, I said!

(The BUTCHER'S HELPER grapples with KEITH who has succeeded in getting close to the doorway through which at that moment CONSUL

CASIMIR enters. HERMANN CASIMIR in the meanwhile has gone to the body; he and the BAKERY WOMAN carry the body to the divan.)

KEITH: *(Defending himself like a desperate man, calls.)* Police!—Police! *(Notices CASIMIR and clings to him.)* For God's sake, save me! They'll hang me!

CONSUL CASIMIR: *(To the crowd.)* All right! That's enough! I refuse to see any more of this!—Leave that woman on the divan!—Get out, I say! Now! There's the door! *(Pulling downstage his son who is about to leave with the crowd.)* Hold on there, sonny! You'll be taking a nice lesson with you on your trip to London! *(The people from the Hofbräuhaus have left the room. To KEITH.)* I was about to invite you to leave Munich within twenty-four hours. But now I think it's best you leave by the next train.

KEITH: *(Still holding the revolver in his left hand.)* I'm not responsible—for this—for this disaster—

CASIMIR: Settle that with yourself! But you *are* responsible for forging my signature on a congratulatory telegram delivered to your founders' party on Brienner Strasse.

KEITH: I can't leave—

CASIMIR: *(Hands him a paper.)* You will sign this receipt. In it you certify that the sum of ten thousand marks owed you by Countess Werdenfels has been received from me. *(KEITH goes to the writing table and signs. CASIMIR counts the money out of his wallet.)* As your successor in the directorship of the Fairyland Palace Company, I request that in the interest of our enterprise's successful development you do not show yourself again in Munich for some time! *(KEITH, standing at the writing table, hands the paper to CASIMIR and mechanically receives the money as CASIMIR pockets the paper.)* Pleasant journey! *(To HERMANN.)* And you come with me!

(HERMANN slips out shyly. CASIMIR follows him.)

KEITH: *(The revolver in his left hand, the money in his right, takes a few steps toward the divan, but recoils in horror. He then looks irresolutely from the revolver to the money in turn. As he lays down the revolver behind him on the center table, with a grin on his face:)* Life is a slippery bitch—

END OF PLAY

CARL R. MUELLER has since 1967 been professor in the Department of Theater at UCLA where he has taught theater history, criticism, dramatic literature, and playwriting. He was educated at Northwestern University, where he received a B.S. in English. After work in graduate English at the University of California, Berkeley, he received his M.A. in playwriting at UCLA, where he also completed his Ph.D. in Theater History and Criticism. He has won many awards, including the Samuel Goldwyn Award for Dramatic Writing, and in 1960–61 was a Fulbright Scholar in Berlin where he attended the Free University, was active at the Berliner Ensemble, and had the dubious historical privilege of having been present at the erection of the Berlin Wall in August of 1961. A translator for almost forty years, he has translated and published works by Büchner, Brecht, Wedekind, Hauptmann, Hofmannsthal, and Hebbel to name only a few. He recently published a translation of von Horvath's *Tales from the Vienna Woods,* which was given its London West End premiere in July, 1999. His most recent published collection of plays are *Arthur Schnitzler: Four Major Plays* and *August Strindberg: Five Major Plays.* Also forthcoming from Smith and Kraus is *Sophokles: The Complete Plays,* a co-translation with a classisist colleague. He is currently at work on translations of both parts of Goethe's *Faust* as well as a second volume of Strindberg plays, and a volume each of Kleist and Schiller. His translations have been performed in every English-speaking country in the world, and have appeared on BBC-TV.